Using Literature to Enhance Writing Instruction

A GUIDE FOR K–5 TEACHERS

REBECCA OLNESS
Black Diamond, Washington, USA

INTERNATIONAL Reading Association
800 BARKSDALE ROAD, PO BOX 8139
NEWARK, DE 19714-8139, USA
www.reading.org

The International Reading Association attempts, through its publications, to provide a forum for a wide spectrum of opinions on reading. This policy permits divergent viewpoints without implying the endorsement of the Association.

Editorial Director   Matthew W. Baker
Managing Editor   Shannon T. Fortner
Permissions Editor   Janet S. Parrack
Acquisitions and Communications Coordinator   Corinne M. Mooney
Associate Editor   Charlene M. Nichols
Administrative Assistant   Michele Jester
Assistant Permissions Editor   Tyanna L. Collins
Production Department Manager   Iona Muscella
Supervisor, Electronic Publishing   Anette Schütz
Senior Electronic Publishing Specialist   R. Lynn Harrison
Proofreader   Elizabeth C. Hunt

Project Editor   Shannon T. Fortner

Cover Design   Linda Steere; photo by Photodisc

Web addresses in this book were correct as of the publication date but may have become inactive or otherwise modified since that time. If you notice a deactivated or changed Web address, please e-mail books@reading.org with the words "Website Update" in the subject line. In your message, specify the Web link, the book title, and the page number on which the link appears.

Library of Congress Cataloging-in-Publication Data
Olness, Rebecca.
  Using literature to enhance writing instruction : a guide for K-5 teachers / Rebecca Olness.
    p. cm.
  Includes bibliographical references and index.
  ISBN 0-87207-560-5
  1. English language--Composition and exercises--Study and teaching (Elementary) 2. Reading (Elementary) 3. Children's literature--Study and teaching (Elementary) I. Title.
  LB1576.O44 2004
  372.62'3--dc22
                                                                    2004020272

For Mother and Daddy, my first and finest teachers.

Contents

Preface

Many good books on writing process and writing workshop are available. Some of them are about the use of children's literature in the classroom, and others explore six-trait analytical writing (Spandel & Stiggins, 1997). In this book, however, I have combined use of the six-trait model with the use of children's literature to show teachers of kindergarten through grade 5 how they can demonstrate good writing techniques and activities that will positively impact student writing. I believe that using literature to show children how writers write, use various styles and techniques, and tell a good story is an effective and efficient way to enhance student writing. I also believe that reading aloud is an essential part of the school day. Teachers often tell me that because of the increased emphasis on academics, they need to justify taking the time to read a book to their class. Tying literature and read-alouds to the writing curriculum reinforces its importance and usefulness. Many teachers are eager to incorporate literature into their writing program, but they tell me they need specific titles, examples, and lessons they can use immediately in their classroom. This book is intended to meet those needs.

The history of this book began in April 2003 when I spoke at a reading conference in Saskatoon, Saskatchewan, Canada, where I was paid the greatest compliment an educator can receive. A teacher who had previously attended my presentation on writing told me, "You changed my life as a teacher of writing." I was gratified—to influence the life of a student or a teacher is the primary reason most of us chose the teaching profession. The subject of that presentation is a large part of chapters 4 through 9 of this book. The first chapters grew out of years of teaching, hearing teachers, researchers, and authors at workshops and conferences, reading professional publications and, of course, children's books.

Early in my teaching career, I was only concerned with reading and did not teach writing. I have always loved children's literature, so that was a part of my teaching from the beginning. I occasionally asked students to write innovations (rewrites of familiar books) or responses to literature, but that was the extent of my writing instruction. Over time, I began hearing more and more about the "reading–writing connection." I read Donald Graves (1983), Nancie Atwell (1987), and Ralph Fletcher (1996) and learned about the writing process, note taking, writing workshop, and journals. These authors' ideas made sense, but I still wasn't convinced that I could (or should) find the time to include writing in my literacy program.

Then I decided to take a weeklong training session titled Six-Trait Analytical Writing, conducted by Vicki Spandel and Ruth Culham. Taking this course is when *my* life changed as a teacher. I learned about the six-trait model, which had emerged from the Northwest Regional Educational Laboratory as an evaluative tool to assess student writing (see Spandel & Culham, 1995). Spandel and Stiggins (1997) propose that six traits, or elements, characterize effective writing: (1) ideas, (2) organization, (3) voice, (4) word choice, (5) sentence fluency, and (6) conventions. Each element (or trait) is evaluated separately, thus allowing for analytic scoring that can best assist instruction. Spandel (2001b) reminds us that the six traits are not an approach to writing in and of themselves—but language used to describe good writing. Although this model was originally intended as an assessment tool, using it in the writing workshop as a model for good writing makes sense. By teaching students to recognize the traits of good writing, teachers can help students infuse these traits into their own writing.

Many writing workshop activities correspond with the six traits. Note taking and keeping a journal, as ways of finding ideas and collecting information for writing, fit perfectly with the first trait of ideas. So does expanding a first draft with details. The drafting process in the workshop corresponds with the second trait of organization. During revision, the third, fourth, and fifth traits of voice, word choice, and sentence fluency are at work to fine-tune the piece. And, finally, editing corresponds with the sixth trait of conventions. By using literature as examples in minilessons, teachers can convey to students specific ways of identifying and using these traits.

For a teacher who uses the writing workshop structure, the traits are easy to include. But teachers who prefer other approaches to writing can also use the six-trait model. My own writing program began with the six traits and was adapted from the original Six-Trait Analytical Writing Model (Spandel & Culham, 1995). I taught students to recognize the traits first in literature and then use them in their own writing. Whatever your writing program, the six traits can be a part of it. My approach puts the emphasis on literature as an example, model, and catalyst for writing. Although chapters 4 through 9 deal specifically with the traits, the first three chapters address the reading–writing connection and using literature as an example for all types of writing.

After my training, I arranged to go into classrooms in the elementary school to teach writing where I served as literacy specialist. I taught writing to children and to teachers, and I learned what worked and what did not. And because of my love for literature, I demonstrated each trait by sharing a book.

I continued to read the works of Lucy Calkins (1994), who outlined instruction in literary nonfiction, poetry, memoirs, and theme studies as a way to expand children's writing experiences; Shelley Harwayne (2000), who advocated having children write their own stories and offered specific links to literature and children's writing; and Regie Routman (1994), who stressed the importance of being a writing model for students. After I read Routman's *Reading Essentials* (2003), I realized that when I approached each trait with demonstration and practice before expecting students to work on their own, I was using her optimal learning model. This model consists of (1) demonstration by the teacher; (2) shared demonstration by teacher and students; (3) guided practice with students and teacher; and (4) independent practice by students, with guidance and support by the teacher. Routman's model, in turn, relies heavily on Don Holdaway's (2000) principles of developmental and social learning, which are an expansion of the "I do it, We do it, You do it" strategy used in many elementary classrooms. With expert assistance and encouragement, learners gradually move from dependence to independence. These researchers' ideas fit in with what I had already learned about writing and the six traits.

I also read innumerable children's books, finding just the right ones to illustrate how good writers use their craft to tell a story. Good books play a strong role in improving the quality of student writing. Lucy Calkins (1994) speaks of the importance of learning from authors and the reading–writing connections that occur in the writing workshop because teachers love and share children's literature. Sharing a book that demonstrates one of the writing traits helps students realize that the effects of literature are achieved because of an author's deliberate craftsmanship. In *Literacy at the Crossroads* (1996), Regie Routman urges teachers to "use excellent literature to notice what authors do: leads, voice, style, interesting vocabulary, format, endings, sentence constructions, powerful adjectives and verbs" (p. 88). This covers the first five traits. "You are teaching the six traits just by reading examples of fine detail, strategic organization, powerful voice, precise word choice, and lyrical fluency" (Spandel, 2001a, p. viii). Chapters

2 through 9 of this book contain annotated bibliographies for use with various writing activities.

I was now able to combine my love for children's literature with what I had learned about writing, and the results were amazing. Teachers were taking the time to read good literature to their students without feeling guilty because the reading had a purpose. Students were commenting on character development, organization, fluency, using just the right words, and discerning the difference between showing and telling in literature. Teachers and students were comfortable with writing, and it became an integral part of the curriculum. Kindergartners and fifth graders alike were commenting on an author's use of voice or word choice; we had "Drop Everything and Write," a block of time when everyone in the school wrote, each trimester; staff devoted one faculty meeting per month to discussion or training in writing; and student writing improved. In the seven years following the adoption of this writing focus in our school, student writing scores improved on both district and state assessments. But best of all, students wrote well and enjoyed it.

An added benefit was the effect on my own writing. I had encouraged students and teachers to think of themselves as writers and to share their work; finally, I realized that by taking the advice I had given to others and by utilizing the techniques and skills I was identifying and demonstrating that I, too, could be a writer. I began sharing my writing with students and colleagues and was able to use the wisdom and experience of those around me to establish myself as a writer.

Exposure to literature has a positive effect on student writing. Eckhoff (1983) analyzed reading texts and writing samples in two second-grade classes. She discovered that literature seemed to have a direct influence on students' writing. Student writing reflected features of the basal reading series used in both groups. Although student writing showed variation, it also showed strong differences—the students reading the more complex text tended to use more elaborate and complex sentence structures than students reading the simpler text. She concluded that children would benefit from texts that help them learn to decode and at the same time provide models representative of literary prose. Dahl and Farnan (1998) found that writers who participate in literature-based reading programs tend to produce writing with the structures and language features of their reading. But, they propose that research consider not only writing *about* literature, but also writing *through* literature, how understandings develop across both reading and writing experiences. Although we know from research that reading literature does influence student writing, what remains unknown are the specific influences of literature on writing. Literature serves as a model for language use, sentence construction, style, and format. Teachers have long recognized the value of quality literature as a critical element in children's literacy development.

This book outlines various ways to enhance and enrich writing instruction through the use of children's literature. Chapter 1 describes the strong reading–writing connection and the value of using literature in the writing program. It also discusses authors as mentors, audience, and the use of writing notebooks.

Chapter 2 discusses shared, guided, and independent writing. It also offers suggestions for books to use in writing activities, including pattern books, alphabet books, and nonfiction.

Chapter 3 addresses finding a topic and encouraging students to write from personal experience or research. It also discusses prompts and assignments. An annotated bibliography offers a selection of books to use with prompts.

In this book I have structured my ideas for writing instruction in the language of the Six-Trait Analytical Writing Model (Spandel & Culham, 1995). Each chapter from 4 through 9 covers one trait of the Six-Trait Analytical Writing Model in depth and offers ideas and strategies to develop the trait in students, sample lesson plans, assessment, and annotated bibliographies of children's literature that can be used to highlight the trait under discussion.

Chapter 10 offers some final thoughts on finding time to read aloud every day and to provide large blocks of time for actual writing. Why teachers must be writers and model writing for their students is discussed.

In this book I hope that just one little idea or example will "change the lives of teachers of writing." I don't have all the answers. I do, however, have years of working with students and teachers who have changed my life.

Acknowledgments

For years I have wanted to write a book. Thanks to a lot of people, my dream has finally become a reality.

First I'd like to thank Sam Sebesta for sharing the beauty and power of literature and showing me that it can also be used as a teaching tool, Vicki Spandel and Ruth Culham for introducing me to Six-Trait Analytical Writing, Carol Santa for convincing me to write this book, Terrell Young for offering assistance and advice, and DeWaundee Green for being a friend and relentless advocate.

I am grateful to many colleagues and workshop participants for encouraging and inspiring me, especially Gary Myers, Gaynell Walker, and the staff and students at Martin Sortun Elementary School for allowing me to teach and learn from them.

I am also grateful to Lori Jamison and Gregg Kurek for their friendship and professional wisdom, and to the Board and staff of the International Reading Association, especially Matt Baker, Editorial Director, and Shannon Fortner, Managing Editor, for their encouragement and expert advice.

Finally, and most of all, I would like to thank my husband, Ron, and children, Michael and Jennifer, who are my support and inspiration.

CHAPTER 1

The Reading–Writing Connection

Nobody but a reader ever became a writer.

—RICHARD PECK

The primary reason for exposing children to quality literature is for its aesthetic value; a secondary benefit is its influence on student writing. Long before writers can create their own text, they can learn what good writing is all about by hearing and loving the work of others (Spandel & Stiggins, 1997). By reading literature often and widely, students more readily learn to write.

Teachers and researchers (Calkins, 1994; Eckhoff, 1983; Harste, Shorte, & Burke, 1988; Lancia, 1997; Tierney & Pearson, 1983) have given increased attention to the connections between reading and writing and to the value of quality children's literature. Reading and writing are similar processes of composing meaning; practice with one contributes to the success of the other. In *The Art of Teaching Writing*, Lucy Calkins (1994) states that reading–writing connections begin when teachers and caregivers help children fall in love with a single poem, book, or essay. When a book means something to a child, teachers can ask, "What did the author do to make us laugh?"; "What does the author tend to do?"; "How did the author create that effect?"; and "Can I borrow any of these techniques in my own writing?" Fletcher and Portalupi (1998) state that "literature may be the most crucial (influence) of all. The writing you get out of your students can only be as good as the classroom literature that surrounds and sustains it. The writing classroom is built on the foundation of literature" (p. 10). Serafini and Giorgis (2003, p. 11) quote an old saying, "Be careful what you read, for that is how you will write," emphasizing that the books teachers read aloud provide powerful models for the types of writing students do. Donovan and Smolkin (2002) found that student writing paralleled what students knew about both narrative (fiction) and expository (nonfiction) text. If students knew and understood the characteristics of the genre, they were able to use those attributes in their own writing.

Spandel and Stiggins (1997) urge teachers to be readers to teach themselves the definition of quality writing. By reading widely and often, we teachers continuously discover examples that we can share with students as we work to teach them about good writing.

While enjoying a story, students hear the language of good writers, are exposed to rich vocabulary, and develop literary awareness, or a "sense of story." They learn the structure and language of books. And they acquire literacy skills that can be transferred to their own writing. For example, having students copy a meaningful passage from a favorite book and look up words from the passage using the classroom library can teach students to look up words to use in their own writing. Having students become aware of the different parts of a book will help them to compose and construct student books that contain different parts, such as dedication pages and illustrations. By leading student discussions about books and stories that focus on characters and plot, teachers will familiarize students with these necessary elements of writing.

Authors as Mentors

Using authors as mentors, students learn a variety of writing styles and elements of craft. When Cynthia Rylant was asked how to teach writing to children, she answered, "Read to them. Take their breath away. Teach your children to be moved and you will be preparing them to move others" (Calkins, 1994, p. 251). As a child, Judy Blume loved the Betsy books by Maud Hart Lovelace. She liked to daydream about each book and make up her own stories about Betsy (Cullinan & Weiss, 1980). Newbery Medal–winning author Sid Fleischman read stories by Jack London and John Steinbeck, and without realizing it at the time, he chose them as his models (Olswanger, 2002) . Author and illustrator Ashley Bryan was fascinated by alphabet and counting books as a young child and discovered he could not only read these books but also create books like these on his own (Cullinan & Weiss, 1980). Author Lois Duncan claims that books were such an important part of her life that from early childhood on, she knew that someday she was going to write them herself (Cullinan & Weiss, 1980).

Share this information with students. Let them know that most authors had mentors and were influenced by the writing of others. Encourage students to investigate and experiment with styles and formats used in books by their favorite authors.

Audience as Focal Point

Even the youngest children realize that books are written for them to read or hear. They are the audience. But many students believe that the teacher is the only audience for their writings. This is understandable, because it is the teacher who usually reads and assesses a writing assignment. The writer needs to know who the audience is to convince the reader to continue reading. Mem Fox (1993) says, "Whenever I write, whether I'm writing a picture book, an entry in my journal, a course handbook for students, or notes to the milkman, there's always someone on the other side" (p. 9).

Consideration of the audience's identity helps the writer to focus on many elements of his or her writing. Writing to different audiences requires attention to appropriate content and tone, depending on the age or experience of the reader. The writer must consider questions the reader might have, then put them in order according to what the reader needs to know first, next, and so on. But most of all, to acquire a sense of audience, the writer must decide what to include, what to leave out (what the reader already knows), and how to present ideas.

It is important for teachers to point out to students the use of audience in literature. As you read stories, directions, bulletins, manuals, or letters to students, ask them to identify the intended audience. Guide them by asking what words in the text helped them make their decision.

In *Once Upon a Golden Apple* (Little & DeVries, 1991), familiar nursery rhyme and fairy tale characters interact with each other in new settings and contexts. After sharing this book with the class, ask students if the story would make sense or be enjoyable if they had never heard of the traditional rhymes and tales referred to in this book. Explain that the author assumed that the audience was familiar with the stories and characters.

After reading *The Berry Book* (Gibbons, 2002), ask students to identify the intended audience (children). Have them explain how they reached this conclusion (illustrations show children; in the recipe section it says, "Always have an adult help you when you bake or cook."). You might also point out that the presentation of oven temperatures in both Fahrenheit and Celsius indicates that the author has written for an international audience.

Or share a school bulletin with the class. Have them identify the audience in a passage like this: "Please wait until your class is called on the intercom and then have them line up and walk to the multipurpose room for the assembly."

Students should immediately know that classroom teachers are the intended audience.

Once students discover the reading–writing connection and the importance of audience to the text, they will begin to write with an audience in mind. Advertisements and "wanted posters" are written in a different style than invitations or a request for a raise in allowance. Journals, anecdotes, and reflections usually have a more informal tone than reports, summaries, or book reviews. The writer's concept of audience can have a strong influence on the style, mood, and format of the piece.

Here are some suggestions for writing activities intended for a specific audience:

- Write a letter to your parents asking for a raise in your allowance or a later bedtime.
- Write a letter to the school board asking for better school lunches.
- Write a thank-you note to school volunteers.
- Write an article for the school or PTA newsletter explaining and describing activities the class has been engaged in or completed during science, social studies, or language arts.
- Write a letter to the principal asking for longer recess time.
- Write a letter to next year's class, explaining what the students should expect of grade 4 and Mr. or Mrs. _____ (the teacher).
- Give directions to a younger child on how to make popcorn or a peanut butter sandwich.
- Give directions to a friend to your home from the school.
- Give directions to a new student to the gym, library, or cafeteria from your classroom.

Notebooks as Sources of Information and Inspiration

In *A Writer's Notebook* (1996), Ralph Fletcher says that a writer's notebook is a place to record things that make you angry or sad or amazed, to write down what you noticed and don't want to forget. He urges, "Write it down in your notebook before it slips your mind" (p. 13).

Helen Lester (1997) describes her "fizzle box" (p. 25) as a place where she stores names, funny words, and wise lessons. Nancie Atwell (1987) defines *territories* as a running list of possibilities for writing. This list can include topics already written about or what a writer might like to write about, genres that a writer has written or would like to try, and potential audiences. Territories are personal and specific, but when shared they may trigger a memory or ring a bell for someone else to add to their own list.

Eve Bunting (1995) writes in a notebook. She says she has written in waiting rooms and in her car during traffic jams. When she gets an idea and doesn't have her notebook, she writes on whatever she can find. She once wrote on the back of a play program and on the motion sickness bag on an airplane. I also keep a notebook handy. If I have an idea in the middle of the night, I turn on the light and write it down so I won't forget about it the next morning. Many writers collect articles from newspapers and magazines that appear odd, interesting, or unusual to them. A bit of news can often spark an idea for writing. Just cut it out and paste it in your notebook.

All writers need a place to keep ideas, thoughts, reactions, and words. As discussed previously, this place can vary in format. There might be lists of names, places, anecdotes, or interesting and unusual words. Phrases and short descriptions of people and events may be included to trigger a memory for future use. One caution, however, is to refrain from calling this place a "journal." Unfortunately, journals have recently received an almost negative connotation. "Do we have to write in our journals?" is often heard in classrooms. We have become overly focused on journal writing, especially with primary-grade students (Routman, 1996). Too often journals are brief and lifeless and, perhaps, overdone in some classrooms. Nevertheless, they can be a place for responses to literature and subject area content, especially mathematics and science, or may be used as a diary, providing a personal record. Personal journals promote fluency in both reading and writing, encourage risk taking, and provide opportunity for reflection. But I recommend that the writer's notebook, box, or collection be kept separate. Writers need a place to record their reactions to the world around them. And it should be readily accessible whenever they are writing.

Genres as Models for Different Styles of Writing

The use of a variety of good books in the classroom can have a profound effect on student writing styles. Saturation with literature directly influences writing by providing important models and a lively interaction between reading and writing (Lancia, 1997).

Reading matters in a writing workshop; when we let the work of other authors affect us in significant ways, we can expect our texts in turn to influence other participants (Calkins, 1994). Most children, either consciously or unconsciously, make use of literary models when they write. As they become familiar with story elements, terminology, and style, students begin to include them in their own writing. A kindergarten student once wrote and illustrated an alphabet book and gave it to me as a gift. He knew that I collected alphabet books so he used that genre, knowing it would be special to me. When I retired, a first-grade student gave me a picture she had drawn. It was patterned after the cover of a book from the Henry and Mudge series by Cynthia Rylant (see Figure 1). In class we had read nearly every book in this series during the course of the year. It was important to her, and she knew it was important to me.

Immersion in literature is one of the best ways to encourage students to write in a particular genre (Routman, 1994). But, students must hear and examine many books before they can be expected to participate in a class book or write one by themselves. As different genres and topics are introduced as read-alouds, they may also appear in student work. A child familiar with folk tales may develop a story in which a character tries unsuccessfully twice to solve a problem and succeeds on the third try. A child who knows many poems and rhymes might experiment with rhyming patterns. Favorite characters, words, and phrases may also appear in student writing. Students who have experience with realistic fiction and fantasy know how to begin and end a story, use plot and character development, and resolve the conflict. Students who have been exposed to nonfiction are able to organize text and illustration to impart information clearly. Students who read "how-to" books and recipes are able to give explicit and sequential directions. Those who read newspapers and magazine articles will be better equipped to compose factual and concise reports.

Reading as a Way to Acquire Vocabulary and Awareness of Style for Writing

Literature is a natural way to explore new vocabulary. One of the areas investigated by the National Reading Panel (National Institute of Child Health and Human Development, 2000) was vocabulary instruction. The Panel's report

FIGURE 1. A First Grader's Re-Creation of a Cover From a Favorite Book

states that most vocabulary is learned through reading or listening to others read. Several studies indicated that story readings helped teach children meanings of unfamiliar words and that read-aloud events helped children learn new words (pp. 4–21). Using new words in writing moves those words into the student's personal vocabulary. After I read Beatrix Potter's *The Tale of the Flopsy Bunnies* (1909) to a group of first graders, the word *soporific* came up in student conversation and writing. So did *bodacious* after *The Cowboy and the Black-Eyed Pea* (Johnston, 1992) and *affronted* after *The Tale of Tom Kitten* (Potter, 1907).

Author's style and story format also have a direct effect on student writing. A child who reads and has been read to will often begin a story with "Once upon a time" and end it with "The end" or "They lived happily ever after." Kindergartners and first graders put an illustration with text on each page; second and third graders begin writing stories with chapters. Alliteration appeared in fourth graders' writing after I read *Four Famished Foxes and Fosdyke* (Edwards, 1995) to the class.

Picture Books as Part of the Writing Curriculum

Because there is such a difference between what fourth- and fifth-grade students read and what they write, it is sometimes more difficult for them to make the reading–writing connection. Their writing is usually one to three pages of narrative or report, yet most are reading book-length novels. This connection is easier to make if students spend some of their time reading, studying, and listening to picture books, alphabet books, and poems (Calkins, 1994). The length of most picture books is similar to what these students are writing, and the time it takes to read them makes them an effective addition to the writing curriculum. Most can be read in five to ten minutes. Usually, only one copy of the book is needed.

Although novels can be excellent examples of good writing, using several picture books is a more efficient way to illustrate writing techniques and style. Many have an ageless quality about them. Teachers, students, and parents need to be reminded that picture books are not only for the very young.

Conclusion

The reading–writing connection is a strong one. Suitable reading material, when used creatively, can enhance the writing curriculum. Students who are exposed to many genres and styles of good literature are very likely to transfer these rich experiences to their own writing. Picture books can be used to acquaint children with a sense of audience, new vocabulary, and various literary devices. Reading aloud should be a daily activity in classrooms, not only for the enjoyment of hearing a good book, but to enrich the writing program. Using literature as an example or catalyst for a shared writing experience can provide students with ideas for class and individual books. In the next chapter, I will explore different writing experiences—shared, guided, and independent—for K–5 students.

CHAPTER 2

Teaching Writing and Genre Literature

Children, like adults, learn best in a supportive context.

—LUCY MCCORMICK CALKINS

Three levels of writing instruction are addressed in this chapter. While they are discussed individually, and are most often a progression, they can also be intertwined and interdependent. Shared writing is frequently the first story-writing opportunity for many children. It can be a relaxed time when teacher and students are gathered informally for a story and often develops naturally as a response to the book. Pattern and alphabet books are often used for shared writing experiences in kindergarten and first grade. All that is learned in shared writing is incorporated by students (with teacher guidance) in guided writing. This can occur as early as grade 1 but is most often the kind of writing that dominates grades 2–4. Nonfiction books, books featuring characters who write, and books used as prompts (see chapter 3) are excellent examples for the reports and stories that students write during guided writing. The ultimate goal is for students to use what they have learned in shared and guided writing and choose to write, taking the responsibility of the writing process, thus becoming an independent writer.

Shared Writing

Shared writing is a powerful approach for developing writing practice. For children in kindergarten and grade 1, especially those with limited literacy experiences, it is effective and nonthreatening to have them write shared stories patterned after books that have been read aloud. Lancia (1997) believes that adapting the ideas of established authors appears to be a significant stage in a child's writing development. In classrooms where students have the opportunity to interact with books every day, imitating and rewriting stories can be an enjoyable learning experience.

In shared writing, the teacher and students compose collaboratively, but it is the teacher who scribes, and thus models the conventions of writing. Although the shared writing technique is usually used in primary classrooms, it can also be effective with students in grades 4 and 5.

Shared writing makes it possible for all students to participate and encourages close examination of texts and words. This technique also utilizes verbal information from students who may be unable to write it themselves. Above all, it gives both the teacher and students confidence in their writing ability (Routman, 1994). Because children are focusing on the thinking–composing process without the additional task of transcribing, shared writing frees their imagination and helps them gain confidence in writing independently.

Shared writing can be used to compose class rules, letters, invitations, and reports. However, one of the most popular uses of shared writing is composing a class book modeled after a book that has been read to the class. The teacher starts by sharing a book with the class, usually an alphabet, counting, or pattern book. Then, the teacher leads a class discussion about how the book was written, pointing out elements such as style, format, rhythm, or rhyme. The class then decides the theme, characters, or focus for the class book. You might prompt students by asking, "What is the pattern in this book?" or "Is there a rhyming pattern? Let's see if we can figure it out, then we can use it in our rewrite." If sharing an alphabet book about frogs, ask, "What will we need to do to write about cats or birds?" The writing of a class book goes beyond the familiar language experience approach in which the teacher takes dictation from students; it is a negotiated process with meanings, choices of words, and topics discussed and decided jointly by students and teacher. Naturally, more teacher direction is needed at the beginning of the school year, especially if the students have never had a shared writing experience before. After the teacher transfers the story to paper, the students illustrate the pages. For kindergarten and the beginning of first grade, the teacher often prints children's words on labels so the children can copy them to their own pages, or the teacher does the writing on each page. Often, a different child illustrates each page of a class book. A variation is to photocopy the pages so that each child can get the entire book and illustrate each page.

Guided Writing

In *guided writing*, the student does the actual writing, and the teacher facilitates, guides, suggests, and encourages. Guided writing takes place any time students have the opportunity to write in the classroom. It may occur as a whole-class, small-group, or individual activity. And it can occur during any type of authentic writing: story, letter, journal, or report writing. Although the holding of the pen or pencil has been switched from teacher to student, collaboration remains a part of the process as long as the student needs it. Yet, the ownership of the writing is always the student's. The teacher's role is to help young writers discover their own abilities by providing opportunities for choice and peer response. Demonstrations and lessons on selecting and narrowing topics, drafting, organizing, revising, and editing, which are addressed in the next seven chapters, will help students move through the guided writing stage and become independent writers. As with all language learning, the role of guidance in writing is to lead the learner toward independence (Murray, 1989).

Independent Writing

The purpose of *independent writing*—like that of independent reading—is to build fluency; establish the writing habit; make personal connections; explore meanings; promote critical thinking; and use writing as a natural, pleasurable, self-chosen activity (Routman, 1994). As with most abilities, children reach the independent stage of writing at different times. Experience, interest, and talent are all factors that lead to independent writing, but teachers who provide rich opportunities to read and write through shared and guided writing can have a huge impact in helping students reach the independent stage. This is especially true in grades K–2. Students who have had shared and guided writing opportunities and many writing experiences are more likely to become independent writers in grades 3–5.

In independent writing, the student takes responsibility for the writing without teacher intervention or evaluation. The student often initiates the writing, while the teacher provides the time or opportunity. Independent writing can only occur after students have had practice, through shared and guided writing, and are able to work out the challenges in the writing process without help from the teacher. Some students will not reach this level during elementary school. For this reason, we must continue to provide instruction and guidance for those students who need it. Independent writing experiences may include journals, response logs, and reflections, as well as freewriting, which is uninterrupted writing of the student's choice.

Genres to Use in Writing Instruction

Discussed in this section are pattern books, alphabet books, nonfiction books, books about the writing process, and books using letters or journals. The first three types of children's literature are found in most classrooms and lend themselves to the different levels of writing described in this chapter. The last two types are worthy additions to the classroom library. At the end of this chapter is an annotated list of book titles that can be used effectively to show the versatility, complexity, and the many uses of writing. The list is organized by genre and offers suggestions for shared, guided, and independent writing experiences.

Pattern Books

By using simple language, rhyme, and repetitive language, *pattern books* allow children to anticipate what is coming next. Their subject matter is often familiar to children, and their text and illustrations are closely related. Use of predictable pattern books facilitates the introduction of writing instruction in kindergarten and grade 1.

Writing instruction in the primary grades often begins with rewrites, or innovations, based on favorite or familiar books, where language patterns are repeated frequently. Usually, innovations begin as whole-class or small-group books that might be based on a story plot or poetry pattern of a book previously read aloud to the class. By changing or expanding on a theme, character, or setting, the teacher and the students jointly construct the text in a shared writing experience, a stepping-stone to independent writing.

Students love to make books. In many schools, the student and class books are the most popular editions in the library. What child hasn't participated in their own version of Bill Martin Jr.'s *Brown Bear, Brown Bear, What Do You See?* (1983). When the class hears *The Popcorn Book* (1978) by Tomie dePaola, they may rewrite the recipe for popcorn with instructions for using a hot air popper or the microwave.

Figure 2 shows the pattern of *No, No, Joan* (1978) by Isaacsen-Bright and Margaret Holland, and Figure 3 provides a sample of a kindergarten class book

FIGURE 2. Pattern for *No, No, Joan*

_____ wants to

_____

_____.

" No, no, _____. "

_____ wants to

_____.

" Yes, yes, _____. "

FIGURE 3. Kindergarten Class Book

(continued)

FIGURE 3 (continued)

(continued)

FIGURE 3 (continued)

Buddy wants to show you his prize.

"No, no, Buddy."

Buddy wants to take a nap.

"Yes, yes, Buddy."

titled "No, No, Buddy," produced in a shared writing experience and based on the pattern book *No, No, Joan*. Figure 4 shows the pattern from *A House Is a House for Me* (1978) by Mary Ann Hoberman. The list of pattern and predictable books is endless. Often, the children themselves are the ones to suggest doing their own version.

Alphabet Books

Alphabet books offer a myriad of writing opportunities for children of all ages. Although they do help young children learn letters and sounds, they also contribute to visual literacy, phonemic awareness, and organization and sequencing

FIGURE 4. Pattern for *A House Is a House for Me*

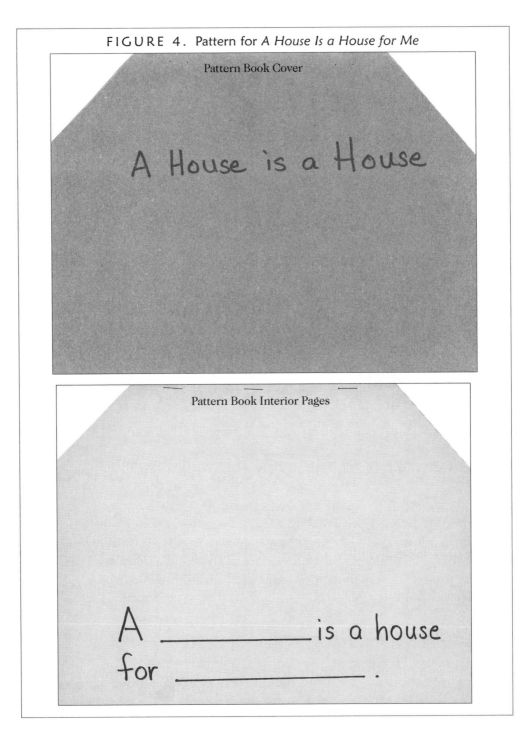

Pattern Book Cover

A House is a House

Pattern Book Interior Pages

A _____ is a house
for _____.

skills. They can be identification books, using key words to label objects or animals, or they can take on a more sophisticated or humorous tone, using information, riddles, and visual puns. Students in kindergarten or grades 1 and 2 can write a themed alphabet book, with each page devoted to a letter, and individual students can make the illustrations. Possible topics include a classroom alphabet book, naming objects in the room; a holiday alphabet book; the Earth Day alphabet; or a toy alphabet book, utilizing catalogs and toy store ads.

For students in grades 3–5, books like *Q is for Duck* (1980) by Mary Elting and Michael Folsom require more advanced skills. The object is to answer the question "why?" (because a duck quacks). (See Figure 5 for the pattern of this alphabet book.) *Alison's Zinnia* (1990), by Anita Lobel, requires an understanding of the pattern as well as research on flowers or whatever theme is chosen to complete each page. "Alison acquired an Amaryllis for Beryl. Beryl bought a Begonia for Crystal." By this time, most students figure out the pattern. On the last page, "Zena zeroed in on a Zinnia for Alison." When using this pattern, be sure to use the names of students in the class. I had read the book many times before a student pointed out that only girls' names are used in this book. We then discovered

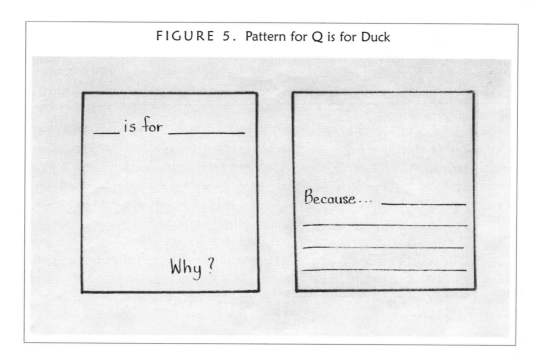

FIGURE 5. Pattern for Q is for Duck

that Anita Lobel gives equal opportunity to boys in *Away From Home* (1994). The pattern is similar. An innovation of this book requires research on the names of cities throughout the world. "Adam arrived in Amsterdam. Bernard ballooned in Barcelona."

A fifth-grade class wrote the "Harry Potter ABC," a favorite to write and read. Each page was devoted to a character, place, or object from the popular series, followed by a two- or three-sentence explanation. This book was one where it was not difficult to find a word for *Q*. "Q is for Quidditch, a game played with seven players on broomsticks, with four balls: a Quaffle, two Bludgers, and the Golden Snitch. Harry was the Seeker and his job was to catch the Snitch."

Writing alphabet books can cover other curriculum areas. For social studies, have students write about a state, province, region, or country. You might create a colonial alphabet book or one on resources or immigrants. Jerry Pallotta's alphabet books, such as his *Icky Bug Alphabet Book* (1986), cover many science concepts. Because traditional alphabet books have little or no information about the word on each page, Pallotta began writing "informational alphabet books," requiring a great deal of research. He has written books about bugs, flowers, insects, snakes, airplanes, fish, and frogs. Students can work individually or in groups to research information for each letter.

Nonfiction Books

Some children, for whatever reason, are unwilling to share a personal story or experience. If this is the case, it is effective to steer them toward expository, or nonfiction, writing. Students with lower literacy abilities also tend to do better with expository text because they can research the topic rather than pull something from personal experience. I believe this is also one of the reasons many struggling readers gravitate to nonfiction books. They can get information but don't have to draw from their own experience. All students need experience with nonfiction books and writing, but it is especially useful for those who struggle with literacy.

Kamberelis (1999) found a relationship between children's classroom contexts and the extent and quality of their expository, or informational, writing. Research by Korkeamaki, Tiainen, and Dreher (1998) suggests that, given appropriate instruction and scaffolding, second-grade children can engage in research using informational texts as a source of data and information for writing. Teachers need to expose students to a wide variety of nonfiction if they expect them to do expository writing.

The simplest form of expository writing is the *concept*, or "all-about," book. It is often a child's first introduction to nonfiction. Specific information is given about an object, food, or animal, accompanied by illustrations. *Food to Eat* (Peters, 1995), a Houghton Mifflin Little Reader, is an example of the concept book, with each page devoted to one food: "This is an orange. This is a banana." Scholastic First Discovery Books and Capstone Press's Pebble Books are series of nonfiction books that give more information, with a few sentences on each page.

As students progress to more complicated nonfiction books in grades 4 and 5, expository text dominates school reading and writing. Expository is different from narrative, or fiction, writing not only in structure, but also in format. Informational books have headings, photographs, captions, charts, graphs, and bold print. Students who are exposed to these books often use some of these details in their own writing. Life-cycle books such as *One Bean* (1998) by Anne Rockwell and *My Puppy is Born* (1991) by Joanna Cole are good models for writing. Short biographies such as David Adler's *A Picture Book of Amelia Earhart* (1998) and *Talkin' About Bessie* (1998) by Nikki Grimes are excellent examples of biographies for grades 3–5 because they offer a "slice of life," an appropriately sized model for children rather than a long birth-to-death account.

Gail Gibbons has written many nonfiction picture books for children, such as *From Seed to Plant* (1999). They are colorful, appealing, and easy to read, and they offer factual information and illustrations about specific topics. They are excellent models for writing reports. Many of us recall elaborate covers, relief maps, and other visual extras from reports we did as students. I loved doing reports on countries because my mother was a travel agent, and I always had access to colorful brochures. I'm ashamed to admit it, but I once latch-hooked a map of Idaho for my daughter's social studies project! Such attempts at nonfiction often result in superficial handling of the material. By using good literature models, teachers can show students that it is the content, organization, and format that are important.

Books About Writing

Don't forget to expose children to literature that features writing. Books about the writing process and the making of a book, as well as biographies of favorite authors, are available for grades K–5. In *If You Were a Writer*, by Joan Lowery Nixon (1988), Melia's mother tells her, "If you were a writer you wouldn't *tell about* what happened in a story. You'd think of words that *show* what is happening. You'd use words that let people see what you see." Hearing about a real author who struggles with revision is often much more effective than anything we as teachers can say to get across that point. In *Author*, Helen Lester (1997) uses the same words to describe her frustrations as a writer in second grade and as an adult. She also compares her teacher to her editor. Children need to know that writing is difficult and that it takes perseverance.

Books Using Letters or Journals

A number of books written for elementary school children feature letter writing, journals, and characters who write. These formats easily lead to student writing activities. For example, Amy Hest (1995) tells the story of 11-year-old Katie Roberts, who uses her private notebook as a diary. No one is allowed to see what's inside. Especially not her mother! Her entries tell the entire story. Student writers can use a similar format. Reading comprehension can be demonstrated by writing letters to and from characters in a book. Social studies can be enhanced by having students write journal entries as an historical figure or by a fictitious character living in a specific era or area. Ideas for writing projects can be borrowed from many of these books.

Conclusion

Once the teacher feels that students are comfortable with shared writing, they can begin guided writing. During guided writing the teacher demonstrates and conducts minilessons that help the students learn to draft, revise, and edit their writing. Only after practice and success with guided writing can the teacher expect students to begin and reach an independent writing level.

The use of pattern books in the early grades is an effective way to introduce young students to writing. Using an alphabet book format provides all elementary-grade students the opportunity to write using themes, information, and curricular areas. Because expository, or nonfiction, text starts to dominate school reading and writing in the upper elementary grades, teachers need to introduce this genre early to all students. The youngest students in kindergarten and grade 1 can write concept books, while students in grades 2–5 begin researching and writing reports and biographies. Books about the process of writing and about characters who write can serve as examples to children of the many uses, importance, and complexity of writing.

Children's literature is often written about topics with which children are familiar. In the next chapter, I will discuss the importance of children using their own knowledge and experiences in their writing.

ANNOTATED LIST OF CHILDREN'S LITERATURE

Pattern Books

Borden, Louise. (1989). *Caps, hats, socks, and mittens. A book about the four seasons.* (Lillian Hoban, Illus.). New York: Scholastic.

> This book starts with winter, goes through the seasons, and ends up again at winter. Have students write about each season during that time of year. I usually have them categorize each page into things to eat, wear, and do during the season, as well as a page for holidays and weather. (Grades K–1)
>
> Winter is hot cocoa, soup, oatmeal, hot cider, and chili.
> Winter is snowsuits, scarves, mittens, hats, and earmuffs.
> Winter is sledding, skiing, skating, snowballs, and snowmen.
> Winter is snow, ice, sleet, wind, and cold.
> Winter is Christmas, New Year's, Martin Luther King, Hanukkah, and Kwanza.

Casey, Patricia. (1994). *My cat Jack.* Cambridge, MA: Candlewick.

> Simple words and large drawings describe Jack as he starts his day: "My cat Jack is a yawning cat./He's a stretching-down cat./He's a stretching-up cat." Students can write innovations using another type of pet or about their own pet. (Grades K–2)
>
> My dog Rags is a barking dog.
> He's a scratching dog.
> He's a curling-up dog.

Charlip, Remy. (1992). *Fortunately.* New York: Trumpet Club.

> The pattern in this book alternates between good (with color illustrations) and bad (black and white) luck. Ned is invited to a birthday party in Florida while he is in New York, but a friend loans him an airplane.... When the plane runs out of gas, he parachutes out: "Fortunately, there

was a haystack on the ground./Unfortunately, there was a pitchfork in the haystack." (Grades K–5)

Use this as a model for opposites. Children can take a familiar story or folk tale and turn it into this format. For the *Three Little Pigs*, students wrote,

Fortunately, the first little pig built a house of straw.
Unfortunately, the wolf blew it down.

Fowler, Allan. (1991). *How do you know it's winter?* Chicago: Children's Press.

This "Rookie Reader" describes winter with simple text and photographs. Using this model, students can write about all the seasons. (Grades K–1) One class wrote the following:

In Spring
The air gets warmer. Snow melts. Grass sprouts. Trees get leaves. Flowers bloom. Baby animals are born. The days get longer. I like spring.

Hoberman, Mary Ann. (1986). *A house is a house for me.* (Betty Fraser, Illus.). Richmond Hill, Ontario, Canada: Scholastic TAB.

This classic describes all kinds of houses or containers, always returning to the refrain. Students must understand the rhyming pattern. "A hill is a house for an ant, an ant./A hive is a house for a bee./A hole is a house for a mole or a mouse./And a house is a house for me!" (Grades K–1)

For innovations I have used a house-shaped pattern for students to write and illustrate on (refer to Figure 4 on page 18).

Isaacsen-Bright and Holland, Margaret. (1983). *No, no, Joan.* (Steve Romney, Illus.). Worthington, OH: School Book Fairs.

On each page, Joan the cat wants something (to eat, to see the yarn, to explore the closet, etc.). Turn the page and Joan has done something very naughty ("No, No, Joan."). At the end, Joan finally finds something to do (take a nap) that won't get her into trouble. (Grades K–1)

I have had students write similar stories about my cats, their cats, even a cat of my mother's that I told them about.

Lee, Dennis. (1974). *Alligator pie.* (Frank Newfeld, Illus.). Toronto: Macmillan of Canada.

This book of poetry patterns invites variations. Students must understand the rhyming pattern in the first poem, "Alligator Pie": "Alligator pie, alligator pie,/If I don't get some I think I'm gonna die./Give away the green grass, give away the sky./But don't give away my alligator pie." (Grades 1–2)

One class wrote,

Alligator jelly, alligator jelly,
If I don't get some I think that I'll be smelly.
Give away the spinach, give away my belly,
But don't give away my alligator jelly.

Martin, Bill, Jr. (1983). *Brown bear, brown bear, what do you see?* (Eric Carle, Illus.) New York: Henry Holt.

In this classic pattern book, originally published in 1967, each answer leads to the animal on the next page. (Grades K–1)

A class innovation was as follows:

Black bird, black bird, what do you see?
I see a brown worm looking at me.

Numeroff, Laura Joffe. (1985). *If you give a mouse a cookie.* (Felicia Bond, Illus.). New York: Harper & Row.

This popular circular story invites rewrites: "If you give a mouse a cookie,/he's going to ask for a glass of milk./When you give him the milk,/he'll probably ask you for a straw." At the end, the mouse is thirsty, so he'll ask for a glass of milk and want a cookie to go with it. (Grades 2–4)

I have had students write,

If you give a kid a book, he's going to read it.
When he reads it, he's probably going to tell his friend about it.

My favorite was written by a group of third graders:

If you give a teacher a class, she'll take attendance.
When she takes attendance, she'll send someone to the office.

Alphabet Books

Bayer, Jane. (1984). *A my name is Alice.* (Steven Kellogg, Illus.). New York: Dial.

"A my name is Alice and my husband's name is Alex./We come from Alaska and we sell ants./Alice is an ape. Alex is an Anteater." This familiar jump-rope rhyme, in alphabet form, is a natural to use for social studies, requiring research on cities or countries. Use names of children in the class. (Grades 1–3)

Cahoon, Heather. (1999). *Word play ABC*. New York: Walker & Company.

Illustrations are visual puns: "bare (bear) feet"; "jay (bird) walk"; "pantry (a tree with pans as branches)". Very funny for the young child, this book offers a challenge for older students to imitate. (Grades 1–5)

Darling, Kathy. (1997). *ABC dogs*. (Tara Darling, Illus.). New York: Walker & Company.

Each page has photographs of puppies and full-grown dogs representing a letter of the alphabet. Fact boxes list each breed's vital statistics as well as information about the job they were originally bred to do. For innovations, students can write about cats, wild animals, or pets. (Grades 3–5)

Elting, Mary, & Folsom, Michael. (1980). *Q is for duck: An alphabet guessing game*. (Jack Kent, Illus.). New York: Clarion.

This book is a unique alphabet guessing game. Facts about animals offer help to solving the riddles ("Q is for duck. Why? Because a duck quacks."). (Grades 1–3)

Grover, Max. (1993). *The accidental zucchini: An unexpected alphabet*. San Diego, CA: Browndeer Press.

Grover makes ordinary objects become fresh and new. "Apple autos" are cars that look like apples. "Ice-cream island" looks like a giant sundae. An innovation of this book requires using two words not usually associated with each other and producing a visual image. (Grades 3–5)

Harrison, Ted. (1982). *A northern alphabet*. Plattsburgh, NY: Tundra Books.

This alphabet book of northern Canada is also a puzzle, story, and game book. The illustrations tell a story, and the author challenges the reader to use the words that border each page to write a story. Students can use one or all of the ideas from this book to make their own about a state, province, or area that they are studying. (Grades 3–5)

Kreeger, Charlene, & Cartwright, Shannon. (1978). *Alaska ABC book*. Homer, AK: Paws IV Publishing.

> Each page describes two things native to or associated with Alaska ("King crab in a kayak"; "Polar bear in a parka"). For social studies, students can write, using a similar format, about their own state or province. (Grades 3–5)

Lobel, Anita. (1990). *Alison's zinnia*. New York: Greenwillow.

> This book is about flowers' and girls' names. The pattern is girl-verb-flower, all beginning with the same letter of the alphabet. ("Alison acquired an Amaryllis for Beryl. Beryl bought a Begonia for Crystal.") For science, students can research different flowers. (Grades 2–5)

Lobel, Anita. (1994). *Away from home*. New York: Greenwillow.

> This book is about cities' and boys' names. The author uses a picture postcard format to journey to various cities of the world. The pattern is boy-verb-city, all beginning with the same letter of the alphabet. Students can research cities of the world. (Grades 2–5)

Pallotta, Jerry. (1986). *The icky bug alphabet book*. (Ralph Masiello, Illus.). Boston: Quinlan Press.

> Colorful illustrations and descriptive paragraphs represent an alphabet of bugs. This, and all of Pallotta's books, are excellent examples of writing for science. Have students use the same format for their own books or have each student do one page for a class book. (Grades 3–5)

Nonfiction Books

Adler, David A. (1986). *A picture book of Amelia Earhart*. (Jeff Fisher, Illus.). New York: Holiday House.

> Interesting, informative picture book about the often unconventional first woman to fly across the Atlantic Ocean. (Grades 2–4)

Cole, Joanna. (1991). *My puppy is born*. (Margaret Miller, Photog.). New York: Morrow.

> From birth to eight weeks, readers follow the development of Dolly, a Norfolk terrier. Simple text accompanies color photographs. (Grades K–2)

Collard, Sneed B., III. (1998). *Our wet world: Exploring earth's aquatic ecosystems*. (James M. Needham, Illus.). Watertown, MA: Charlesbridge.

> Each page describes an aquatic ecosystem (salt marsh, seagrass meadow, coral reef). Information includes location, plants, and wildlife of the system. Use this as a model for report writing. (Grades 4–5)

Curtis, Neil, & Greenland, Peter. (1992). *How bread is made*. Minneapolis, MN: Lerner.

> Photographs and text describe the making of bread, from the wheat on the farm to the bakery. Use as a model for "how-to" books requiring research. (Grades 2–3)

Freeman, Marcia S. (1999). *Pine trees*. Mankato, MN: Pebble Books.

> Each page has a photograph and a description of a pine tree (cone, bark, etc.) While the text is very simple, this book has a table of contents, index, and glossary. Students can use this format for reports. (Grades 1–2)

Gibbons, Gail. (1999). *From seed to plant*. New York: Scholastic.

> Text and illustrations describe seeds, plants, and how they grow. Pollination and seed scattering are also explained. Additional information about plants and a project are included at the end. Students can model life-cycle reports on this book. (Grades 1–3)

Grimes, Nikki. (2002). *Talkin' about Bessie: The story of aviator Elizabeth Coleman*. (E.B. Lewis, Illus.). New York: Orchard Books.

> Biography of the first African American female pilot, told in imagined monologues. The form is fiction, but the story itself is based on fact. This is a format that students can use for biographies. (Grades 3–5)

Marzollo, Jean. (1993). *Happy birthday, Martin Luther King*. (J. Brian Pinkney, Illus.). New York: Scholastic.

> This picture book biography has a simple, informative text. The author includes a foreword for parents and teachers. Although the book begins with Dr. King's birth and very briefly describes his childhood, the main focus is on his inspirational leadership. Use this book to illustrate a "slice of life" biography. (Grades K–3)

Rockwell, Anne. (1998). *One bean*. (Megan Halsey, Illus.). New York: Walker & Company.

> This concept book shows and explains the development of a bean seed. Use as a model for life cycles. (Grades K–1)

Sandler, Martin W. (1995). *Presidents*. New York: HarperCollins.

> From George Washington to Bill Clinton, both the public and private lives of the presidents are described, with photographs from the Library of Congress and presidential libraries. Rather than a section on each president, biographies are within categories based on groups of the youngest, those with pets, number of children, and so forth. Use this book as a model for including personal anecdotes with facts in report writing. (Grades 4–5)

Simon, Seymour. (2000). *Seymour Simon's book of trucks*. New York: HarperCollins.

> Each page describes a type of truck and what it is usually used for. Large, color photographs make this a favorite. Students can do innovations of this book on cars, airplanes, boats, or machinery. (Grades K–2)

Thimmesh, Catherine. (2000). *Girls think of everything. Stories of ingenious inventions by women*. (Melissa Sweet, Illus.). Boston: Houghton Mifflin.

> This collection of stories tells of ingenious inventions by women, what inspired them, and how they turned their ideas into innovations that have made our lives simpler and better. Each story can be used as a model for report writing. (Grades 4–5)

Wynn-Thomas, Nell. (2001). *The farm* (Little Readers Series Book 3: Early Emergent Collection). Boston: Houghton Mifflin.

> This concept book of farm animals ("A cow is on the farm. A horse is on the farm.") can be used as a model for innovations. Students can write about the zoo, the ranch, the rain forest, or the jungle. (Grades K–1)

Books About the Writing Process

Borden, Louise. (2001). *The day Eddie met the author*. (Adam Gustavson, Illus.). New York: Margaret K. McElderry.

When an author visits his school, third-grader Eddie hopes he will be able to ask his question, "How do you write books that have parts meant for me?" This picture book sends an important message about how we all have stories inside us. (Grades 2–4)

Bunting, Eve. (1995). *Once upon a time*. (John Pezaris, Photog.). Katonah, NY: Richard C. Owen.

Eve Bunting shares her story of becoming an author in this easy autobiography. She tells how she gets and organizes ideas, and she explains why she writes "sad" books. (Grades 1–3)

Christelow, Eileen. (1995). *What do authors do?* New York: Clarion.

In cartoon style, this picture book includes discussion of writer's block, revision, and creativity while showing the details of how a book gets illustrated and published. It also recommends sharing writing with others and belonging to a writers' group. (Grades 3–5)

Clements, Andrew. (1999). *The Landry news*. (Salvatore Murdocca, Illus.). New York: Simon & Schuster.

In this novel, a fifth-grade girl posts a note on the bulletin board challenging her burned-out teacher to *teach* them. Realizing that he hasn't been really teaching for years, Mr. Larson challenges the class to create a newspaper. As the class learns about freedom of the press, their teacher nearly loses his job. Students can get ideas from this book about publishing a class newspaper. (Grades 4–5)

Clements, Andrew. (2002). *The school story*. (Brian Selznick, Illus.). New York: Scholastic.

Sixth-grader Natalie's mother is an editor, whose firm is looking for a school story to publish. Natalie, feeling that she probably knows more than most adults about school, decides to write one. With the help of her friend Zoe, she assumes a pen name, gets a post office box, and the fun begins. Of course she sends the manuscript to her mother. This novel offers good advice about writing. (Grades 4–5)

Creech, Sharon. (2001). *Love that dog*. New York: HarperCollins.

> Jack is supposed to write a poem about a pet, but he doesn't have a pet and he hates poetry. With the subtle help of his teacher and a poem by Walter Dean Myers, Jack learns to love and write poetry. (Grades 3–5)

Danziger, Paula, & Martin, Ann M. (2000). *Snail mail no more*. New York: Scholastic.

> In the sequel to *P.S. Longer Letter Later*, the two authors again assume the characters of Tara and Elizabeth, best friends who no longer live in the same area. The girls correspond by e-mail now. The authors of this book actually wrote it by sending chapters back and forth to each other. (After Danziger wrote one chapter, she sent it to Martin, who wrote the next chapter.) This is an excellent format for student writers. After pairing up and deciding on characters and plot focus, they can use this method to write a story. (Grades 4–5)

Duke, Kate. (1996). *Aunt Isabel makes trouble*. New York: Dutton.

> In this second book about storyteller Aunt Isabel and her niece Penelope, Kate Duke not only outlines a story plot but also throws in some twists and turns. This is an excellent example of story grammar (a predictable structure or pattern of events that create the properties of a story) and predictability. It can also be used as a minilesson on story grammar. (Grades 2–3)

Kehoe, Michael. (1993). *A book takes root: The making of a picture book*. Minneapolis, MN: Carolrhoda.

> This book focuses on the actual production of a book after the author submits it to the publisher. Color photographs show printing plates, the press, and explain the four-color process. A glossary is included. (Grades 3–5)

Kropp, Paul. (2002). *What a story!* (Loris Lesynski, Illus.). Markham, ON: Scholastic Canada.

> Sara can only come up with excuses when her teacher gives a writing assignment. Finally her teacher lets her write about a topic of her choice. This easy reader has an important lesson about prompts and free choice. (Grades 1–2)

Lester, Helen. (1997). *Author: A true story*. Boston: Houghton Mifflin.

> The author draws parallels between her struggles with writing as a young child and the struggles many writers have. She gives writing tips, including a wonderful visual example of revision. (Grades K–5)

Nixon, Joan Lowery. (1988). *If you were a writer*. (Bruce Degan, Illus.). New York: Four Winds Press.

> The mother in this picture book is an author. When asked how she writes a story, she describes finding ideas, using words that show rather than tell, and finding the right words. This book covers many of the six traits of writing. It is useful in emphasizing the vocabulary of literacy. (Grades 1–4)

Ryan, Pamela. (1993). *Chasing the alphabet: The story of children's author Jerry Pallotta* (an About the Author Book). Boston: Shining Sea Press.

> In this biography of Jerry Pallotta, readers discover that he was frustrated with alphabet books when reading to his young daughter and decided he could write different ones. So, at age 32 he became an author, starting out with a book based on his childhood experiences on the beach in Massachusetts. He went on to write many more and also designed author and illustrator trading cards. This book offers valuable information about the importance of careful research, as well as ideas and tips for writing alphabet books. (Grades 3–5)

Stevens, Janet. (1995). *From pictures to words: A book about making a book*. New York: Holiday House.

> Illustrator Janet Stevens puts herself in this picture book, surrounded by imaginary characters, as she walks the reader through the process of writing and illustrating a book, from ideas and sketches to the finished product. Although humorous, this book offers valuable suggestions about writing, including story grammar and organization. (Grades 2–5)

Books Using Letters or Journals

Ada, Alma Flor. (1994). *Dear Peter Rabbit*. (Leslie Tryon, Illus.). New York: Atheneum.

> This picture book goes behind the scenes and provides glimpses into the lives of favorite folk tale characters through the letters they write.

Students should be familiar with *The Three Pigs*, *The Three Bears*, *The Tale of Peter Rabbit*, and *Little Red Riding Hood* to enjoy this story. (Grades K–2)

Ada, Alma Flor. (2001). *With love, Little Red Hen.* (Leslie Tryon, Illus.). New York: Atheneum.

Lives of folk and fairy tale characters intermingle as they write letters to each other. Did you know that Goldilocks is Farmer McGregor's daughter? Students should be familiar with *The Little Red Hen*, *The Tale of Peter Rabbit*, and *The Three Bears* to fully appreciate this picture book. (Grades K–2)

Ahlberg, Janet, & Ahlberg, Allan. (1986). *The jolly postman, or, other people's letters.* Boston: Little, Brown.

This is another book of letters. Students should be familiar with *The Three Bears*, *The Gingerbread Man*, *Hansel and Gretel*, *Jack and the Beanstalk*, *Cinderella*, and *Little Red Riding Hood*. This format can be used during a folk tale unit. Children can find similarities or differences in tales, then write letters to and from characters. For instance, I have had students suggest that the wolf in *Little Red Riding Hood* and *The Three Pigs* is the same wolf. Little Red and the pigs can then correspond with each other about their experiences. (Grades K–2)

Ahlberg, Janet, & Ahlberg, Allan. (1995). *The jolly pocket postman.* Boston: Little, Brown.

This book features real letters in pockets written to and from nursery rhyme, folk, and fairy tale characters. To fully understand and enjoy this book, students should be familiar with *Alice in Wonderland*, *Little Miss Muffet*, *The Wizard of Oz*, and *The Gingerbread Boy*. (Grades K–2)

Cleary, Beverly. (1984). *Dear Mr. Henshaw.* (Paul O. Zelinsky, Illus.). New York: Yearling.

Cleary uses humor and letters to an author in this Newbery Medal–winning novel to tell the story of a young boy who is struggling with his feelings for his father, who left the family. There are also some good writing tips. (Grades 3–5)

George, Jean Craighead. (1993). *Dear Rebecca, winter is here*. (Loretta Krupinski, Illus.). New York: HarperCollins.

> In letters from a grandmother to her granddaughter, George explains the winter solstice in simple, poetic terms that are easily understood by children. (Grades K–2)

Hest, Amy. (1995). *The private notebook of Katie Roberts, age 11*. (Sonja Lamut, Illus.). Cambridge, MA: Candlewick.

> Katie's journal entries, drawings, and letters reveal feelings about her father's death, her mother's remarriage, and having to leave New York to live on a ranch in Texas. (Grades 4–5)

Hest, Amy. (1998). *The great green notebook of Katie Roberts: Who just turned 12 on Monday.* (Sonja Lamut, Illus.). Cambridge, MA: Candlewick.

> Third in a trilogy, Katie's journal reveals that, although she is adjusting to a stepfather and twin brothers, she is struggling with growing-up pains. Then an accident dramatically changes things. (Grades 4–5)

Teague, Mark. (2002). *Dear Mrs. LaRue: Letters from obedience school.* New York: Scholastic.

> Feeling that he has been unjustly punished, Ike the dog writes hilarious letters to his owner, Mrs. LaRue, from the Igor Brotweiler Canine Academy. Younger children will enjoy the slapstick humor, while older students will appreciate the word and visual puns. (Grades K–5)

Williams, Vera B. (1989). *Stringbean's trip to the shining sea*. (Jennifer Williams, Illus.). New York: Scholastic.

> Each page is a postcard sent by Stringbean Coe, his older brother Fred, or both, as they take a car trip from Kansas to the Pacific coast. For fourth- or fifth-grade social studies, students can use this format to write an account of a trip through their state, province, or country. This requires research on key areas and points of interest, as well as utilization of map skills. (Grades 2–5)

CHAPTER 3

Writing From Experience

Writing is more than living...it is being conscious of living.

—ANNE LINDBERGH

Choosing a Topic

"I don't know what to write about." Sound familiar? Many students are stuck before they get started. They need encouragement and, often, a suggestion for a topic. The best advice teachers can give students is to write about what they know. That is the recurring theme of all the author talks I've attended. Mr. Ratburn gives Arthur the same advice in *Arthur Writes a Story* (Brown, 1996). When students choose their own topics, about real interests and experiences, their writing becomes personal and meaningful. When the topic matters to them, students will be more willing to invest their time and effort.

Most authors say they get their ideas from personal experiences or observations. That's not to say that everything is based on a real situation, but the idea came from an event, word, or something that sparked a question or idea. Each of Patricia Reilly Giff's books is based on personal experiences or tales students related during her 20 years as an elementary school teacher (Pope & Michael, 2003). Cynthia Rylant put many memories of her childhood in her first book, *When I Was Young in the Mountains* (1982), based on her life as a young girl living with her grandparents in West Virginia. According to his website, www.paulkropp.com, Canadian author Paul Kropp draws most of his characters and situations from real life. Then he uses his imagination to fill the gaps when reality and research can't provide what's needed. Eve Bunting (1995) gets most of her ideas from interesting things she's read about in newspapers, magazines, or books and then she researches them. According to Richard Peck (2002), Newbery Medal–winning author of *A Year Down Yonder* (2000), "We get our ideas from memories, usually of other people—and even from other people's memories and books" (p. 73).

Finding Out More About a Topic

Teachers know that children come to school with different levels of experience and background knowledge. Some children have more access to a variety of topics than others. A child who has a parent, relative, or friend who is an artist or musician will be able to write what they know about art and music; a child who has experience with animals will have an easier time writing about them than the child who has not had that experience. Students who have a great deal of difficulty finding the right topic may benefit by a one-to-one conversation with the teacher. Ask questions such as, "Do you have any hobbies? Are you interested in any particular animals or insects? What kinds of activities or sports do you like?" If the student tells you that riding his bike is something he enjoys, then ask, "Where do you like to ride? How do you feel while riding? Can you tell about a specific incident (trip, race, crash, etc.) that was special or exciting?" Have students tell you about something that really interests them—it could be anything from turtles to hockey. If the topic is self-selected, they most likely already know something about it.

To help students find more information about a topic, you may want to use a K-W-L graphic organizer to increase understanding and provide a framework for writing (Ogle, 1986). This technique models for students the active thinking involved in reading for information (what they know about a topic, what they want to know, and what they learned after reading/listening) in three vertical columns (see Figure 6). Students often find that using notes or charts is an easy way to organize material for writing.

Another way to find out more about a topic is to interview classmates or family. There may be an expert in the room or at home. Interviewing helps the writer to explore questions that the reader might want answered. Have children share topics with classmates. If a student is interested in hedgehogs, a classmate might share that she or someone else in the school has a hedgehog, giving the student an opportunity to ask questions, and perhaps even visit and observe the animal. When family members or neighbors are interviewed as a source of information, students can take notes and bring their ideas to class, or even write part of their composition at home.

FIGURE 6. K-W-L Graphic Organizer		
K—What we know	W—What we want to find out	L—What we learned and still need to learn

Reprinted from Ogle, D. (1986). K-W-L: A teaching model that develops active reading of expository text. *The Reading Teacher, 39,* 564–570.

Providing Prompts

A *prompt* is a broad idea or suggestion intended to spark a memory or incident for the writer. It must be broad enough so that all students will be able to connect with it and write from their own experience. It must also be free of bias and allow all students to respond, regardless of gender, ethnic, or socioeconomic status. For instance, the prompt "Favorite Place" could be a park, store, restaurant, or grandma's porch. "The Perfect Vacation" could be an account of an actual trip or one the writer dreams of.

Teachers may need to provide prompts to students, after rewrites and innovations, to help them write original text. Providing prompts is part of the natural progression from shared writing to guided writing, with the teacher encouraging, supporting, and monitoring student writers. Prompts are helpful for students who are not yet able to find their own writing topics—those with limited background experience and those who claim they don't have anything to write about. Although most proponents of writer's workshop advise against giving topics for writing, I feel prompting is appropriate for students who sit and stare at a blank page. Teachers can help these students get started by providing suggestions. The ultimate goal is to have students think of themselves as authors and go through their day looking for possible writing ideas (independent writing). But for many, we must provide help along the way. (Prompts are also discussed in chapter 4, but there they are used as examples of narrowing topic and finding important details.)

Use your imagination in creating writing prompts and remember to be open to student suggestions. It is important to have students choose one event or object and then expand it—by describing why it was important, how they felt, and the resolution if there was a problem—to avoid merely having a list of things. Kindergarten and first-grade students may have only a few sentences, while those in grades 2 and 3 write one or two paragraphs. Students in grades 4 and 5 should have an introduction, followed by two or three paragraphs with pertinent and related details, and a conclusion. The following are examples of writing prompts that I have used with students:

- Think of a friend. Tell a story about him or her. Focus on one incident. (Grades 1–5)

- Stories of my life. Remember when you were happy, angry, proud, or scared. Describe the event, reactions, and why it is important to you. (Grades 2–5)

- My favorite place (Grades K–5), teacher (Grades 3–5), or food (Grades K–1).

- I'll never forget the time…. Describe the event, how you felt, and why it was memorable. (Grades 3–5)

- My most valuable possession that was not bought in a store. Emphasize value in nonmonetary things. (Grades 3–5)

- Things to do on a rainy day. (Limit to one thing for grades K–1 and to two or three things for grades 2–5.)

- Things I've learned in school (or in grade ___). This is useful at the end of the school year. (Grades K–5)

- One invention I could never live without. Describe it and explain why it is so important to you. (Grades K–5)

- My worst food (or trip, movie, present, etc.). Why didn't you like it? (Grades K–5)

- If only it (pet, refrigerator, playground) could talk…. Give the object's point of view. (Grades 3–5)

The most beneficial way to set the stage for a prompt is by sharing literature that relates to the prompt. At the end of this chapter, I have provided an annotated list of books that are effective sources of writing ideas. After a brief description of each book, I have offered a writing prompt that relates to the book.

Introducing Assignments

Students are at times required to write on a specific topic for assessment purposes. Therefore, they need to be able to recognize the difference between a *prompt,* which is a general stimulus, and an *assignment*, which is a specific request for information. In my classroom, a prompt was a very broad idea to use as a starting point. In fact, if students wanted to write about something completely different, I nearly always allowed it. In contrast, to fulfill an assignment, students must closely adhere to the given topic. For example, our school district gave a prompt to specific grade levels each year and then assessed student writing results. If a student wrote about something else, the rater might comment "off prompt," but the writing was assessed and the topic choice did not affect the assessment. The district was interested only in the quality of the writing. On the other hand, for our required state assessment in language arts, the writing portion was an assignment. If the writing was "off topic," the entire writing sample was scored as zero.

Give students practice with an assignment after they are comfortable writing original text, with or without a prompt. Because most formal writing assessments begin in grade 4, I usually introduce assignments by grade 2. Knowing that students would be required to write on a specific topic, I gave them at least one writing assignment each trimester. The following examples of assignments are similar to ones that may be found on some tests:

Assignment 1: Choose one kind of animal you know something about. It might be a pet, an animal you have seen at the zoo or on television, or an animal you have read about. Think about it for a while. Write a description of the animal including what it looks like, what it eats, and where it lives. Be sure to include what makes this animal interesting to you.

Assignment 2: All of us have broken a rule at some time in our life. We have done something we wish we had done differently. Choose one time when you broke a rule. Describe what you did, why you did it, and what happened afterward.

Include what you would change if you had the opportunity to do it over again. What have you learned and how are you different as a result of breaking that rule?

Assignment 3: Imagine you found a box on your way home. The box was sealed tight, so you took it home. When you got home, you opened the box and found something unusual. Describe what you found and what you did.

Assignment 4: Imagine that you drank a magic potion, and then suddenly you started to become smaller and smaller. Finally, you were no larger than a fly. What did you do?

Do you notice a pattern in these? They are wordy, which makes them more confining and difficult for many children. I do not recommend using these more than occasionally, because they do not allow for individual interest or choice and require the writer to respond to a specific, narrow situation. They are especially difficult for students with limited experience and abilities, and the number of words in the instructions is simply overwhelming for some. However, because they are similar to ones that may be found on some tests, we have to prepare children by practicing assignments once in a while.

Sharing Writing With Others

Children need to share their writing with other students. Inform students that many writers say that they belong to a writers' group. Let students know that they should be able to get constructive criticism and suggestions from classmates. You must set specific guidelines so that sharing remains nonthreatening and nonjudgmental. The teacher must model genuine and helpful responses to the content of writing, so that students will know how to conference effectively with each other. Show writing samples on the overhead projector, read them aloud, and offer appropriate comments. The following are examples:

- This is a great beginning sentence. It makes me want to read more.
- The part about the dog eating the roast made me laugh, but I wonder how he got it off the counter.
- The ending surprised me. I can't figure out how they found the book. Maybe you need to add some clues.
- I could almost smell that apple pie in the first paragraph.

- I'm really confused about how the turtle got out of the bowl. Could you add some details?

Then ask students to comment on other pieces of writing on the overhead. Always practice together with the class before you have students work in groups or pairs. Eventually, students should be able to share writing with a partner and get constructive comments, suggestions, or questions about their work. Change pairs often. Good friends may be familiar with the event that is written about and, therefore, may not be able to make helpful comments. And some students are just better than others at giving suggestions. By changing partners, you can give all students the opportunity to work with someone who can genuinely help them.

Conclusion

Most authors write about what they know. They get their ideas from personal experiences, memories, and observations, and they record these ideas in a specific place. Their advice to students is nearly always to "write what you know and care about."

Some students need suggestions for writing topics. Broad ideas, or prompts, are intended to trigger a memory of a person, place, or event that students can write about. Sharing literature with students that is related to the prompt is especially helpful. Assignments are more specific than prompts; these should be practiced occasionally because students are sometimes expected to write within more strict parameters for required assessments. Students benefit by sharing what they have written with others, and teachers can provide nonthreatening formats for doing so.

The following six chapters will provide a closer look at teaching the writing process through the six traits of writing, as identified by Spandel and Stiggins (1997). In each chapter, I explain one of the six traits and then present examples, activities, student writing samples, assessment guidelines, and lesson plans for each trait. An annotated bibliography of children's literature accompanies each chapter. The next chapter discusses the trait of ideas and shows how teachers can help students find good ideas and details.

ANNOTATED LIST OF CHILDREN'S LITERATURE
TO USE WITH WRITING PROMPTS

Ackerman, Karen. (1989). *Song and dance man.* (Stephen Gammell, Illus.). New York: Knopf.

> Grandpa relives his vaudeville days by putting on a show for the children. Though he loved that time he says he wouldn't trade a million good old days for the days he spends with them. (Grades 1–4)
>
> **Prompt:** Think about an older person you know (grandparent, neighbor, friend). Write a story about some special time you have had together.

Allard, Harry. (1977). *Miss Nelson is missing.* (James Marshall, Illus.). Boston: Houghton Mifflin.

> The kids in Room 207 were misbehaving so Miss Nelson was forced to do something drastic. The next day, instead of the sweet Miss Nelson, the class was met by the wicked Miss Viola Swamp. (Grades 2–4)
>
> **Prompt:** Write about a time you had a substitute teacher.

Beard, Darleen Bailey. (1999). *Twister.* (Nancy Carpenter, Illus.). New York: Farrar Straus Giroux.

> Lucille and Natt brave the twister alone in the cellar while Mama goes to help their elderly neighbor. The storm passes as quickly as it came, and although there is damage, the family is thankful they are safe. (Grades K–3)
>
> **Prompt:** Think about a time when there was a storm. What did you do? How did you feel?

Birdseye, Tom.(1988). *Airmail to the moon.* (Stephen Gammell, Illus.). New York: Holiday House.

> Ora Mae is a strong-willed girl who finally loses her first tooth. But then she really loses it, or did someone steal it? (Grades 2–5)
>
> **Prompt:** Write about losing your first tooth.

Buehner, Caralyn. (2002). *Snowmen at night.* (Mark Buehner, Illus.). New York: Phyllis Fogelman.

What do snowmen do at night? Do they look the same the next morning? The illustrator adds to the mystery by hiding pictures in the paintings. (Grades K–3)

Prompt: Write a story explaining what you think snowmen or snow angels do at night.

Carlson, Nancy. (1999). *Look out kindergarten, here I come*. New York: Viking.

Henry is looking forward to his first day of kindergarten, but when he gets there he's not so sure anymore. Soon he realizes that it really is going to be fun. (Grades 1–3)

Prompt: Think about your first day of kindergarten. Write about how you felt and what you did.

MacLachlan, Patricia. (1994). *All the places to love*. (Mike Wimmer, Illus.). New York: HarperCollins.

On the day Eli is born, his grandmother holds him up to the window of the farmhouse so he will see all the places to love. Everyone in the family has a favorite place, and Eli discovers that they all have to do with home, family, and love. (Grades K–5)

Prompt: Write about your favorite place.

MacLachlan, Patricia. (2001). *The sick day*. (Jane Dyer, Illus.). New York: Random House.

Emily is sick, and her father stays home to care for her. Nothing seems to help her feel better until Father finds a way to turn the sick day into a special day. Then, Father gets sick. (Grades 1–5)

Prompt: Think about a sick day. What makes you feel better?

Oram, Hiawyn. (1998). *Badger's bad mood*. (Susan Varley, Illus.). New York: Arthur A. Levine.

Badger is in a bad mood for no reason, and his friends try to cheer him up. Mole figures out that everyone needs to be told they are appreciated, so he arranges a wonderful awards ceremony. Guess who gets all the awards? (Grades K–2)

Prompt: Tell about a time you were in a bad mood. What caused it? How did you get out if it?

Polacco, Patricia. (1998). *Thank you, Mr. Falker*. New York: Philomel.

Tricia has a terrible secret. No matter how hard she tries, letters get jumbled up and she can't read. By fifth grade, her classmates tease her and call her "dummy." Then her fifth-grade teacher recognizes her problem and is able to help her overcome it. (Grades 3–5)

Prompt: Think about a person who helped you learn how to do something. Write a story about it.

Russo, Marisabina. (1993). *Trade-in mother*. New York: Greenwillow.

Max's mother always says "no." He tells her about the mother he'd like to trade her in for. But his mother tells him she'd never trade him in. (Grades K–3)

Prompt: Describe the perfect mother.

Schwartz, David M. (1989). *If you made a million*. (Steven Kellogg, Illus.). New York: Lothrop, Lee & Shepard.

This picture book demonstrates the concepts of million, billion, and trillion in terms that children can understand. (Grades 1–4)

Prompt: If I had a million dollars....

Steig, William. (1995). *Grown-ups get to do all the driving*. New York: HarperCollins.

A child looks at the sometimes ridiculous world of adults. (Grades 2–4)

Prompt: What do grown-ups get to do that you would like to do? Why?

Stevenson, Suçie. (1987). *Do I have to take Violet?* New York: Dodd, Mead.

Elly resents having to take her little sister Violet for a walk. At first Violet pesters and annoys her, but they eventually have a very good time together. (Grades 3–5)

Prompt: Tell about a time you had to take a small child somewhere with you.

Viorst, Judith. (1972). *Alexander and the terrible, horrible, no good, very bad day*. (Ray Cruz, Illus.). New York: Atheneum.

Alexander is having the worst day ever. Everything goes wrong. Some days are just like that. (Grades K–5)

Prompt: Tell about a very bad day that you have had.

Waber, Bernard. (1972). *Ira sleeps over*. Boston: Houghton Mifflin.

> Ira is eager for his first sleepover at Reggie's until his sister keeps asking if he's going to take his teddy bear along. (Grades 2–5)
>
> **Prompt:** Write about your first sleepover or about a time when you were homesick.

Winch, John. (1997). *The old woman who loved to read*. New York: Holiday House.

> An old woman moves from the noisy city to the country so she will have peace and quiet to read. But country life is busier than ever, and she has so much work to do that it is winter before she finally has time to sit down and read. (Grades K–5)
>
> **Prompt:** Write about your favorite book.

Wyeth, Sharon Dennis. (1998). *Something beautiful*. (Chris K. Soentpiet, Illus.). New York: Doubleday.

> A little girl living in a ghetto has a hard time finding something beautiful in her neighborhood. But then she realizes that the friends, food, and music in her community are all beautiful. (Grades K–5)
>
> **Prompt:** Tell about something or someone beautiful in your neighborhood.

CHAPTER 4

Finding Good Ideas and Details

When you get a good idea, stay with it.

—JACQUE WUERTENBERG

The trait of ideas is the first of the six traits, each of which should be taught one at a time and covered thoroughly. Ideas are the foundation or starting point for writing, so it makes sense to start with them. Vicki Spandel (2001b) advises beginning with ideas and also explains that ideas will take the most time of all the traits. I always begin with ideas, and then have students work on the second trait, organization. It is then relatively easy to weave in the other traits (voice, word choice, sentence fluency, and conventions).

Every teacher knows the needs of her own class, but a rule of thumb for the amount of class time to take on each trait is one to two weeks. (More specific time frames are given under Sample Lessons in this chapter.) And remember that, although you will have your students actually write stories or reports at the end of the two weeks, the only trait that will be scored is ideas. Never score a paper for a trait that has not at least been introduced. After another trait is studied, you will score it along with ideas. You are building on past experience; therefore, once a trait has been introduced, you will always be scoring it.

When I first began using the traits with writing instruction, I went into classrooms for 30–45 minutes for five consecutive days, and then had the classroom teacher follow up on the lessons for as long as necessary. Because I was visiting many classrooms, by the time I came back to a particular class, the students were ready for another trait. Students need at least a basic understanding of each trait before moving on to another. Of course, if the entire school uses this approach, students will need only a review rather than an introduction at each grade level. It is important, however, to fully explain each trait to accommodate students who are new to the school and those needing extra help. This is a good time to enlist the help of members of the class who have knowledge of the traits to assist in instruction and demonstration.

The Role of Ideas in the Writing Process

Ideas are the reason for writing. They are what the author has to say: the purpose, central idea, or topic. If a prompt or assignment is given, the writer needs to look for a way to connect it to personal experience. The topic must be manageable, have a focus with quality details, and go beyond the obvious. The writer needs to show, rather than tell, these details and to use images and anecdotes to hold the reader's attention.

The writer's task is first to identify information important enough to capture in writing and then to make that information accessible, understandable, and penetrable to a range of key audiences (Spandel & Stiggins, 1997). Student writers often do not realize how important accurate information is to good writing. If they've done their research (whether it's based on reading, interviewing, or personal experience), drafting is relatively easy; if they have not, it's all but impossible. Further, seeking good information isn't just for research writing; it's also for fiction (Spandel, 2001b).

When teaching the trait of ideas, try to picture students looking at the world through a magnifying glass. You are trying to teach them to write with detail, with a sharp eye, with clarity, and with focus (Spandel, 2001b). Have students ask questions such as "What is the purpose?" and "Who is the audience?" when you read stories to them. Point out that good authors start with an idea, and then expand on it with relevant details and anecdotes. When students are writing, have them ask themselves what the reader will want to know.

Narrowing the Topic

Once the prompt, or general topic, for writing is established, that idea needs to be narrowed down to a more specific topic. Small topics work best. Small, focused topics are not only easier to write about but are more interesting (Spandel, 2001b). Both Barry Lane (1999) and Ralph Fletcher (1993) encourage writers to *write small*, but Fletcher also advises writers that in order to do that, they must also *think small*. The best things to write about are often the tiniest things. Not just a story about your puppy, but about the day you got him or the time he bolted out the front door and was lost for three hours.

In the elementary grades, a typical piece of student writing might be from three to five paragraphs or two to three pages in length. Using this length as a guideline, I ask the class if I can do a good job writing about my trip around the United States. Unfortunately, some will answer, "yes." I then explain that I could not give enough important details to make it interesting if I tried to tell about the entire trip. I then ask them to help me narrow it down. Could I write about traveling through Texas? Again, some will think this smaller topic will work, but I explain that Texas is very large and that perhaps I should focus on one city, San Antonio, or better yet, my visit to the Alamo. That is something I can tell in a few paragraphs by describing what I saw, felt, and experienced. I also might include short anecdotes about how small the Alamo looked surrounded by the city, or about how surprised I was that there were still fresh flower wreaths placed in remembrance of the fallen heroes.

Another question for students is, Can I write about my trip to the Alamo if I've never been there? Of course not. I have to experience it to write about it. However, could I write a report on the Alamo if I've never been there? Yes, but I have to do research to get the facts straight. This writing will take a different form, though, because it will not relate a personal experience.

The key to helping students narrow their topic is to demonstrate, then practice together and in groups, before expecting them to do it on their own. This is similar to Regie Routman's (2003) Optimal Learning Model: demonstration, shared demonstration, guided practice, and independent practice. For every strategy I introduce, I first demonstrate on the overhead projector, then I have the class participate in the activity while I write on the overhead. When I am confident that they understand, I have them work in pairs or groups. Only after they demonstrate the ability to do the task will I expect them to work independently. When you reach the point at which students are to begin writing, always check to make sure each one has a manageable topic. This may seem tedious, but it is a waste of their time and yours if you let them proceed with something that is too broad. In time, they will be able to confer with classmates and, eventually, be able to succeed on their own.

The following exercises show how to narrow the topic:

Pets (too broad)

Dogs (still too broad)

How to train a dog (maybe)

How I taught my dog to fetch (just right)

State (too broad)

City (still too broad)

Grandma's house (maybe)

Grandma's porch (just right)

Washington State (too broad)

Seattle (still too broad)

Pike Place Market (maybe)

Shop where they throw the fish (just right)

Winter Sports (too broad)

Skiing (too broad)

Sun Valley (maybe)

My first chair lift ride (just right)

Vacations (too broad)

Camping (too broad)

Cooking over a campfire (maybe)

The first time we made s'mores (just right)

To better illustrate the narrowing-down process, refer to local or regional areas, events, or sports that most of the class will be familiar with.

Selecting the Important Details

Ralph Fletcher (1996) urges writers to select the details that capture what's really important. Barry Lane (1999) writes, "When I was in school I thought details were just extra words to add in a story to make it better. I thought detail was decoration or wallpaper.... Details are not wallpaper; they are walls" (p. 42). Donald Murray (1984) explains that no matter what type of writing is being done—a science report, poem, term paper, business letter, short story, essay exam, film script, argument, newspaper story, or personal letter—the writer will capture the reader if the reader is given writing that is filled with concrete details.

Once the topic has been narrowed down, the writer must decide which details are important to include. If a student is describing a favorite doll and it is on a shelf with 20 other dolls, I should immediately be able to recognize it. Some distinguishing feature should set it out from the others. The skill lies in being able to choose between what's really important and what's not. I don't need to know that it is a toy and has arms and legs. But if a leg is broken, or is unique in some way, that's important. If a student is giving directions on how to plant corn or go to the gym, I should be able to follow those directions and get the desired result. Good writers anticipate questions the reader might have. Don't tell the obvious, but do tell what the reader wants or needs to know.

A surefire technique for getting important details is to clock the time for listing associations with a topic. To demonstrate to the class, appoint a timekeeper to tell you when one minute has gone by. When the timekeeper tells you to begin, start writing on the overhead projector as many words or phrases that come to mind about your topic. Stop when the minute is up.

During one class session, for the topic "Grandma's Porch," I wrote down the following details:

red squares	rocky chairs
fuchsias	snow angels
hummingbirds	white flowers
porch swing	railing
Grandpa	iced tea
flower box	

The rationale for this technique is that when students think of a detail immediately, it is an important one. What if students remember something later that is really important? That's okay. Let them know they can use it, that this listing is only a starting point. Do student writers have to use everything on the list? No. Some things might not fit with what they want to tell. Let them know that they can save it for another time or forget it. What if there are only a few words on a student's list? Give the student time to rethink the topic. Maybe the student really doesn't know enough or care enough about it to do a really good job.

Some teachers and students may prefer to use webs, outlines, or other brainstorming methods. The object is to list the important details. For the student who didn't know what to write about, this is a definite beginning. (The next chapter will discuss how to organize these details.)

Sticking to the Topic

Educator Mary Bigler says, "The main thing is to keep the main thing the main thing." This is good advice. After the topic is focused, stick to it. The best way I know to teach sticking to the topic (and also main idea) is with Margaret Wise Brown's *The Important Book* (1949). The pattern (see Figure 7) for the following text is simple:

> The important thing about a spoon is that you eat with it. (topic sentence)
>
> It's like a little shovel. You hold it in your hand. You can put it in your mouth. It isn't flat, it's hollow and it spoons things up. (supporting details)
>
> But the important thing about a spoon is that you eat with it. (restate the topic sentence)

I demonstrate on the overhead projector, using the following example:

> The important thing about Mrs. Olness is that she loves to ski. (I usually give them a choice of two or three topics)

The next step is to give at least three, but no more than five, supporting details. As I add a detail, I ask the class if it supports my topic.

> She skis nearly every weekend during the winter. (they approve)
>
> She was a ski patroller for 26 years. (they approve)

Then I throw in a zinger:

> She has a cat named Nicky.

They all say "No!" Then I argue by telling them it is true. I really do have a cat named Nicky. I have never had a class allow me to include this sentence. The point, of course, is that even though I do have a cat named Nicky, I am writing about skiing. We then agree on something such as the following:

> Every year she takes a ski vacation.

We then add the last line:

> But the important thing about Mrs. Olness is that she loves to ski.

THE IMPORTANT BOOK

The important thing about_____

is that he/she _____

_____

_____

_____

_____

But the important thing about _____

is that he/she _____

_____

Now I ask students to write an important thing about themselves. Some may need suggestions such as helper at home, good student, friend, kind person, big brother or sister, athlete, musician, and so on. Following the *The Important Book* pattern is a wonderful activity for a class book at the beginning of the school year. Each page describes an important thing about a member of the class. Don't forget to add your page, too. One year, when the principal at our school retired, I had a fourth-grade class write "The Important Thing About Mr. Myers." It was one of his most treasured gifts. This format also works for social studies and science (water, cities, regions, or industry), but it requires careful research. The possibilities are endless, and it really works!

Another way to illustrate sticking to a topic is to bring in easy chapter books. The books in the Henry and Mudge (1987) series by Cynthia Rylant have a central theme and characters. But each of the three to four chapters is about a specific incident. *Three Stories You Can Read to Your Cat* (1997) by Sara Swan Miller has three separate stories about the same cat. Picture books have been produced by taking one incident or chapter from a classic novel, such as those based on Betty MacDonald's Mrs. Piggle-Wiggle (1947) series and the Little House (1932) books by Laura Ingalls Wilder. These all feature one concise story, or one event, with relevant details.

Showing, Not Telling

Good writers use specific examples, not general terms. When they describe something, they use the five senses. "Writing from the heart is not just about writing from the heart. It's about writing from and *for* all the senses. Readers want to feel, they want to taste, they want to smell" (Aronie, 1998, p. 143). Not, "I liked going to Grandma's after school," but, "Grandma met me at the door with a smile and a hug, and the aroma of freshly baked cookies filled the room."

Students need to be taught to recognize *telling* statements and to change them into *showing* ones. This skill is invaluable when revising ones own writing. After much practice, all you'll need to do is tell them to check their work for *telling* and they'll know what and how to revise.

To demonstrate this skill to students, put a *telling* statement on the board or overhead:

My room was messy.

Ask students to describe what a messy room might look like. (unmade bed, clothes and toys on floor, etc.). Have them help you turn this into a *showing* statement.

I had to force open the door because a football and backpack blocked it. How am I ever going to find my soccer shirt in that mountain of clothes on the unmade bed?

Put another telling statement on the board or overhead:

> The store was crowded.

Ask students if it tells or shows. Then have them describe what a crowded store might be like and help you revise the statement:

> It was impossible to move through the aisles. I was bumped into three times before finally finding the end of the checkout line.

After many examples, have students work in pairs or groups, turning telling statements into showing ones. Remind them to start by listing what it would look, sound, smell, or feel like, and what people would say or do in order for it to show, rather than tell. I also add that the *telling* word cannot be used in the revision. Following are several examples:

Original statement:	It was stormy. (can't use *stormy*)
Description:	rain, wind, dark, no electricity, lightening, thunder
Revision:	Rain pelted against the windows as branches from a nearby tree brushed the side of the house. All of a sudden there was a loud boom, a flash of light, then the entire house was dark.
Original statement:	Harry was forgetful. (can't use *forget*)
Description:	late, forgot his lunch or trumpet, no homework
Revision:	At least twice a week Harry's mother ran down the street to the bus stop, bringing his lunch or backpack. He rarely had his trumpet on band days, and one time he actually wore his pajama top to school!
Original statement:	The movie was boring. (can't use *boring*)
Revision:	I heard whispers, yawns, and even snoring. Then a few people started leaving the theater.
Original statement:	We had a good time. (can't use *good time*)
Revision:	First we played cards. Then we had pizza and watched movies of when we were little. We laughed till we cried!
Original statement:	She looked weird. (can't use *weird*)
Revision:	Nothing seemed to match or fit. Fashion was obviously not important to her.

Original statement:	Bill was a terrible cook. (can't use terrible)
Revision:	The hamburgers were either raw or charred. Even the dog wouldn't eat most of what Bill cooked.

And one of my favorite student responses:

No one ever asked Bill to a potluck.

(More examples of showing rather than telling are given in chapter 6.)

Using Books as Examples of Ideas

The only way to raise the quality of writing in a school is to create, share, and celebrate the specific criteria for that quality with everybody on a regular basis (Lane, 1996). Even very young children can listen and look for one colorful word or the most exciting sentence or a line that has interesting sounds or the scariest phrase (Frank, 1995). According to Fletcher and Portalupi (1998),

> Many of us have proceeded with the assumption that students will eventually internalize the qualities of good writing if we keep exposing them to the best books around. This may be true. But...we argue that teachers need to take it one step further. In order to help young writers make the most of the literature they read, teachers also need to use explicit language to address specific issues of craft. (p. 10)

That is why it is important to share literature that exemplifies the trait you are teaching.

When focusing on the trait of ideas, look for books filled with details that have a clear and focused message, theme, or moral. Read books that have one central idea or an easy-to-follow story, with interesting images. As you read, ask students to tell you what they picture in their minds. And don't forget the illustrations. True picture books have important details in the pictures. You need both illustrations and text to tell the story. One cannot stand alone without the other. Alphabet books with a specific topic are examples of ideas (*The Flower Alphabet Book* [Palotta, 1988] or *Guinea Pig ABC* [Duke, 1985]). Nonspecific alphabet books are examples of word choice.

It is important to remember that these titles are ones that one person chose as examples of ideas. You might want to use some of them to illustrate other traits. Most books are strong in all traits or they would not have been published. But in some, the trait seems to "jump out at you." I once did a workshop for a school district on an island. Because I had to fly on a very small plane, I couldn't take the books to use as examples. Using the bibliography I sent, the principal purchased the books for the school library and had them available for me to use in my presentation. Imagine my surprise when I saw that each book had been marked on the cover with the trait I had designated in the bibliography. Although it is true that a book can illustrate a certain trait well, I caution against labeling a book for one trait. As I said before, you may want to use a book to emphasize a different trait. Over the years, I have switched books from one trait to another. Once, while reading a story aloud that I had read several times before, it occurred to me to use it for another trait. As you become familiar with the traits and using books to illustrate them, I guarantee this will happen to you. At the end of this chapter is an annotated list of books to use for the trait of ideas.

Assessing Writing

Because of its strong link to instruction, analytic assessment has soared in popularity over the past 10 years and is used widely. An analytical scale, scoring guide, or rubric is an attempt to define components or *traits* and to describe, using *criteria*, what each one would look like at each level of proficiency, ranging from beginning performance through strong performance. (Figure 8 presents a rubric for six-trait writing.) Analytical scoring also provides the strongest foundation for instruction because it affords a complete picture of writing and allows students to focus their revision on particular problems (Spandel, 2001b). Rubrics can do something grades alone have never accomplished: They can define quality. They give students the criteria and the terminology to respond to their own and others' work (Strickland & Strickland, 1998).

Many rubrics are available to use in evaluating student writing. Northwest Regional Educational Laboratory has rubrics for the 6 + 1 Trait Writing model on their website (see www.nwrel.org/assessments/scoring.asp), with number 5 being the highest rating and number 1 the lowest. Spandel (2001b) also describes a 6-point scale, explaining that "many educators prefer an even-numbered scale to avoid the 'midpoint dumping ground' associated with a score of 3" (pp. 56–57). But, she argues that whatever the numbering system, there will always be a great percentage of writers who will produce samples that fall into the midlevel, or developing, range.

FIGURE 8. Rubric for Six-Trait Writing

Rating scale	5	3	1
Ideas	Interesting, creative, makes you think; exciting, important details evident; topic not too wide	Creative, but doesn't catch your attention as much as it could; some important details, but needs more	Shows no originality; not interesting to read; no sense of adventure; doesn't make you think or want to read more
Organization	Events are well ordered; good use of time words (*then, next, finally*); catchy beginning, strong ending	Events are difficult to follow at times; has a good beginning but a weak ending, or vice versa	Events are not ordered at all; beginning and ending are both weak
Voice	Feelings are expressed well; voice matches tone of story (depending on what story is trying to do, scientific writing, etc.); good use of dialogue and dialects where needed	Some feelings are expressed well; switches between first and third person; voice doesn't match purpose of story very well	Cannot hear the writer's voice at all; no use of dialogue or dialect; no match between voice and purpose of story
Word choice	Strong words chosen, good use of adverbs and adjectives without overdoing it; age-appropriate words	Some strong words, but could have more; too many or too few adverbs and adjectives; words not appropriate for age of intended audience	No strong words; use of adverbs or adjectives is nonexistent or inappropriate
Sentence fluency	Good mix of short and long sentences; sentences don't all start with same word; variety of sentence structures used (statements, questions, quotations, and exclamations)	Lack of variety in sentence length and structure; many sentences start with same word	No variety in sentence length or structure; all sentences start with same word; when read out loud, there is no flow or rhythm to the piece
Conventions	Presentation is excellent; spelling and grammar rules are all followed; punctuation is near perfect	Some errors noted, but not too many; presentation is a little messy	Errors are extreme in number; presentation is messy, many cross-outs, no attempt made to make it look nice

Reprinted from Smith-D'Arezzo, W.M., & Kennedy, B.J. (2004). Seeing double: Piecing writing together with cross-age partners. *Journal of Adolescent & Adult Literacy, 47,* p. 400.

I have found it beneficial to have students use a simple checklist for evaluating their own work. The checklist can be on a chart in the room, on student desks, or in notebooks. Then I use a similar checklist for each trait. You may want to assign numbers 1–5 with 1 being the lowest and 5 the highest, or use a continuum beginning with *emerging* and ending with *capable*. Whatever you do, make sure that students understand how you assess their work. Students who know the traits are less confused when they receive feedback. If you have thoroughly covered the trait of ideas, students will understand what you mean if you tell them their paper needs more or less detail or suggest that they change telling statements to showing statements. It is most important for teachers to use the same writer's vocabulary in comments that they use during instruction. Share sample papers and demonstrate how you score or evaluate. Students need to know what a strong or weak paper looks like so they can recognize strengths and weaknesses in their own writing.

Sample papers may be obtained from the Northwest Regional Educational Laboratory website (see www.nwrel.org/assessment/scoringpractice.asp) or by trading with other teachers. If you choose the latter route, be sure that the papers used in your class do not reveal the writers' identities or are about an event or someone the students will recognize. This caveat is especially true for weak papers. Bring in other examples of writing such as directions, brochures, newspaper articles, and letters. Score them for the trait of ideas, and point out their strengths and weaknesses to students.

Another helpful way for students to become familiar with language that is used to assess writing is to have students review a book that has been read aloud. Have them tell what the book was about (not just a summary, but the theme or message). Have them find a phrase or sentence that comes closest to telling what the story was about. Once they are familiar with this activity, they can do the same with student samples and, eventually, with their own writing.

Student Checklist

- Is my topic narrow enough?
- Do I know and tell enough about my topic?
- Do I have important details?

- Did I show, rather than tell?

- Is my message clear?

When evaluating a paper for ideas, look for quality, not quantity. It is not the actual number of ideas or details but the effective use of information that makes a good piece of writing.

Evaluator Checklist

RATING: STRONG (5)

- The message is clear and concise.

- Writing is knowledgeable or from experience.

- Details are accurate and interesting.

- The writer shows, not tells.

- Most readers will learn something new by reading this.

Following is a student example from grade 5:

> Gillman Village (my favorite place)
> My favorite place is Gillman Village, in Issaquah. I go there with my grandma. When we go there the first shop you see is the Red Balloon. This place has many different things and gadgets to look at. When we're finished shopping there we go to the Stamp Shop, my favorite. Every wall has hundreds of stamps and inkpads, and when I see the colored paper, a big grin covers my face. I always find something I need in that store! Then Grandma wants to go to the yarn and craft store, for she's a crafty lady. Sometimes I laugh at her because she nearly buys out the whole store.
>
> By then our stomachs are growling so we stop at the Greek Café. After a delicious lunch, the sweet smell of the candy shop next door lures us in. I pick out a treat and Grandma always buys something to take home to my sisters and brother. Then it's time to shop some more. When grandma's purse is finally empty, and we have so many bags we can hardly carry them, we walk to the car. When we get to my house, Grandma tells me how much she loves me, gives me a kiss and a warm hug, and says that next time we will bring my sister, too.

Although the writer could still elaborate on some events, the composition has interesting details and shows, rather than tells. I would score this 4–5 in ideas.

RATING: DEVELOPING (3)

- Too general. Needs more details.

- The reader still has some questions.

- Predictable. No new information.

- Tells, but doesn't show.

- Equal strengths and weaknesses.

Following is a student example from grade 4:

> Michigan (favorite place)
> My favorite place is Michigan because I was born and raised there. Another thing is that my dad and all his family lives there. I like to go swimming in the lake that is close to our house. It's fun. You can have a barbecue.
>
> My favorite thing is to fish and I like to swim. I also like to run with my dog in the sand.
>
> One day my dad called to tell me that my dog died. I was so sad. I didn't want him to die because he was my favorite dog. I couldn't believe it. Now I have another dog at my mom's house but I still remember my other dog. My new dog is fine. I love him, too, but he won't replace my old one.

There is more telling than showing in this piece. The composition starts out like a list and is somewhat confusing. The writer needs to focus on one thing, perhaps the dog, and add details. I would score this 2–3 in ideas.

RATING: WEAK (1)

- Topic is random.

- Information is limited.

- A list of things.

- Message is not clear.

- Reader is confused.

Following is a student example from grade 3:

My favorite place

My favorite place to go is my friend's house, because he has a game boy and a Nintendo and his mom is nice. I like to ride bikes. He has a scooter. He gets to stay up late. We stay at my house a lot. It is fun at his house. Sometimes we go to my house. Once we got in trouble and I couldn't go to his house anymore. I miss him. We walk to school together and have fun.

This composition is a list, without a clear message. The writer does not focus on one incident. Most statements tell, rather than show. I would score this 1–2 in ideas.

Sample Lesson Plans

Although the needs of students are varied, and the teacher is the one who knows best how long it takes for most of the class to understand a concept, a suggested time frame might be to spend one or two days on narrowing the topic exercises and activities; at least one day brainstorming for important ideas; and one or two days on *The Important Book* and supporting details. Another week might be spent on the various activities aimed at showing, rather than telling. Read at least one book each day to illustrate your teaching objective. And remember to have students recap or recall the previous day's lesson before proceeding with a new activity.

Following are two sample lesson plans that I have used after introducing the trait of ideas, and covering the material previously outlined. The sample for grades 2–5 is intended to take from three to five days to complete. Remember to read a story related to the topic and have students work on their own writing each day.

Sample Lesson Plan (Grades K–1)

DAY 1

1. To develop a sense of favorite food, read *More Spaghetti, I Say* (1987) by Rita Gelman.

2. Have students list as many favorite foods as they can. Record on a chart.

3. Brainstorm and record on chart words used to describe food (*delicious, sour, tart, spicy, crunchy, smooth*).

4. Have students pick a favorite food to write about. Encourage them to think about why they like it, who cooks it the best way, and when they like to eat it.

5. Have students use these details to write about their favorite food (depending on the age and ability of students, some may have a word or a sentence with a picture).

DAY 2

1. Share another book on favorite food such as *Lunch* (1992) by Denise Fleming.

2. Have students return to their draft and make revisions (refer to chart from Day 1 for spelling).

3. Depending on their ability, students can copy and illustrate their draft. These can be individual works or can be put into a class book ("Favorite Foods of Room 3").

For students in kindergarten and grade 1, it is best to focus on growth and change, rather than numbers. Look for details in illustrations such as facial expressions, petals on flowers, clothing, and so on.

Sample Lesson Plan (Grades 2–5)

DAY 1

1. To develop a sense of place, read *All the Places to Love* (1994) by Patricia MacLachlan. Discuss places that are important to each of us. Ask students what the book makes them picture in their minds.

2. Have students list as many memorable places as they can. They can be public or private, but should be personally important to the individual.

3. Share lists with the class. Encourage *borrowing* (all good writers do this).

4. Have students pick one place from the expanded list that they would like to write about and list all the details (words and phrases) they can in one minute. Remind them to write down what they see, hear, smell, and feel.

5. Have students use their details to write a draft of their memorable place, writing on every other line to save room for revision and addition.

DAY 2

1. Share another book on the topic of place such as *The Cabin Key* (1994) by Gloria Rand.

2. Share sample papers on overhead (not from your class). Assess each one for ideas. What makes the strong ones work? What could make each paper stronger?

3. Have students help you revise one of the weaker papers.

4. Share another piece of writing (sample or one of yours). Have students work with partners to create a revision.

5. Have students return to their own draft from Day 1. They should actually assess their own work for ideas and revise.

DAY 3

1. Read aloud a book about a special place, such as *Homeplace* (1995) by Anne Shelby.

2. If you feel the class still needs practice with revision, share a different sample and have them help you revise it.

3. Have students share their own revised draft with a partner. Partners should point out questions they may have or what they would like to know more about. Students should double-check for telling statements.

4. Have students finish their revisions.

Conclusion

Teach the traits separately, take adequate time on each one, and begin with the trait of ideas. By using activities aimed at narrowing the topic, focusing on important details, and using showing statements, students will learn to apply these strategies when writing. When students understand the vocabulary of the traits and have had practice evaluating sample papers, they will be better equipped to revise their own writing. One of the best ways to demonstrate the trait of ideas to students is to share literature that has the criteria of the trait. Books that have a central theme, focused details, and a strong message are excellent examples to use for the trait of ideas.

For ideas, students should automatically think *narrow topic* and *details*. They should write about what they know and care about or have carefully researched. Their writing should have a purpose. They should also be able to check their work for telling statements and be able to revise them to show, rather than tell.

With new rubrics and other evaluation guides for teachers, considerable progress has been made in recent years toward improving writing evaluation in the classroom. The use of a student checklist that corresponds to the evaluator's checklist is helpful to students, both for checking their writing and for understanding teacher comments.

ANNOTATED LIST OF CHILDREN'S LITERATURE TO USE FOR IDEAS

Brett, Jan. (1997). *The hat*. New York: Putnam.

Using both text and detailed illustrations, Brett tells the story of a hedgehog who finds a woolen stocking, and the fun begins. Young children will enjoy the picture clues given by Brett on each page. This picture book shows the importance of details in illustration as well as in text. (Grades K–2)

Bunting, Eve. (1998). *Your move*. (James Ransome, Illus.). San Diego, CA: Harcourt Brace.

Knowing that he is a role model for his younger brother, James decides that being part of a gang is not the right choice to make. Although in picture book format, the longer text and subject matter make this title more appropriate for older students. The message is very strong and clear. (Grades 3–5)

Carlson, Nancy L. (1991). *Take time to relax*. New York: Viking.

Tina and her family are always rushing in all directions. But one morning it snows, and all the roads are closed. They find that they really enjoy just being together. Although the word *relax* never appears in the text, the message is obvious. (Grades K–4)

Cole, Joanna. (1987). *The magic school bus: Inside the earth*. (Bruce Degen, Illus.). New York: Scholastic.

This picture book and all the magic school bus books are excellent examples of writing about one topic and using details, in both text and illustration. Actual student reports are also featured. (Grades 2–4)

Fox, Mem. (1985). *Wilfrid Gordon McDonald Partridge*. (Julie Vivas, Illus.). New York: Kane/Miller.

Making connections is the theme of this picture book that tells the story of a young boy and his best friend, an elderly woman. By trying to help her, he learns about memories. This is a fine example for a prompt on "Something I'll always Remember." (Grades 1–3)

Gibbons, Gail. (1997). *The honey makers*. New York: Morrow Junior Books.

The author uses a picture book format to inform readers about beekeeping. The beekeeper's duties are described in a yearbook in the back of the book. A page of interesting facts is placed at the end. Use as an example of researching and writing reports. (Grades 3–5)

Gibbons, Gail. (2000). *Cats*. New York: Holiday House.

Readers learn about the history of cats and the many types of breeds, as well as how they communicate with others and how to care for them. This picture book includes diagrams and labels. Another example for report writing. (Grades 1–3)

Gibbons, Gail. (2002). *The berry book*. New York: Holiday House.

Berries are eaten by humans and many birds and wild animals. Facts about berries, as well as a recipe for jam, pie, and ice cream are included in this picture book. Use as a model for reports and including important details about a specific topic. (Grades 1–3)

Howard, Ellen. (2002). *The log cabin church*. (Ronald Himler, Illus.). New York: Holiday House.

Elvirey can't understand why building a church in the Michigan woods is so important to Granny. But when the neighbors arrive and everyone joins in to help, she realizes what she's been missing. The church itself isn't as important as the friendship of neighbors. This book is an example of one story about one event, and it is also an example for a "Favorite Place" prompt. (Grades 2–4)

London, Jonathan. (2002). *Loon lake*. (Susan Ford, Illus.). San Francisco: Chronicle.

> The author and illustrator intersperse facts about loons and other lake creatures in this gentle story about a father and daughter on a camping trip. This picture book is a good model for writing about a specific incident or place. (Grades 1–3)

MacDonald, Betty. (1997). *Mrs. Piggle-Wiggle's won't-take-a-bath cure*. (Bruce Whatley, Illus.). New York: HarperCollins.

> Adapted from the *Mrs. Piggle-Wiggle* books, this picture book tells about one incident, from one chapter, when the lovable Mrs. Piggle-Wiggle advises Patsy Brown's parents how to get her to take a bath. Another example of one event or incident. (Grades 1–3)

Martin, Jacqueline Briggs. (1998). *Snowflake Bentley*. (Mary Azarian, Illus.). Boston: Houghton Mifflin.

> This Caldecott Medal–winner tells the story of Wilson Bentley, who spent his life finding a way to take photographs of snowflakes. Although the main text is a fictionalized account of Bentley's study of snowflakes, factual information is inserted in the borders on most pages. This book exemplifies both a story and a report. (Grades 2–5)

Meddaugh, Susan. (1995). *Hog-Eye*. Boston: Houghton Mifflin.

> In this picture book, a little pig gets on the wrong bus and doesn't make it to school. Instead, while taking a shortcut through the woods, she is kidnapped by a hungry wolf. Realizing that this wolf cannot read, she outsmarts him and gets away. The underlying message in this book is the importance of knowing how to read. (Grades K–5)

Miller, Sara Swan. (1997). *Three stories you can read to your cat*. (True Kelley, Illus.). Boston: Houghton Mifflin.

> An easy reader with three chapters, this book tells separate events about the same cat. This is a good example of writing about one incident. (Grades 1–2)

Potter, Beatrix. (1902). *The tale of Peter Rabbit*. New York: F. Warne.

> In this classic, Peter faces many dangers. The moral is obvious. Obey your mother, and you won't get into trouble. (Grades K–2)

Powell, Consie. (1995) *A bold carnivore: An alphabet of predators*. Niwot, CO: Roberts Rinehart.

> This alphabet book is about predatory animals. Each page has details in text and illustrations about a carnivore. This book is an excellent example for report writing. (Grades 2–5)

Pringle, Laurence P. (1997). *Naming the cat*. (Katherine Potter, Illus.). New York: Walker & Company.

> When a stray cat adopts the family, everyone tries to think of a name for the new pet. As the cat gets into one predicament after another, the reader realizes long before the family that they should name it "Lucky." This picture book explains how the cat got its name. (Grades K–2)

Rahaman, Vashanti. (1997). *Read for me, Mama*. (Lori McElrath-Eslick, Illus.). Honesdale, PA: Boyds Mills Press.

> Joseph wants nothing more than to have Mama read to him. But he and the reader both discover that it isn't because she is too busy, but because she cannot read. The underlying message of this picture book is the importance of literacy. (Grades 2–4)

Rand, Gloria. (1994). *The cabin key*. (Ted Rand, Illus.). San Diego, CA: Harcourt Brace.

> A description of the family cabin in the woods, this picture book includes details and anecdotes. The book is an example of the kind of writing we would like to see from students writing about their favorite place. (Grades 2–5)

Shelby, Anne. (1995). *Homeplace*. (Wendy Anderson Halperin, Illus.). New York: Orchard Books.

> This picture book tells the story about the importance of a house built in 1810 and how it and the generations that lived in it grew and changed. Use as an example for a "Favorite Place" prompt. (Grades 2–5)

Schoenherr, John. (1995). *Rebel*. New York: Philomel.

> A true picture book, the text and illustrations both tell the story of a Canada Goose family with one gosling who turns out to be a rebel. Factual information is given in the text, while the illustrations show the rebel getting in dangerous situations. The actions of the rebel are never explained, but the underlying message is apparent. (Grades 1–3)

Wilder, Laura Ingalls. (1994). *Dance at Grandpa's*. (Renée Graef, Illus.). New York: HarperCollins.

> Adapted from one chapter of *The Little House* books, this picture book tells the story of a trip to Grandpa's house in the big woods. The text has details and events about the trip and the dance. (Grades 1–3)

CHAPTER 5

Organizing Ideas

Writing a first draft is like trying to build a house
in a strong wind.

—WILLIAM FAULKNER

After the topic has been narrowed and important details have been established, these details must be organized. *Organization* is the internal structure, the "skeleton of a piece" (Spandel & Stiggins, 1997, p. 35). Ideas and organization provide the foundation of writing. Once students have an idea and details, they are ready to proceed with the actual organization of their writing. This stage of the six-trait model corresponds to prewriting and drafting in the writing workshop.

Basic Framework: Beginning, Middle, and Ending

The writer must find a beginning place that both entices the reader to continue reading and provides an understanding of what is to come. Details should be put in an order that will help the reader follow a logical sequence. And, the writer must craft a conclusion that both provides a resolution and invites the reader to think about what might happen next (Spandel & Stiggins, 1997). When teaching the trait of organization, I always start by telling students to think "good beginning, middle, and end." The beginning and the end are the two most important parts. Think about the universality of "Once upon a time" and "They lived happily ever after." I often tell students that organization is the framework for writing. They must take their ideas (details) and place them in a framework that best tells the story or gives the information. The details should be linked, built to a turning point, and then resolved.

When writing expository text, the following model is useful: State what you're going to explain. Tell in sequence. Include all the essential information, leaving out details that are not necessary. It is important to note that this framework is a starting point and may change as the piece is written. Patricia O'Conner (1999) advises writers to "expect their organization plan to stretch and change as they go along. It's supposed to. If it doesn't, there's something wrong" (p. 25).

Using Organizing Techniques

Many organizing techniques are available to teachers and students. I like to teach a number of these techniques and then let students choose one that works best for them. A simple technique for primary-grade students is to fold a blank piece of paper into thirds. (I can tell you from experience that it is easier for you to fold 25 papers than to instruct young children how to do it.) The first column on the left is for the beginning. A picture, word, or sentence can be placed there. The middle column is for recording what happens in the middle, and the column on the right is for the end (see Figure 9). This page can then be used by the student

---

FIGURE 9. Sample Graphic Organizer for the Basic Framework for Writing: Beginning, Middle, and End

Beginning	Middle	End
getting up in the dark	putting boat in the water	cleaning and cooking the fish
long car ride	catching three fish	

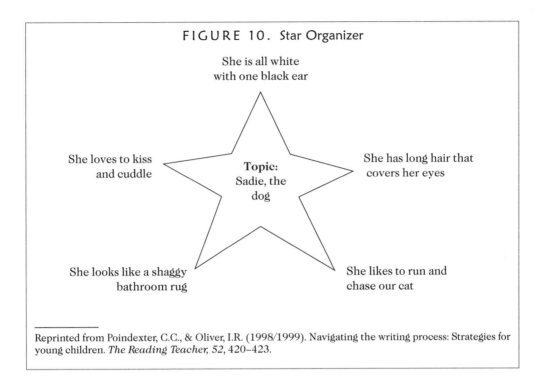

FIGURE 10. Star Organizer

She is all white
with one black ear

She loves to kiss
and cuddle

Topic:
Sadie, the
dog

She has long hair that
covers her eyes

She looks like a shaggy
bathroom rug

She likes to run and
chase our cat

Reprinted from Poindexter, C.C., & Oliver, I.R. (1998/1999). Navigating the writing process: Strategies for young children. *The Reading Teacher, 52,* 420–423.

as the framework or outline for his or her story. A variation of this technique is to take the words that have been brainstormed for important details and place them in the appropriate column. Sorting designates that the words or phrases will be in the beginning, middle, or end of the story.

For younger students, Poindexter and Oliver (1998/1999) offer the star organizer, which helps students organize their thoughts when writing a description (see Figure 10). When the teacher asks them to describe something or someone, students write on a blank star form. They write the topic in the middle of the star and their descriptions at each of the five points. Then they use their descriptions, or notes, around the star as a guide for the paragraph they write.

Another writing framework application for primary grades presented by Poindexter and Oliver is the step map, which is useful for writing directions or sequencing (see Figure 11). For example, children observe while the teacher makes a peanut butter and jelly sandwich. Then they describe what they saw, and the teacher fills in the step map with their descriptions. Finally, the students use the step map as a guide to write a paragraph about making the sandwich.

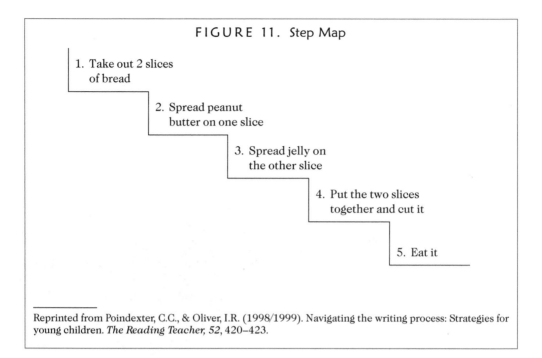

FIGURE 11. Step Map

1. Take out 2 slices of bread

2. Spread peanut butter on one slice

3. Spread jelly on the other slice

4. Put the two slices together and cut it

5. Eat it

Reprinted from Poindexter, C.C., & Oliver, I.R. (1998/1999). Navigating the writing process: Strategies for young children. *The Reading Teacher, 52,* 420–423.

Fifth-grade teacher Gregg Kurek has students design a book jacket for their story and write a summary as it would appear inside the jacket (see Figure 12). Creating the book jacket requires students to organize the story, taps the artistic skills of many who do not always have a chance to show their talent, and demonstrates how summaries are written to sell books. Then, using the summary as an outline, the story is written.

Yet another effective organizing technique is the storyboard, a large piece of paper that is divided into sections or panels, usually by folding (see Figure 13). It is used to show the plan of action for a story using pictures, words, or sentences. After brainstorming ideas about their topics, students roughly sketch out stories on the storyboard frames, remembering to think through their beginnings and endings first. Harrington (1994) describes using a storyboard as a prewriting technique that features children's drawing. When the children were satisfied with the story lines they created, they were ready to put words on paper. This technique is especially useful for remedial students who often have a lot to say, but have trouble putting thoughts into words. Drawing pictures provides both motivation and the framework for the story they want to tell. In an author talk, I once

FIGURE 12. Sample Book Jacket

Front Cover

THE GIANT AND THE CORN STALK

By: George Brown

Back Cover

George Brown is a sixth grader at Reed Middle School located in Bridgman, Michigan. Next year he will be attending seventh grade in Colorado and living with his grandparents. George has been to Colorado many times and really likes all the mountains.

George was born on November 22, 1984. He has two younger brothers, Matt and David, and Patti is his mother. He also has two cats, a dog, and a couple of rabbits.

When he is not writing stories, George likes to draw and paint. This is his first book. He has written two stories and three poems when he was younger, and these have been printed in other books. His friend, Ryan Wolf, inspired him to write this story after their teacher, Mr. Kurek, taught them how authors fracture fairytales and make them seem like new stories. He is now writing a Readers' Theater script based on the story of "Moss Gown" in a cooperative group with his friends.

Inside Front and Back Flaps

The Giant and the Corn Stalk

One day, a long time ago, there lived a young girl whose name was Ruth. Ruth was a poor young thing. She lived with her mother, and they had very little money.

Out of desperation, Ruth's mother called her aside one day and said, "Go out and sell the cow, who could no longer give milk, for some flour and eggs and maybe a bit of meat. Ruth went out and sold the cow, but instead of getting the things her mother asked for, Ruth traded the cow for a bag of magical seeds.

When Ruth returned home, her mother was angry and threw the seeds out the window...and sent Ruth off to bed with no dinner.

The next morning when Ruth awoke, the seeds had grown into a five foot stalk of corn. She was amazed. The next day the stalk was over fifty feet high, and the following day the stalk was well over one thousand feet tall.

Ruth finally figured out that it was a corn stalk and a really big one too. She knew it must be a magical stalk and wondered where it went. Because it was so high, she decided to climb it.

She start to climb and was soon above the clouds when all of a sudden she saw...

Read this exciting story to find out what Ruth found and what happened to that poor little girl and her mother. The story is by the magnificent author, George Brown.

FIGURE 13. Sample Storyboard

StoryBoard

1. Jake starts to play sports.

2. Jake sees his dad's cards of himself.

3. Jake gets teased because kids find out he's different.

4. Jake walks home thinking if he should tell his dad.

5. (Next day) Jake's Dad comes in at recess and shows the kids his jersey.

6. ...was like Jake again.

Reprinted from Heffernan, L. (2004). *Critical literacy and writer's workshop: Bringing purpose and passion to student writing* (p. 55). Newark, DE: International Reading Association.

heard author Jack Gantos (1989) describe how he uses a storyboard to write the popular Rotten Ralph books. Using a large sheet of plain paper (poster board size), he folds it into 16 squares. He can then use a sticky note in each square, mapping out the events of the entire story, allowing for movement and change. This technique can be used by students of all ages, using fewer squares depending on the age and ability of the writer.

The organization of events in a story line is known as a *plot*. In author talks that I've attended, authors have discussed plot. Betsy Byers shared the following formula for realistic fiction: A plot with possibilities. Characters to make the plot happen. A believable setting. Lots and lots of good scrapes. Jane Yolen says that "the main plot line is simple: Getting your character to the foot of the tree, getting him up the tree, and then figuring out how to get him down again." And I feel that any graphic organizer for story grammar will work as an outline for older students.

To illustrate one organizing technique, let's begin by looking at the list of words I came up with in one minute for the topic "Grandma's Porch." By using that same list, I can organize the details by using numbers. (A variation would be using colored dots to signify details that belong together.)

1 red squares	1 rocky chairs
2 fuchsias	3 snow angels
2 hummingbirds	white flowers
1 porch swing	1 railing
2 Grandpa	iced tea
2 flower box	

The numbers indicate the things that go together. They can also, as they do in this case, indicate the paragraph they will be in. In the first paragraph I am going to describe the porch, what it looked like and the furniture it held.

> Grandma's porch was made of big red cement squares. You went up three steps to get on it, and it had a black wrought-iron railing around it so you wouldn't fall off. There was a big blue porch swing on one end of the porch with a white fringed canopy. I spent hours sitting there with Grandpa, swinging. On the other end there were some metal chairs with legs that were curved in one piece. I loved to rock those chairs, but that made big scratch marks on the porch so I'd get in trouble for doing that.

In the second paragraph I will tell about the time a hummingbird, attracted to the fuchsias in the flower box, flew into the window and how Grandpa revived it.

> There was a big window box on the porch full of fuchsias that Grandma planted every spring. Hummingbirds loved to hover there, drinking the nectar from the blossoms. One day we were inside and heard a "thump". A hummingbird had flown into the window. It was lying motionless in the dirt around the flowers. Grandpa and I went outside and he picked up the little bird, cradling it in his big hands. We sat in the swing together and he just held the little guy. It must have been the warmth of his hands that brought the bird around because it started moving. When Grandpa opened his hands the bird flew away.

Paragraph three will tell about the time Grandma and I made snow angels on the porch.

> One January morning, Grandma and I looked out the picture window and saw snow. About six inches of white, fluffy stuff formed a big cloud on the porch. Grandma was the youngest of seven children and always said it wasn't fair that I had no brothers or sisters to play with. So, guess what we did? Dressed in our warmest clothes, we put on hats, mittens and boots and went out the back door. We walked around the yard, carefully tiptoeing up the edge of the porch steps. Plopping in the snow in front of the window, we made snow angels. Getting up carefully, we left the same way we came. When Grandpa got home from work we took him into the living room and had him look out the window. There were two perfect snow angels, one big and one little. Grandma and me.

To complete this piece, I would probably write a concluding paragraph about how important those events and the porch were to me. Notice that I did not put a number in front of "white flowers" or "iced tea." I decided not to use them in this piece. They didn't fit. But, I can write them in my notebook for future use.

I have included samples of my own writing in this and the next four chapters for two reasons. The first is for demonstration purposes. They are actual examples that I have used in classrooms. I wrote them during class sessions, modeling the process and steps for finding a topic, organizing the ideas, and then, through revision, fine-tuning the piece. The second reason is to show students that we can all become writers. Teachers need to be writers in order to teach writing (see chapter 10). Students need to see that we, as teachers, are not asking them to do something that we cannot do ourselves. We need to model and demonstrate the writing process.

Developing Sequencing Skills

Good writers use time as an organizer if the topic changes or evolves over time. They also use clue words such as *first, next, then, before, after that,* and *finally* to help readers follow the sequence of events. If the story is focused on time, phrases like *the next day, later that day, in the morning,* and *after awhile* help the reader understand the sequence. Transition words, such as *however, in fact, nevertheless,* and *therefore,* indicate that a change is about to occur and are also an aid to understanding. Each ending sentence of a paragraph should point the way to the next. Donald Murray (1984) recommends listing the main points (sequences), then moving them around until they are in a natural order in which each point leads to the next one. Student writers are capable of following Murray's recommendation.

Share books that use time as an organizer: *Sunday Morning* (1968) by Judith Viorst, in which time is essential to the story, and *Jack's Garden* (1995) by Henry Cole, which explores growth and change of living elements by describing one boy's garden from seed to harvest. Share books with natural units of time: a day, seasons, rituals, and holidays. Read *Pond Year* (1997) by Kathryn Lasky and point out how authors often slow down and focus on one brief time. They don't tell the whole story on the first page. Introduce students to the use of *flashback,* an interruption in action to insert an event or episode that took place at an earlier time. Flashback is used to give readers information from the past that allows them to better understand the present situation or explain a character's motivation. A good example of flashback is *One Small Blue Bead* (1992) by Byrd Baylor, which moves immediately from the present to the distant past and back to the present again.

Wordless picture books are excellent ways for young children to practice sequencing skills. They can dictate or write a sentence to explain what is happening on each page. Books like *Carl Goes to Daycare* (1993) by Alexandra Day are excellent for this activity. The text at the beginning and end of the story gives a framework, and students can use the illustrations to fill in the events in between.

Another sequencing activity is to take a short story or article, copy or retype it, then cut it apart or write it on sentence strips and have students use time and word clues to put it in the correct order. This activity shows them the importance of using logical sequence. For first or second graders, use a simple text like *From Egg to Robin* (1998) by Susan Canizares and Betsey Chessen. Write the following sentences on sentence strips:

This is a robin.

The robin builds a nest.

The robin lays eggs.

Then the eggs hatch.

The robin feeds her babies.

The babies get bigger.

Now they are grown-up robins.

Mix up the strips and have children put the sentences in the correct order. Discuss how they knew this was the proper sequence. The book can then be used to confirm the order.

For older students, take a paragraph from a story or article like *The Army of Emperor Qin* (1987) by Patricia West, and write the sentences on sentence strips:

In the summer of 1974, farmers near Xian in China needed more water for their fields.

They dug wells deep in the ground but found no water.

Instead, they discovered a huge underground room.

The surprised farmers found themselves looking into the faces of six-foot-tall soldiers holding sharp swords.

The farmers did not run, though.

The soldiers were made of clay.

Mix the sentence strips up, then have students put them in the correct order. When students are proficient in ordering sentences, you can take whole paragraphs from a story or article and do the same sequencing activity with them. For example, the following are paragraphs from *Sarah, Plain and Tall* (1985) by Patricia MacLachlan:

We waited and watched. I rocked on the porch and Caleb rolled a marble on the wood floor. Back and forth. Back and forth. The marble was blue.

We saw the dust from the wagon first, rising above the road, above the heads of Jack and Old. Bess. Caleb climbed up onto the porch roof and shaded his eyes.

"A bonnet!" he cried. "I see a yellow bonnet!"

The dogs came out from under the porch, ears up, their eyes on the cloud of dust bringing Sarah. The wagon passed the fenced field, and the cows and sheep looked up, too. It rounded the windmill and the barn and the windbreak of Russian olive that Mama had planted long ago. Nick began to bark, then Lottie, and the wagon clattered into the yard and stopped by the steps.

"Hush," said Papa to the dogs.

And it was quiet.

Sarah stepped down from the wagon, a cloth bag in her hand. She reached up and took off her yellow bonnet, smoothing back her brown hair into a bun. She was plain and tall.

In discussing the solutions, always ask students to explain how they decided on the order and what transitional or clue words within the text helped them.

Beginnings and Endings

First Lines

The first line sets the tone for the whole piece. It is often referred to as a lead, grabber, or hook. The reader is being baited and lured into reading the paper. The opening line sets up the piece and pulls in the reader. The reader wants to read more. And, the author has got to engage the reader by getting into the material right away. I share first lines with students and then ask them what they want to know. For example, if the first line is "I'll never forget my sixth birthday," students will usually tell me that they want to know what was unforgettable about it. Another might be "Dr. Green was the best teacher I ever had." The class will want to know what was special about her. What did she do and say? Why was she better than other teachers?

Newbery Medal–award winning author Kate DiCamillo demonstrates her understanding of the power of the first line in *Because of Winn-Dixie* (2000): "My name is India Opal Buloni, and last summer my daddy, the preacher, sent me to the store for a box of macaroni-and-cheese, some white rice, and two tomatoes and I came back with a dog." Another one of my favorites is the first line of Richard Peck's *Fair Weather* (2001): "It was the last day of our old lives, and we didn't even know it."

When I do presentations for schools, we usually meet in the library or in a classroom. I ask teachers to take a book from a shelf or from a desk and read the first line aloud. The randomly chosen book is almost always an example of a good lead that entices the reader to read more. We find good first lines often in fiction, both picture books and novels, but also in nonfiction. I have never had this approach to demonstrating the importance of first lines fail.

To illustrate the power of first lines to students, I type several first lines and put them on the overhead. Showing them one at a time, I ask the class to tell what they want to find out. Following are examples of first lines and the questions they evoked:

First line: The war came and took my father forever. (*The Private Notebook of Katie Roberts, Age 11* [1995] by Amy Hest)

Questions: What war? Did he die? Did he stay and not come home?

First line: The day we brought Lucy home she was so tiny she could have fit in my mother's coat pocket. (*Lucy Comes to Stay* [1994] by Rosemary Wells)

Questions: What or who was Lucy? Was she a puppy or kitten or a premature baby?

First line: The fog clears at about ten o'clock every morning at Chestnut Cove. (*Chestnut Cove* [1995] by Tim Egan)

Questions: Is it always foggy? Why does it always clear at ten o'clock? What can you see when it clears? What and where is Chestnut Cove?

First line: I am in my room and I am never coming out. (*Now Everybody Really Hates Me* [1993] by Jane Read Martin)

Questions: Why? What happened? What is she mad about or afraid of?

First line: He sleeps in a little gray bed at the back of the cookie store and each morning, around six A.M., the cookie bakers come to wake him and kiss him and tell him hello. (*The Cookie-Store Cat* [1999] by Cynthia Rylant)

Questions: Who is he? Why do they kiss him?

First line: Miss Tizzy always wore a purple hat with a white flower in it and high-top green tennis shoes. (*Miss Tizzy* [1993] by Libba Moore Gray)

Questions: Who is Miss Tizzy? Why does she dress like that? How old is she?

First line: Mr. Lincoln was the coolest principal in the whole world, or so his students thought. (*Mr. Lincoln's Way* [2001] by Patricia Polacco)

Questions: What was he like? Why did the students think he was cool?

First line: Stanley collected pets. (*Pet Boy* [2001] by Keith Graves)

Questions: What kind of pets? Who is Stanley?

First line: It all started with one little string of tiny white Christmas lights. (*The Amazing Christmas Extravaganza* [1995] by David Shannon)

Questions: What started? Why one little string of lights?

First line: Nelia Batungbakal was too excited to sleep. (*A Very Important Day* [1995] by Maggie Rugg Herold)

Questions: Who is Nelia? What is she excited about?

First line: I had a tantrum today. (*The Tantrum* [1993] by Kathryn Lasky)

Questions: Why? What kind of tantrum? What happened after she had the tantrum?

Following are some additional first lines you might want to use with your class:

There's a silly old saying that if you hold a guinea pig up by its tail, its eyes will drop out. (*I Love Guinea Pigs* [1994] by Dick King-Smith)

One morning when Sarah woke up, Rotten Ralph was swinging on her chandelier. (*Worse Than Rotten, Ralph* [1978] by Jack Gantos)

Horace P. Blumpoe was a grump. (*Blumpoe the Grumpoe Meets Arnold the Cat* [1990] by Jean Davies Okimoto)

The day she was born was the happiest day in her parents' lives. (*Chrysanthemum* [1991] by Kevin Henkes)

My dad and I live in an airport. (*Fly Away Home* [1991] by Eve Bunting)

Solomon Singer lived in a hotel for men near the comer of Columbus Avenue and Eighty-fifth Street in New York City, and he did not like it. (*An Angel for Solomon Singer* [1992] by Cynthia Rylant)

Miss Elizabeth felt troubled. (*Dear Willie Rudd* [1993] by Libba Moore Gray)

My grandfather was a young man when he left his home in Japan and went to see the world. (*Grandfather's Journey* [1993] by Allen Say)

Out where coyotes serenade the moon and sagebrush grays the land, there lived a young woman of bodacious beauty. (*The Cowboy and the Black-Eyed Pea* [1992] by Tony Johnston)

Someone had dropped the cat onto old Regis sleeping in his bed by the stove. (*Tulips* [1992] by Jay O'Callahan)

Your great-great-great-great-grandpa built this house. (*Homeplace* [1995] by Anne Shelby)

When students are exposed to good first lines in literature, it is easier for them to understand the importance of using them in their own writing. Let them choose from two or three leads from a piece of your own writing. Point out the effectiveness of "I'll never forget the day the helicopter landed on the playground" as opposed to "I am going to tell you about an exciting day." Have students write two or three leads as options. They can share with others to see what the reader thinks is the best choice.

For expository writing, Fletcher and Portalupi (2001) advise writers to bring the reader to the place where they can see the subject in its natural environment. When writers begin by describing the setting, they are inviting the reader in for a closer look at the subject. In *Disappearing Lake* (1997), author Debbie S. Miller sets the stage on the first page:

> In a wooded valley, the snow begins to melt. Sparkling beads of water trickle together, growing into rivulets, brooks, and streams. They speak to you in the language of water. A snowy meadow laced with the tracks of moose and caribou, wolf and bear, fox and raven, is changing.

Her words create a visual image that is enhanced by the illustration. It isn't until the middle of this picture book that the message emerges: the importance of vernal ecosystems and a description of Disappearing Lake in Alaska's Denali National Park.

Another effective technique for expository writing is to think of the most unusual and exciting fact about your topic and turn it into a question. Then answer it. Move from the most general to the most specific. For a report on emus, the writer might begin with "Do all birds fly?" The next line answers the question with general information: "Although all birds have wings and most of them fly, there are a few who don't." Then more specific information is added: "The Australian emu is a large, flightless bird, second in size only to the African ostrich. Emus cannot fly, but they can run up to 30mph." The report continues with more facts about emus.

Ending Lines

Good writers tie up loose ends and leave you thinking at the end of a story. Only fairy tales end with "And they lived happily ever after." After kindergarten, I discourage students from using that ending unless they are writing a fairy tale. Most of us want resolution. Authors often resolve the most pressing problem in a story, but leave room for interpretation, imagination, or even a sequel in the ending. In discussing his young adult novel *Close Enough to Touch* (1981), author Richard Peck (2002) says, "The story ends at a new beginning. What will happen after the final page is to be written in the minds of the reader" (p. 102). In the second of the Boston Jane trilogy (2002), author Jennifer L. Holm sets the stage for the next book in the last line. After months in the wilderness, Jane sees a boat coming ashore. As it docks, she sees her nemesis from the East, Miss Sally Biddle of Philadelphia.

Endings can be difficult for young writers. Often, the writer is so concerned with telling the story or including information that, by the end of the piece, they simply run out of things to say. Using one of the organizing techniques discussed earlier in this chapter can help students gain greater control of their material by laying out the structure before actually writing. The writer should have a general idea of the ending before starting and be thinking about the ending while writing. I like to show students ending lines on the overhead projector and ask them what the author has given them to think about. The following are examples of ending lines and the question(s) they evoked:

Ending line:	They never found out who it was that stole the feast—can you? (*The Eleventh Hour* [1988] by Graeme Base)
Question:	How do you steal a feast? Who is the thief?
Ending line:	And I'm happy, too. (*Jin Woo* [2001] by Eve Bunting)
Question:	What would happen next?
Ending line:	And so began a journey that would happen every year until forever. (*The Reindeer Christmas* [1993] by Moe Price)
Question:	Every year?
Ending line:	Did you ever hear the story of the Girl Wonder? (*Girl Wonder* [2003] by Deborah Hopkinson)
Questions:	What story? Who is the Girl Wonder?
Ending line:	Someday. (*The Other Side* [2001] by Jacqueline Woodson)
Questions:	What does that mean? Is something going to happen?
Ending line:	And although Hare and Bear learned to live happily as neighbors, they never became business partners again! (*Tops & Bottoms* [1995] by Janet Stevens)
Questions:	Did they really get along? Did Hare ever find another business partner?

Matching First and Ending Lines

Until I started teaching writing and investigating beginning and ending lines, I really didn't realize that good writers almost always tie the first and last lines together in some way, often with repetition of words. I looked at many picture books and novels. I took first lines and printed them to be shown on the overhead projector one at a time. Then I printed the ending lines and cut them apart, distributing them to students or workshop participants. I tell them that when I read a first line, I guarantee that they will know if they have the last line, even though they have no idea what book the line comes from. I have done this with third graders through adults, and it always works. In the examples that follow, I have numbered the lines so you can use these with your own students.

First Lines

1. There was a time, long, long ago, when the cottage stood sturdy and strong on a bluff overlooking the ocean.

2. My name is Ora Mae Cotton of Crabapple Orchard, and last night somebody stole my tooth.

3. The village children called him Mr. Gloomy.

4. Even on the boat they had to practice.

5. Just let me say right off the bat, it was a bike accident.

6. "If you were a smart dog, you'd chase that rabbit."

7. Pirates are robbers of the high seas.

8. When Amanda walked into a room, her hair seemed to enter first.

9. This is the wall, my grandfather's wall.

10. Two men walked into the rain forest.

11. Poulette was an unusual hen.

12. Honey cocks her ears and peers through the fence.

13. This is the pot that Juan built.

14. Once upon a time, there was a nanny goat who lived in a little house in the forest with her children, seven little kids.

15. Grace lived with her ma and her nana and a cat called Paw-Paw.

Ending Lines

1. It was a fisherman's cottage, but it was no longer deserted. (*Newf* [1992] by Marie Killilea)

2. I wonder if the tooth fairy ever sends motor-mouth kids like me airmail to the moon. (*Airmail to the Moon* [1988] by Tom Birdseye)

3. No one ever called him Mr. Gloomy again. (*The Christmas Miracle of Jonathan Toomey* [1995] by Susan Wojciechowski)

4. "But Papa, you must practice, practice, practice!" (*The Amazing Felix* [1993] by Emily Arnold McCully)

5. I just thought you ought to know. (*Mick Harte Was Here* [1995] by Barbara Park)

6. "I guess you're smarter than I thought." (*Smart Dog* [1993] by Ralph Leemis)

7. Today, treasure hunters still search for the long-hidden treasures of the pirates. (*Pirates* [1993] by Gail Gibbons)

8. And anyhow, thought Amanda, I can always grow it back. (*Amanda 's Perfect Hair* [1993] by Linda Milstein)

9. I'd rather have him here. (*The Wall* [1990] by Eve Bunting)

10. Then he dropped the ax and walked out of the rain forest. (*The Great Kapok Tree* [1990] by Lynne Cherry)

11. An ordinary hen can be anything she wants to be, but under all those fancy feathers, a peacock is just a long-necked chicken. (*Hen Lake* [1995] by Mary Jane Auch)

12. As each day goes by, Anne and Honey will continue to learn from each other, and they can look forward to many happy years together. (*A Guide Dog Puppy Grows Up* [1991] by Caroline Arnold)

13. The beautiful pot that Juan built. (*The Pot That Juan Built* [2002] by Nancy Andrews-Goebel)

14. From that day on, the nanny goat and the seven little kids never had to worry about the big bad wolf again and they lived happily ever after. (*Nanny Goat and the Seven Little Kids* [1990] by Eric A. Kimmel)

15. "Just like families," said Grace. (*Boundless Grace* [1995] by Mary Hoffman)

In the following example of an organization lesson that I have used with third- and fourth-grade students, the structure is based on a first line and an ending line. I wrote about a cat that I once had. For the brainstorming technique, in one minute I wrote the following, and then I used numbers to organize the ideas.

Julius

1 orange	1 rain
1 wet	4 big
2 chocolate cake	fish
3 car	roof
trees	

I presented the following possible first lines to the class:

1. I'll never forget the first time I saw Julius. He was a little ball of orange fur.

2. Julius was the best cat I ever had.

3. One day I got a tiny orange kitten.

The class chose the first one. Then, after I explained more about the weather and described how Julius looked, the students helped me revise the beginning of the piece:

I'll never forget the first time I saw Julius. He looked like a drowned rat. After bringing him in the house and drying him off, I could see that he was really a fluffy ball of orange fur.

I then explained that the second paragraph will tell the story of how Julius jumped up on the kitchen counter and landed in the middle of a chocolate cake. Paragraph three would describe how he got into my friend's car and ended up going home with her. The last paragraph would tell about how big he grew to be and how long we had him. The class helped me with an ending that would not only complete the story, but tie in with the beginning.

Who could have guessed, on that soggy August day when he came into our lives, that he would rule our house for the next 19 years?

Involving the class in an activity like this helps the students to revise their own writing.

Using Books as Examples of Organization

Sharing literature is a most effective way to illustrate organizational techniques. Students can analyze patterns in books and compare organization in different types of texts, letters, instructions, and booklets (Spandel, 2001b). After reading a book to the class, have the students go back and find the turning point in the plot or point out the clues and events that lead to the resolution. In stories with a mystery or a surprise ending, go back through the story and have students identify clues to the solution or ending that good writers scatter throughout the piece, in both text and illustrations. Many of these clues appear insignificant or are completely overlooked until the ending is revealed.

When focusing on the trait of organization, look for well-paced books with a definite beginning, middle, and end. Spandel (2001a) describes the qualities key to good organization as

> leads designed to hook readers and keep their attention, sequencing that makes sense, strong transitions that link sentences or ideas together, and a solid conclusion that ties things together in the reader's mind but often leaves the reader with something to think about, too. (p. 39)

Books using time sequence, life cycles, and flashbacks illustrate the effectiveness of good organization. At the end of this chapter is an annotated list of children's literature to use for the trait of organization.

Assessing Organization

When evaluating a paper for organization, look for a strong beginning, middle, and end, with a powerful lead linked to an insightful ending. Spandel (2001b) advises that

> if you look deep within, you should find a pattern—a skeletal structure that holds the body (the ideas) together. We don't want to be overly conscious of the skeleton, but we want the comfort of knowing it is there and that things are not going to fall apart. When the writer has a strong point to make or the need to share a story, the ideas drive the organization. (p. 60)

The writer must connect the ideas to a larger theme, set up a problem, and then solve it. Details need to link to the main topic, and transitions should be smooth and lead to a strong ending with a sense of resolution. And "like" bits of information should be grouped together. This is similar to the example of *The Important Book* (Brown, 1949) in chapter 4. The sentence about my cat did not belong in the paragraph about skiing. All sentences must relate to the paragraph's main idea. Sharing and scoring many samples of writing with students is an excellent way to increase their awareness and understanding of the trait of organization. Remember to score each trait separately. At this point, you will be scoring papers for ideas and organization.

Student Checklist for Organization

- Do I have a good beginning?
- Did I tell things in the proper order?
- Do all details relate to my main point?
- Is it easy to follow?
- Does the ending make you think?

Evaluator Checklist for Organization

RATING: STRONG (5)

- There is a definite pattern or order that makes sense.
- The beginning grabs your attention and makes you want to read more.
- The piece has good pacing.
- Strong transitions link the ideas.
- Conclusion is strong, with a sense of resolution.

Following is a student example from grade 4:

> Odie (pets)
> The day we got Odie, he weighed 3 1/2 pounds. Now he weighs ninety! He is a Golden Retriever. Golden Retrievers make great pets because they are friendly and like kids and other dogs. They like to play ball and fetch and run. But what they really love to do is swim. They actually have webbed feet like ducks so that's one reason they are such good swimmers.
>
> When Odie was a puppy, he did some pretty funny things. He'd jump up on the bed and grab my sister's hair in his teeth and then start to shake his head back and forth. She'd really scream at that. He also chewed up anything he found so the whole family had to be careful not to leave anything important on the floor. He had a little pen on the patio where he stayed while we were gone. One day I was the first one home and when I went to get him, he wasn't there. One of the boards was knocked down so I knew he got out of the pen. But where was he? I was so scared. But then I hear "yip, yip, yip" from above. He had climbed all the way up the stairs to the deck but couldn't figure out how to get back down. Wow! That was a close call. We could have lost him.
>
> Odie loves to go in the car and the boat. One time he swam after the boat when our whole family went out in it. A fisherman asked us if we knew that a dog was fol-

lowing us and sure enough, there he was swimming right behind us. So we went over to an island so we could get him in the boat with us. From then on we either had to tie him up or take him with us when we went out in the boat.

Odie loves to eat. That's why he weighs so much. One time he got into my sister's and my Halloween candy and he ate a bunch of it, wrappers and all. Another time he followed some kids from the bus stop and took a cookie out of a girl's hand. He didn't hurt her though. He just wanted that cookie.

If you are thinking of getting a dog, you should get a Golden Retriever. I think Golden Retrievers make the best pets for families. Odie is the best kind of dog for our family. He's the best dog ever.

The writer sticks to the topic and tells relevant anecdotes. I would score this 5 in ideas. For organization, although the beginning and ending are not particularly strong, they are present, and the beginning and ending are tied together. There is a logical sequence and the topic in each paragraph is supported with details. I would score this a 4–5 in organization.

RATING: DEVELOPING (3)

- Beginning is present but not outstanding.
- The ending needs work.
- Generally easy to follow.
- Some ideas don't seem to fit.
- Equal strengths and weaknesses

Following is a student example from grade 3:

Buddy (pets)
Cats are my favorite animal. I have a cat named Buddy. He is black and really big. Sometimes he comes when you call him. Sometimes he just ignores you. Cats make great pets because they can sleep with you and they don't make much noise. Some cats claw the furniture. My friend's cat wrecked their couch and stereo speakers but Buddy only scratches his scratching post.

Most cats like cat food. Buddy eats special food because he's so fat. My friend's cat eats Little Friskies but there are all kinds of dry cat food. Some cats like Purina cat chow. There is cat food in cans, too. It stinks. Wild cats eat mice and snakes and birds. They eat garbage, too.

Cats can live a long time. My grandma had a cat that was nineteen years old. It died. Cats can die young if they get run over or get sick. I hope Buddy lives a long time.

The writer generally sticks to the topic. The beginning is not strong, although the ending is adequate. Sequence is a bit difficult to follow. Some details might need to be moved around. I would score this a 3 in ideas and a 3 in organization.

RATING: WEAK (1)

- Beginning is weak or not present.

- Ending is weak or not present.

- Sequencing seems random.

- Transitions are missing.

- No identifiable structure.

Following is a student example from grade 5:

Dogs (Pets)
Most dogs are nice but some are mean. There are many types of dogs like poodles, cocker spaniels, wiener dogs, husky, chows, and labs. I like black labs but once a mean one scared me. I have a cocker spaniel mix named Penny. She is so sweet. But once she bit the mailman and got in trouble. She likes me the best in my family. Some dogs are little and some are big. I like big dogs but Penny isn't all that big. Some dogs have long hair and some are almost bald. I don't like skinny dogs. Penny likes to sleep on my bed. She sheds lots of hair on the carpet. Once she got on the couch. I take Penny on a leash but she doesn't like it. I think it's mean when people don't take care of their dog. There are lots of starving dogs in the world. People shouldn't get a dog if they are going to be mean to it. When we picked up Penny from the vet she was so glad to see us she peed on the floor. Next I'd like to get a Great Dane.

The writer does not focus on one incident. Topic and sequence are random. Beginning and ending are both weak, and there is no identifiable structure. I would score this paper a 1–2 in ideas and a 1–2 in organization.

Sample Lesson Plans

For organization, I usually spend one or two class sessions on organizing techniques. For grades K–1, use the three-sectioned paper for beginning, middle, end; the star organizer; or the step organizer. For grades 2–5, number the ideas previously brainstormed or use one of the storyboard activities. I would not introduce more than one technique at a time. I also recommend at least one day for beginning lines and one day for ending lines. Make sure students understand the author's purpose in choosing these lines before doing the activity that matches the first and ending lines. Another week might be spent on sequencing activities. Be sure to read at least one book each day to illustrate the trait of organization. Additional time might be spent analyzing authors' organizational techniques in these books.

Following are two sample lesson plans that I have used for the trait of organization.

Sample Lesson Plan (Grades K–1)

DAY 1

1. Read *The Three Little Pigs* to the class and discuss the beginning, middle, and end of the story. Explain that this is part of good organization.

2. Divide the class into three groups. Have each group act out or draw the first part of the story, the middle, and the end.

DAY 2

1. Read *The Gingerbread Man* to the class.

2. Discuss the beginning, middle, and end of the story with the class, using the word *organization*.

3. Using paper with three sections, or that has been folded in thirds, demonstrate that the first section (left) is for the first part of the story, the middle section is for the middle of the story, and the last section (right) is for the end of the story.

4. Have students draw a picture of the beginning, middle, and end of the story in the appropriate space. Depending on the age and ability of the student, a few words or sentences can be added.

5. Encourage children to share their finished papers with a neighbor.

Sample Lesson Plan (Grades 2–5)

1. Read *Rotten Ralph* (1976) by Jack Gantos.

2. Ask students if the story was easy to follow. Explain that authors often use clue or transition words to guide the reader and help order the sequence of events.

3. Go back through the book (use a Big Book; give students a copy if you have a class set; or make a photo copy of each page and show on an overhead projector).

4. Have students look at page 6. Ask what the clue words are. (One afternoon)

5. On page 7, have students identify the clue words. (The very next day)

6. Continue in the same manner for the following pages:

page 10	one day
page 12	the next evening
page 14	after dinner
page 16	one evening
page 18	so
page 20	then
page 22	next
page 26	when
page 28	then
page 30	after that
page 32	the next day
page 38	during the night
page 40	in the morning

7. If you think students need more practice with this activity, any of the Rotten Ralph books can be used.

8. Encourage students to use words and phrases like the ones they identified to make the organization of their writing more clear.

Conclusion

Along with ideas, organization is the foundation for writing. Once students have established and narrowed their topic (ideas), they need to organize the details and develop an outline or structure for writing (organization). Sharing literature with students is an ideal way for them to see organizational patterns and techniques that authors use. When students see how the beginning line hooks the reader and ties to the ending, how the story line is easy to follow with the use of transition words, and how details give clues to the resolution or ending, they will be more apt to apply these techniques to their own writing.

For organization, students should automatically think *beginning, middle,* and *end.* They should use clue or transition words to facilitate logical sequence and focus on effective ways to ensure that the organization is sound. When students have become comfortable with organizational concepts, they are ready to go on to the trait of voice, the subject of chapter 6.

ANNOTATED LIST OF CHILDREN'S LITERATURE TO USE FOR ORGANIZATION

Adler, David A. (2003). *Mama played baseball.* (Chris O'Leary, Illus.). San Diego, CA: Gulliver Books.

> Amy's parents are both in uniform. Her father is off fighting a war, and her mother plays in the first professional women's baseball league. The story has an easy to follow sequence, leading up to the end of the war and the end of the league. (Grades 3–5)

Bunting, Eve. (1996). *Sunflower house.* (Kathryn Hewitt, Illus.). San Diego, CA: Harcourt Brace.

> The life cycle of sunflowers is featured in this story of young children and their adventures in their house, made by planting sunflowers in a circle. (Grades K–2)

Gantos, Jack. (1998). *Back to school for Rotten Ralph.* (Nicole Rubel, Illus.). New York: HarperCollins.

> Ralph, the rotten cat, accompanies Sarah to school. Each page begins with a sequence word. (Grades K–2)

George, Jean Craighead. (1997). *Look to the north. A wolf pup diary*. (Lucia Washburn, Illus.). New York: HarperCollins.

Using time frames young students can understand (When you see dandelions turning silver, look to the north. Wolf pups are being born), the author follows the lives of wolves, from birth to adulthood. (Grades K–3)

Herold, Maggie Rugg. (1995). *A very important day*. (Catherine Stock, Illus.). New York: Morrow Junior Books.

On a cold, wintry day, 12 families of different nationalities prepare for something important. It is not until the end of the book that the reader realizes they are all going to the United States Courthouse to become citizens. Then the reader can recognize that there were clues throughout the story, leading to the surprise ending. A glossary of names and countries is included at the end of the book, as well as information on becoming a U.S. citizen. (Grades K–5)

Johnston, Tony. (1996). *The wagon*. (James E. Ransome, Illus.). New York: Tambourine Books.

A chronological account of a slave's birth and the wagon that he and his Papa made. It is that same wagon that takes the family to freedom and to the funeral of Abraham Lincoln. (Grades 2–5)

Locker, Thomas. (1995). *Sky tree: Seeing science through art*. New York: HarperCollins.

Text and paintings show the changes in a tree from season to season. Specific information about each tree is included at the end of the book. (Grades 3–5)

Maestro, Betsy. (1996). *Coming to America: The story of immigration*. (Susannah Ryan, Illus.). New York: Scholastic.

The story of immigration to America from the first nomadic settlers to the present. A timeline and facts about immigration are included in the back of this book. (Grades 1–3)

McGeorge, Constance W. (1999). *Boomer's big surprise*. (Mary Whyte, Illus.). San Francisco: Chronicle.

Readers learn the surprise when they start reading this book, but the sequence of events lead to an unexpected ending. (Grades K–2)

Moss, Marissa. (2001). *Brave Harriet: The first woman to fly the English Channel*. (C.F. Payne, Illus.). San Diego, CA: Harcourt.

Based on the life of Harriet Quimby, the first American woman to receive a pilot's license and the first woman to fly solo across the English Channel, the story unfolds through newspaper articles she wrote as a reporter for the *New York Herald*. Time is most important in this account of her aviation feat. (Grades 3–5)

O'Callahan, Jay. (1996). *Tulips*. (Debrah Santini, Illus.). Atlanta, GA: Peachtree.

Every spring and fall, Pierre, the prankster, visits his Grand Ma Mere, who has the most lovely gardens in all of Paris. One fall, Pierre dares to play his grandest trick of all. My favorite book to show the power of clues leading up to a surprise ending. (Grades K–5)

Pinkney, Gloria Jean. (1994). *The Sunday outing*. (Jerry Pinkney, Illus.). New York: Dial.

Ernestine and Aunt Odessa usually just pretend that they are riding on a train, but Ernestine finds a way to take a real trip on the Silver Star. Details link to the resolution. (Grades K–3)

Polacco, Patricia. (1996). *Aunt Chip and the great Triple Creek Dam affair*. New York: Philomel.

Everyone in Triple Creek loves TV so much that they only use books for propping doors, fixing fences, and repairing the dam. Confined to her bed for 50 years, Aunt Chip teaches her nephew Eli how to read, and he and his friends nearly cause a disaster in their quest for books. Clues to Aunt Chip's identity abound and make perfect sense once the surprise ending is revealed. (Grades 2–5)

Polacco, Patricia. (2002). *Christmas tapestry*. New York: Philomel.

With their first Christmas in Detroit about to be ruined, a boy and his father meet an old Jewish woman, whose story changes their life and saves their Christmas. A truly astonishing ending makes sense when one looks back at all the details. (Grades 3–5)

Rand, Gloria. (1997). *Baby in a basket.* (Ted Rand, Illus.). New York: Cobblehill Books.

> Based on a true story of the first kindergarten teacher in Alaska, this book has a very definite beginning, middle, and end. Clue words and strong transitions make the sequence easy to follow. (Grades K–3)

Rockwell, Anne. (1998). *One bean.* (Megan Halsey, Illus.). New York: Walker & Company.

> With simple text and illustrations, the life cycle of a bean is explained. Additional information about beans and activities are included at the end. (Grades K–2)

Say, Allen. (2002). *Home of the brave.* New York: Houghton Mifflin.

> Flashbacks and sequence tell the story of a Japanese internment camp during World War II. (Grades 3–5)

Tunnell, Michael O. (1997). *Mailing May.* (Ted Rand, Illus.). New York: Greenwillow.

> There is a definite beginning, middle, and end to this true story of a 5-year-old girl who was actually mailed from Grangeville to Lewiston, Idaho, because the train fare was too expensive. (Grades K–3)

Waddell, Martin. (1992). *Owl babies.* (Patrick Benson, Illus.). Cambridge, MA: Candlewick.

> From beginning to end, Bill, the littlest owl, worries that his mother will not come home. Time is important to this story as the owls anxiously await their mother's return. (Grades K–2)

CHAPTER 6

Expressing Feelings Through Voice

Voice separates writing that is read from writing that is not read. Voice is the writer revealed.

—Donald Murray

Now that the foundation of ideas and organization has been laid in chapters 4 and 5, the writer's personality can take over. Just as each individual has a unique speaking voice and ways of expressing him or herself verbally in language, a writer has a distinct *voice* in writing. It is this quality of voice, more than any other, that allows us to recognize excellent writing. Writing that we read for entertainment in books and magazines appeals to us largely because of its voice. Voice is present because the author is personally invested in the work. All students have an individual voice and something important to contribute.

In an author talk, Jan Brett explained that the story starts to work when you put some of your own personality into it (voice). Donald Murray (1985) says that "we all rehearse what we are going to say...the how is voice" (p. 22). Ralph Fletcher (1996) defines voice as "the writing you do because your heart will burst if you don't write it" (p. 92). Voice is another reason for allowing students to self-select their writing topic. If it's something the student cares about, the student's voice will come through. And to Vicki Spandel (2001b),

> voice is the presence of the writer on the page. When the writer's passion for the topic and sensitivity to the audience are strong, the text virtually dances with life and energy, and the reader feels a strong connection to both writing and writer. (p. 51)

I tell students that the key word for voice is *feelings*. It is the voice in writing that makes you feel something, makes you mad, or makes you laugh or cry. While reading, have you ever wanted to stop a character from doing something foolish or dangerous? If you have, the writing is full of voice because you actually care about the character and what happens to him or her. Dialog can also add voice to writing. Often you can tell exactly what characters are feeling by what they say.

Voice is personality on paper. Writing with voice includes opinion, persuasion, and point of view. A fractured fairy tale is an example of writing with voice, because a familiar story is retold from the perspective of a different character. All forms of advertising contain voice.

Showing Feelings in Writing

Good writers describe characters by using specific examples of how they look and feel, what they say, and what they do. This is exactly like showing, rather than telling, but it has to do with feelings. You can do activities with students (similar to those shown in chapter 4 for revising telling statements to showing statements) to help them recognize *general* statements and change them to *specific* ones by showing how someone feels. I like to start by having the class help me generate a list of *forbidden words*. Words like *mad, glad, sad, happy, nice, mean, afraid, sorry, liked, good, bad, scared,* and *fine.* Post the list in your classroom so that students can check to see if these words occur in their writing. Good writers don't use general terms like these to describe characters' feelings. In *Stranded* (1995), by Ben Mikaelsen, the author does not say that Koby is happy, but that "every inch of Koby's body smiled." When Mudge gets lost and Henry can't find him in *Henry and Mudge* (1987b), I tell students that Cynthia Rylant could have written "Henry was sad." But she's a good writer, so she writes, "Henry's heart hurt and he cried for an hour." That's really showing the reader exactly how Henry feels.

To illustrate showing feelings in writing to students, write the word *mad* on the board or overhead projector. Have students describe what a person would do, act, or say if they were mad:

- Stamp his feet
- Slam a door
- Get red in the face
- Clench her fists
- Yell

The following are additional words that can be used in student activities in which students describe what a person would do, act, or say:

Excited
- Jump up and down
- Sweat
- Squeal
- Speak in a higher voice

Nervous
- Wring hands
- Talk fast
- Shake
- Blush

Unhappy
- Pout
- Hang head
- Cry
- Frown

Embarrassed
- Blush
- Whisper
- Hang head
- Shake

Be sure to point out that often the writer must include more than one thing to make it clear how a person feels. For instance, people can shake when they are cold, afraid, nervous, or embarrassed; the presence of other words determines exactly why they are shaking and how they are feeling.

When the class is comfortable with going from a general word to more specific words, you can begin to use phrases and sentences that need to be changed to describe how characters feel and what they do.

Original statement: John and Bob were happy their team won.

Revision: John and Bob jumped up and gave each other a high five. They could hardly wait for the pizza party the coach had promised them.

Original statement: Harry was grateful for his new bike.

Revision: "You're the best parents ever," Harry told his Mom and Dad as he hugged them. "I know it cost a lot of money, so I'll do extra chores and take a cut in my allowance."

Original statement: Sue's kitten loved her.

Revision: The kitten followed Sue everywhere. With a room full of people, the kitten always jumped up on Sue, purring as it curled up on her lap.

Original statement: Tom felt bad that his friend was sick.

Revision: Even though his other friends were playing ball, Tom went straight to Greg's house after school to see how he was and to take him his homework. Since Greg couldn't go outside, Tom played cards with him.

Original statement:	Barbara was disappointed that she would miss the field trip.
Revision:	"I've waited all year to go to the zoo with my class," Barbara sobbed, as her mother helped her into bed. "Why did I have to get Chicken Pox today?"
Original statement:	Joey was afraid of dogs.
Revision:	Breaking out in a sweat, Joey had a look of panic on his face as he walked faster and faster past the barking Collie.

The following are some additional sentences to use with your class:

Sam was excited about the vacation.

Jane hated to practice the piano.

Giving an oral book report made Ed nervous.

Maggie loved to read.

Remember to demonstrate these activities, and then have students work in groups or pairs, before expecting them to work on their own. After practicing this, students should be able to check their own writing for forbidden words and phrases and revise to describe specific feelings.

Persuasive Writing

Intended to influence others, *persuasive writing* emphasizes the reader (audience). The purpose is to convince the reader to adopt a given point of view or to urge the reader toward some specific action prompted by good evidence (Spandel & Stiggins, 1997). Persuasive writing requires the writer not only to be aware of the audience and their probable position, but also to consistently present a particular point of view. Students often struggle to build or elaborate an argument. Many simply state a conclusion and support it with one or two claims. Encourage students to weigh the pros and cons. Have them draw a vertical line down the center of a page and list the pros on one side and the cons on the other (see Figure 14). Another tactic is to anticipate possible arguments of the reader, and discuss them openly to change the reader's opinions. Giving some time to arguments on the other side will strengthen one's position in the long run.

One activity for teaching persuasive writing is to have students write letters to parents, teachers, the principal, or school board in which they present their case to the readers to allow them to have something or to change some rules. (For suggestions for writing persuasive letters, see chapter 1 under Audience as Focal Point.) The writers must anticipate reactions, responses, and arguments to fully state their position. They will have to use their voice in writing to get their point across.

Another activity to teach persuasive writing uses advertising, an excellent example of voice and persuasion. Have you ever watched cartoons on a Saturday morning? I was appalled at the tactics used to convince young children that they need certain products. Because children are familiar with advertising, it is an excellent example to use when teaching about persuasion. Have them review ads

FIGURE 14. Sample Graphic Organizer for Pros and Cons of School Uniforms

Pros	Cons
Those without a lot of clothes or certain brands won't feel bad	Can't wear what you want
Less expensive for some	Lots of clothes that we can't wear to school
No distracting clothing	Too expensive for some
Don't have to worry about what to wear each day	Not everyone looks good in certain colors or styles
	Hard to tell everyone apart
	Can't buy at thrift store

from the newspaper or magazines and identify what the writer wants the reader to do and the methods used to convince them to do it. Then have students write advertisements aimed at convincing the reader to buy a product.

By fourth or fifth grade, students are frequently required to write a persuasive letter for a state or provincial writing assessment, so it is wise to expose them to this writing genre in the early grades. Here is an example of a persuasive letter that I wrote for use with a group of fifth-grade students. (In chapters 7 and 8, I will show you how they helped me revise it for word choice and sentence fluency.)

Dear Mom,

Before you say no, just listen to what I have to say. Let me begin by saying how lovely you looked this morning. Your new hairdo is most becoming and that outfit you wore makes you look even slimmer than you are.

I've been thinking that Nicky really needs a friend. I read recently in Cat Fancy that cats need companionship just as much as people do. With you at work and me at school, what does that poor animal have to do all day? I'm afraid we're not providing him with the kind of environment that is best for his well-being.

My friend Jennifer told me about a shelter for cats that she and her mom went to. There are hundreds of cats who don't have a home. She said it was the most depressing place she's ever been to. What in the world is going to happen to all those poor kitties? If we adopted a friend for Nicky, we would be saving one of those poor creatures from a life of misery, or even worse, no life at all. I think it's our duty to rescue one of those cats.

Now, there's something else I want you to think about. I know how upset you are about all the furniture Nicky has wrecked with those claws of his. I also read that if a cat has a playmate and something to do all day, it won't bother scratching furniture. We could also get one of those cute scratching posts for both of the cats to play on. Think of all the money you'll save on furniture by just investing a little bit of money now on another cat and a scratching post.

Speaking of money, I'd be willing to contribute some of my allowance to buy extra cat food. And of course I will feed and brush and do everything to take care of the cats. I know I haven't done much to take care of Nicky but I'll change. This is the new me!

Oh, one more thing. Since you are the sweetest, kindest mother in the whole world, when we get this cat I've decided to let you name it. Start thinking of a name because we have to act soon. I'm the luckiest girl in the world to have such a wonderful mother.

Love,
Becky

P.S. Let me know when we can go pick out a cat.

Explaining Point of View

To explain point of view to students, contrast traditional folk tales and fairy tales with newer versions that are based on them but told from the point of view of a different character, usually the antagonist. Perhaps the most familiar is *The True Story of the 3 Little Pigs!* (1989) by Jon Scieszka. In this book, the wolf tells the story and claims his innocence. Other variations of this tale include *The Fourth Little Pig* (1990) by Teresa Celsi and *The Three Pigs* (2001) by David Wiesner, the latter of which won the 2002 Caldecott Medal. Alvin Granowsky has written a series of books titled *Another Point of View* that includes the original tale and a new story from a different point of view, when the book is flipped over. Titles include *Henny Penny/Brainy Bird Saves the Day* (1996a), *Cinderella/That Awful Cinderella* (1993a), *Rumpelstiltskin/A Deal is a Deal* (1993b), and *The Little Red Hen/Help Yourself, Little Red Hen* (1996b). These books are useful in explaining point of view to students in primary grades and can serve as models for student writing. I have had students rewrite the story of *Snow White* from the stepmother's point of view and *Little Red Riding Hood* as told by the wolf.

Using Books as Examples of Voice

Voice is "confidence, enthusiasm, personality, individual expressiveness, a desire to reach out to the reader through language, and a way of revealing a writer's feelings or attitudes toward a subject" (Spandel, 2001a, p. 61). Writing with strong voice begs to be shared. Start by reading personal favorites that you love. Favorite books always have voice. That's why they become favorites. Ask students what they feel as they listen or read. Help them find the words or phrases that made them laugh or feel sad or empathize with a character. Children need to understand that the things that make Roald Dahl's or Mem Fox's writing successful are the same things that will make their own work successful. Point out that illustrations are another way of showing voice. Often, a picture conveys the message and words are not required. Young children show voice in illustrations by putting smiles, frowns, or tears on the faces of figures. And, of course, teachers have traditionally shown students that their work makes them happy by putting a smiley face on it. Share several books by the same author and have students look for similarities in voice. Look at books by the same illustrator and discover how the artist conveys voice through the pictures.

When teaching the trait of voice, look for books that make you feel something. Ask yourself if you will love reading it aloud to the class, especially more than once. Would you give it as a gift? Look for books that are honest and from the heart. Read books to your class that make you laugh, like *Officer Buckle and Gloria* (1995) by Peggy Rathmann, *Thomas' Snowsuit* (1985) by Robert Munsch, and *Trick or Treat, Smell My Feet* (1998) by Diane deGroat. Read books that make you proud, like *O Canada* (1992) by Ted Harrison, *The Flag We Love* (1996) by Pam Muñoz Ryan, and *My Great-Aunt Arizona* (1992) by Gloria Houston. Read books that inspire you, like *Tomás and the Library Lady* (1997) by Pat Mora, Mem Fox's *Whoever You Are* (1997), and *Thank you, Mr. Falker* (1998) by Patricia Polacco. Share books that convey magic or a tradition or memories of childhood, like *Polar Express* (1985) by Chris Van Allsburg, *One Candle* (2002) by Eve Bunting, and *More Than Anything Else* (1995) by Marie Bradby. Read books that bring tears to your eyes, regardless of how many times you have read them, books like *Faithful Elephants* (1988) by Yukio Tsuchiya, *Toby* (1994) by Margaret Wild, and *The Christmas Miracle of Jonathan Toomey* (1995) by Susan Wojciechowski.

National and world tragedies often inspire books of letters by children that convey their feelings about the event. *Dear Oklahoma City, Get Well Soon* (1996), edited by Jim Ross and Paul Myers, is a collection of children's letters to the people of Oklahoma after the Federal Building was bombed. One young child writes, "When I heard about the explosion I was a puddle of tears" (p. 9). This child writes with voice. After the tragedy of September 11, 2001, Shelley Harwayne and the New York City Board of Education collected letters written from young people's point of view about the event for *Messages to Ground Zero* (2002). At the end of this chapter is an annotated list of children's literature to use for the trait of voice.

Assessing Voice

When evaluating writing for voice, look for honesty, enthusiasm, and conviction and, as Regie Routman (1996) states, a paper that "aches with caring" (p. 87). Is it something you want to share with a colleague? Does it make you understand the author's intent and feelings? Can you tell that the writer really cares about the topic? Does it appeal to your emotions? Does the writer show with specific examples what the narrator or characters in the story think and feel, rather than using general terms? If so, it is most likely high in voice. For persuasive writing, the writers must present their case with supporting details and anticipate the reader's questions and arguments. Are all arguments supported, not just the ones she believes in? The point of view should be apparent and backed up with relevant details. Look for humor, compassion, and memorable moments that provide visual images in your mind. Spandel (2001b) defines a paper strong with voice as one where the writer's energy and passion for the subject drive the writing, making the text lively, expressive, and engaging. Sharing many books and papers, discussing their voice, and scoring papers for voice will familiarize students with the trait and make it easier for them to revise their own work.

Student Checklist for Voice

- Do I care about the topic?
- Does this sound like me?
- Do I make the reader feel something?
- Did I show feelings rather than tell about them?
- Do my illustrations show voice?

Evaluator Checklist for Voice

RATING: STRONG (5)

- Writing is honest and convincing.
- The piece is full of feeling.
- Tone fits the purpose and audience.
- I want to hear or know more.
- There is a connection between writer and reader.

Following is a student example from grade 4:

> Divorce (Something I'll Never Forget)
> When your parents divorce it makes you feel like you're split in two. Who am I with this weekend? Who gets me on Thanksgiving or Christmas Eve? My dad didn't just leave my mom, he left me, too. I was sent to my grandma's the weekend he moved out. I guess they thought it would be easier for me but they were wrong. Kids aren't as dumb about things like that as grown-ups think. I was only six but I knew something was going on. I know it sounds silly, but the thing I miss most is how he'd say, "Hey, Sport" when he came home from work and gave me a big bear hug. When I got home his stuff was gone, just like he'd never been there.

At first my mom tried to do special things with me like play games and rent movies but after a while we didn't do that as often and it was go to school, eat dinner, do homework, watch TV, and go to bed. And sometimes she'd cry or I'd hear her on the phone saying mean things about my dad to her friends or my grandma.

Every other weekend I went to my dad's but his apartment was tiny and he never had anything good in the refrigerator. Kids don't like TV dinners so we'd usually have frozen pizza or go to MacDonald's. There was only one bedroom so I'd sleep in a sleeping bag on the couch. It was fun at first, kind of like camping, but pretty soon I started wishing I was in my own bed with sheets and stuff.

There are some good things about having divorced parents. Like on my birthday my mom would let me have a party or a sleepover and then my dad would do something special, too. And you get twice as many presents. But at Christmas, just when I was ready to play with my new stuff at my mom's, it was time to go with my dad. But, more presents!

Now my dad has a girlfriend and she has two kids. If they get married they'll live with him and see him every morning and have dinner with him every night. Maybe he'll call them "Sport" and hug them. When I get married, I'm never going to get a divorce. Sometimes I wish I was five again. Then it was me, my mom, and my dad.

The topic is clearly defined, with relevant details. I would score this a 4–5 in ideas. The organization needs work. Sequence is not always clear. The beginning is strong, as is the ending. I would score this a 3–4 in Organization. The writer is honest about his feelings. It is obvious how he feels and what he worries about. It touches your heart. I would score this 5 in voice.

RATING: DEVELOPING (3)

- Writing is pleasant, but not individual.
- There are brief moments that amuse or move the reader.
- There is more telling than showing feeling.
- Some parts are vague.
- There are equal strengths and weaknesses.

Following is a student example from grade 5:

My Best Friend (Friendship)
Jamie and I have been friends since preschool. We liked each other from the moment we met. We are so much alike. The first time I slept over at her house we discovered that we both still sucked our thumbs!

We were in the same class in first grade but not in second. That was awful but we still walked to the bus stop together and played together at recess. We were in the same class in third and fourth, and now fifth. That rocks!

Sure, we have fights once in a while but we know we'll be friends forever. The longest time we were ever mad was three days. That was because she laughed at me when I fell off my bike in the mud so I threw a mud ball at her and called her a nasty name. I even call her mom "mom" sometimes and she doesn't care.

I know that she will always be there for me and that I will always be a friend to her. We plan to go to the same college and then get an apartment together. When we get married, we'll be each other's maid of honor and our kids will be friends, too.

The writer starts out with specific details, but then gets too general. I would score this 3 in ideas. The beginning and end are present, but not strong. Some things could be moved around. I would score this 3 in organization. The voice is not strong. There are a few memorable moments (thumb-sucking, mud ball) but more telling than showing. I would score this 3 in voice.

RATING: WEAK (1)

• Writing is not personalized.

• I can't tell how the writer feels.

• No risk is taken.

• No memorable moments.

• Writer doesn't care or know enough about topic.

Following is a student example from grade 3:

Soccer (Favorite Thing)
I like to play soccer. It is fun. Once I made a goal. It was neat. But we lost the game. I wear shin guards. Sometimes they fall down.

My coach is nice. We practice on Wednesdays. The games are on Saturday. Sometimes it rains and we get wet. Once it snowed at a game. It was cold. It was hard to see the white ball in the snow. We slipped and slid.

My soccer clothes get really dirty so my mom has to wash them. Maybe I'll play basketball next year.

Although a few details are given, there is no elaboration, and not all details are relevant. I would score this 2–3 in ideas. The organization is weak: no definite beginning or end, and the sequencing is random. I would score this 1 in organization. This piece does not convey or elicit feelings. I would score this 1–2 in voice.

Sample Lesson Plans

For voice, I recommend spending at least one day on "forbidden words," compiling a list with the class and posting it in the room. Then, take two or three sessions for showing, rather than telling, feelings. Persuasive writing and point of view can take only one day for grades K–2 (brief explanation) and up to a week each for grades 3–5. And, of course, every day share a book that exemplifies the trait of voice. You may also want to compare the works of one author or illustrator and identify his or her "voice." Following are two lesson plans that I have used for the trait of voice.

Sample Lesson Plan (Grades K–2)

DAY 1

1. Read *Love You Forever* (1986) by Robert Munsch. Explain that this is a story about the love between a mother and her son. Discuss the voice in the book and how it makes you and the class feel.

2. Read *Guess How Much I Love You* (1995) by Sam McBratney. Discuss all the ways Little Nutbrown Hare told his father that he loved him. Remind students that showing feelings is a form of voice.

3. Have the class name other words and phrases you could use to tell someone how much you love them ("more than anything in the world," "more than chocolate candy," "more than winning a soccer game"). Record answers on the board or a chart.

4. Have students copy one of the phrases or have them write one of their own and illustrate it. You might prepare a template for them: "I love you more than _____."

DAY 2

1. Read *I Love You As Much—* (1993) by Laura Krauss Melmed. Explain that in this story a mother is telling her child how much she loves him. This is a form of voice.

2. Using the pattern in the book ("said the mother camel to her child, 'I love you as much as the desert is dry.'"), ask students to think of some other mother animals and how they might tell their child how much she loved him (animals that are not in the book: cow, pig, chicken, duck, squirrel, dog, cat, deer). You might also want to do a theme, such as farm animals, wild animals, zoo animals, or pets. Record on board or chart.

3. Have students choose an animal mother and write a sentence telling how much she loves her child (some children may need to copy from the chart). Have students illustrate their sentence.

4. These pages can be put together into a class book.

Sample Lesson Plan (Grades 3–5)

DAY 1

1. Read *Fly Away Home* (1991) by Eve Bunting. Explain that this story takes place in an airport in Chicago where homeless people really do live. Discuss the feelings that are described in the book: fear of being caught, worry about the bird, hoping for an apartment, sad that the mother died, anger that rents are too high and that others have homes, and hope that they will find a way out.

2. Have students work in pairs or groups to find the words used to convey these identified feelings. You will have to have several copies of the book or reproduce appropriate pages for each pair or group.

3. Ask students why they think the author chose *Fly Away Home* as the title. (The bird found a way out of the airport, and Andrew hopes that he and his dad will, too.)

DAY 2

1. Read *Smoky Night* (1994) by Eve Bunting. Explain that this story is based on the Los Angeles riots.

2. Discuss the feelings described in this book: fear, confusion, panic, concern, worry, and hope.

3. Have students work in pairs or groups to find the words used to convey these feelings.

4. Have students compare this book with *Fly Away Home*. They look very different because they have different illustrators, but has the author used the same or similar ways to tell the story? (In both, there is a "story within a story," there is a single parent and one child who have a major problem, and the story ends with hope.)

Conclusion

Voice is writing from the heart. Once the foundation for writing (ideas and organization) is in place, the writer's personality can come through. Writers must know and care about their topic, and they must use specific examples to show and describe feelings. They must form a connection with the reader, and their tone must match the purpose and the audience. If the reader laughs, cries, or reacts in any way, the piece has voice. Persuasive writing, advertisements, and point of view are all forms of voice.

For voice, students should automatically think *feelings*. They should check their work for vague or general statements and be able to revise to show, rather than tell. Literature is an ideal way to explore how authors use voice to convey their message. Sharing and scoring many sample papers will help students understand what is needed in their own writing.

In the following chapter on word choice, I will discuss how teachers can build on the students' ability to recognize the *forbidden*, or general, words we've discussed in this chapter and to replace them with more specific words.

ANNOTATED LIST OF CHILDREN'S LITERATURE TO USE FOR VOICE

Alderson, Sue Ann. (1999). *Wherever bears be: A story for two voices*. (Arden Johnson, Illus.). Berkeley, CA: Tricycle Press.

> Two young girls go berry picking and imagine that bears are everywhere—friendly bears, of course! Text and illustrations show what's in the girls' minds in this whimsical, "feel-good" story. (Grades K–2)

Atkins, Jeannine. (1999). *A name on the quilt: A story of remembrance*. (Tad Hills, Illus.). New York: Atheneum.

Lauren remembers the good times with Uncle Ron as she and her family make a quilt panel in his memory to be part of the NAMES Project AIDS Memorial Quilt. Through words, the author shows how the family feels and how making the quilt helps the family members cope with their loss. (Grades 2–4)

Brutschy, Jennifer. (1993). *Winter fox*. (Allen Garns, Illus.). New York: Knopf.

On a cold winter night, Rosemary's beloved rabbit disappears. Fearing what happened, she accompanies her father on a hunt for the fox that has been raiding the chicken coop. Rosemary's point of view changes completely when she sees the ragged, lean, and hungry fox. (Grades 3–5)

Bunting, Eve. (1995). *Dandelions*. (Greg Shed, Illus.). San Diego, CA: Harcourt Brace.

Zoe has never seen her Papa so happy, or her Mama so sad, as they leave the comfort of a house in Illinois for the Nebraska prairie. Bunting shows two opposite points of view about this journey to a new place. After a trip to a small town with Papa, Zoe finds a way to make Mama smile. (Grades 3–5)

Bunting, Eve. (2001). *Jin Woo*. (Chris K. Soentpiet, Illus.). New York: Clarion.

Illustrations as well as words show voice in this story of a family who is adopting a Korean baby. David isn't sure how he feels about the newcomer, but his mother helps him understand just how important it is to be a big brother. (Grades K–3)

Bunting, Eve. (2000). *The memory string*. (Ted Rand, Illus.). New York: Clarion.

Laura's memory string represents her family history, most of all her dead mother. Laura doesn't give her new stepmother a chance until she is there to comfort her when the string breaks. Bunting uses words and symbolism to show the relationship between the string and the girl's broken heart, and how both might be mended. (Grades 2–4)

Bunting, Eve. (1996). *Train to somewhere*. (Ronald Himler, Illus.). New York: Clarion.

Based on the orphan trains, carrying homeless children from New York to the Midwest in the mid-1850s, Bunting captures the feelings of a young girl who is sure her mother will return to get her. This is a wonderful example of the power of showing rather than telling about feelings. (Grades 3–5)

Cannon, Janell. (1993). *Stellaluna*. San Diego, CA: Harcourt Brace.

A baby fruit bat is separated from her mother and adopted by a family of birds. Information about the differences in these species is conveyed in an often humorous way. Voice is displayed in illustrations as well as words. The facial expressions on both the bat and the birds show the reader exactly how they feel. (Grades K–3)

Coerr, Eleanor. (1993). *Sadako*. (Ed Young, Illlus.). New York: Putnam.

Ed Young's beautiful paintings show the courage of Sadako, adapted by the author from her novel about the young girl with the "atom-bomb" disease. Both the author and illustrator, through words and pictures, convey a powerful plea for world peace. (Grades 3–5)

Coles, Robert. (1995). *The story of Ruby Bridges*. (George Ford, Illus.). New York: Scholastic.

The first black child to attend an all-white elementary school, 6-year-old Ruby Bridges faces challenges, hatred, and danger every day when she is escorted to and from first grade at William Frantz Elementary School in New Orleans. Through both words and pictures, the reader can see Ruby's courage and dignity. (Grades 1–5)

Curtis, Christopher Paul. (1995). *The Watsons go to Birmingham: 1963*. New York: Delacorte.

This Newbery Honor Book is full of voice. The author uses words to create vivid images, which show both humor and suffering. Often hilarious, the family trip from Michigan to Alabama, so that Grandma can straighten out oldest child Byron, soon involves a tragedy that affects not only the family but also the nation. (Grades 4–5)

Dahan, Andre. (2000). *Squiggle's tale*. San Francisco: Chronicle.

An adventurous pig, Squiggle goes to visit his cousins in Paris and writes letters home to his parents assuring them that he is being good. That is from his point of view. The illustrations show what Squiggles is really doing. (Grades K–3)

Hall, Donald. (1994). *I am the dog, I am the cat.* (Barry Moser, Illus.). New York: Dial.

> This book shows different points of view. On alternating pages, the dog and the cat describe their life and feelings for various things, including each other. (Grades K–5)

Johnson, Paul Brett & Lewis, Celeste. (1996). *Lost.* New York: Orchard Books.

> On a camp-out in the Arizona desert, the family dog, Flag, chases a rabbit and gets lost. The little girl and her father spend the next few weeks searching for him. Color illustrations on the left-hand pages show the perils that Flag faces, while the right-hand pages have text and pictures of the girl and her father in their search for the dog, telling the story from two different perspectives. (Grades 2–5)

Martin, Ann M. (1996). *Leo the magnificat.* (Emily Arnold McCully, Illus.). New York: Scholastic.

> Based on the life of a real church cat, this story tells how Leo touched the lives of young and old and how the congregation found a special way to remember him. Although Leo doesn't belong to anyone, the author's words show the reader how much he was loved by many. (Grades 1–4)

McKissack, Patricia C., & McKissack, Frederick L. (1994). *Christmas in the big house, Christmas in the quarters.* (John Thompson, Illus.). New York: Scholastic.

> Christmas is celebrated in Virginia in 1859. This story shows contrasting points of view. The text and illustrations alternate between what is happening at the big plantation house and at the nearby slave quarters. (Grades 3–5)

Okimoto, Jean Davies. (2002). *Dear Ichiro.* (Doug Keith, Illus.). Seattle, WA: Kumagai Press.

> Henry says he'll hate his friend Oliver forever when they have a fight. Later, at a baseball game he learns a lesson in forgiveness when his great-grandfather, a World War II veteran, tells him he can't believe he's cheering for baseball players from Japan. This story brings a message of healing and hope by looking at the feelings of Henry and his grandfather. (Grades 1–5)

Polacco, Patricia. (2001). *Betty Doll*. New York: Philomel.

> Betty Doll was always there when Mary Ellen needed her. Knowing that she is about to die and that her daughter, Trisha, will need comforting, she leaves Betty Doll and a letter where Trisha will find them. It is the words in the letter that help Trisha deal with her loss. (Grades 2–5)

Say, Allen. (1999). *Tea with milk*. Boston: Houghton Mifflin.

> Although she was born and raised in San Francisco, May's parents decide to return to Japan when she graduates from high school. She goes with them and struggles with the two cultures. Words and illustrations show how she feels like an outsider, but finally discovers the true meaning of "home." This is a true story about the author's mother. (Grades 3–5)

Tunnell, Michael O. & Chilcoat, George W. (1996). *The children of Topaz: The story of a Japanese-American internment camp*. New York: Holiday House.

> Based on the classroom diary of a third-grade class, life in a Japanese-American Internment Camp in Utah is told from the students' point of view. (Grades 3–5)

Turner, Ann. (1994). *The Christmas house*. (Nancy Edwards Calder, Illus.). New York: HarperCollins.

> The house has seen many Christmases and several generations of the same family. Special memories are told from the point of view of various people and by the house itself. (Grades 2–5)

CHAPTER 7

Choosing the Right Words

I do not choose the right word. I get rid of the wrong one.

—A.E. HOUSMAN

Word choice is precision in the use of words—wordsmithery. This trait involves the love of language, a passion for words, combined with a skill in choosing words to create just the right mood, meaning, impression, or word picture the writer wants to instill in the heart and mind of the reader (Spandel, 2001b). Skill in word choice is not just choosing a correct word, but finding the best word to make meaning clear and to create a particular feeling.

In learning to choose words, students need to be reminded that it is not always best to use the most unusual or the longest word, but the one that suits the mood and the topic best. Trying to impress the reader with "big words" often skews the meaning and diminishes, rather than enhances, the piece. The vocabulary needs to be natural, and the audience must always be considered. Every word or phrase must be crystal clear, or defined for the reader. Strong word choice is not so much an exceptional vocabulary, but a skill requiring the writer to use everyday words precisely.

When checking a piece for word choice, the writer must often revise by finding a better way to get the message across. I once heard author-illustrator Jan Brett tell the audience at a conference, "It takes an hour for an inch. Words have to be simple. Illustrations do not." Point out to students the intricacies of her illustrations and the simplicity of her text in *The Mitten* (1989). Another way to show students that precision is best is to share pieces that are overwritten. Menus, travel brochures, and descriptions in catalogs often use superfluous words and phrases intended to impress and influence the reader. Have students help you revise them with simple language.

115

Increasing Vocabulary

Words are invaluable pieces in the writing process. The larger a student's collection of words, or vocabulary, the greater the variety of words the student has to choose from in writing. The National Reading Panel (NICHD, 2000) concluded that vocabulary can be acquired through incidental learning. This conclusion suggests that students who are exposed to words through wide reading will increase their vocabulary. Teachers can make a list of interesting words and add to it as the class finds new ones from literature. Megan Sloan (1996) has pairs of students look through a book, recording the interesting words they find. Next to the interesting word, students write the common word the author could have used. She also has students dramatize several words that differ by shades of meaning (*raced, crept, tiptoed, sauntered*). First-grade teacher Anne Veer has a word value chart in her classroom (see Figure 15). As new words are found, they are placed in the appropriate column. Students can check their own writing using this chart. The object is to have some high value words in a piece. Whenever Ralph Fletcher (1996) encounters an unusual new word, he adds it to a list in his notebook. He lists words like *persnickety, succotash,* and *scuppernong*. Georgia Heard (1995) haunts used-book stores, searching for books that contain unusual words. Teachers can have students write favorite words in personal dictionaries or notebooks so they can access them easily for future use in their writing.

Gaining Precision

Research has shown that the teaching of grammar in isolation (repetitive drills and exercises) does not lead to improvement in students' writing, and that in fact, it hinders development of students' written language (NCTE, 1985). But students do need to know how to write with more powerful nouns and verbs (Routman, 1996). In order to do this, they must be able to identify and use nouns, verbs, and other parts of speech. Beginning in first grade, teachers should point out and call nouns, verbs, and adjectives by their names when talking about them in reading and writing. In first and second grade, we often refer to nouns as *naming* words, verbs as *action* words, and adjectives as *describing* words. I think this is fine as long as we also call them by their correct names. Another way to make sure students understand these parts of speech is to share books like *A Mink, a Fink, a Skating Rink* (1999), about nouns; *To Root, to Toot, to Parachute* (2001), about verbs; and *Hairy, Scary, Ordinary* (2000), about adjectives, all by Brian P. Cleary.

$ .01	$ .10	$ .25	$.50	$1.00	$2.00	$5.00
mad	angry	cross	annoyed	furious	enraged	
				irate	incensed	
	tired	sleepy	drowsy	weary	fatigued	soporific
				exhausted		
glad	happy	pleased	cheerful	delighted	elated	ecstatic
sad	unhappy	depressed	gloomy	dejected	broken-hearted	melancholy

FIGURE 15. Word Value Chart

Verbs

I tell students to think *strong verbs* for word choice. Verbs are more powerful than modifiers. Teach children to develop a critical eye for verbs, looking for action, energy, and power, as you share stories with them. Patrick O'Connor (1999) defines a wishy-washy writer as one who uses weak nouns (like *destruction*) instead of strong verbs (like *destroy*). The wimp writes, "'The storm resulted in the *destruction* of the building,' instead of 'The storm *destroyed* the building'" (pp. 151–152). Some good writers regard adjectives as signs of weak sentences. They use precise, strong nouns and verbs rather than adjectives and adverbs to prop up weak nouns and verbs. For example, they would use not the *young horse*, but the *colt*; not *walked lively*, but *pranced* or *trotted*; and *whispered* instead of *talked softly*. Other good writers use the different parts of speech with care. Le Guin (1998) describes adjectives and adverbs as "rich and good and fattening" but admonishes not to overindulge (p. 61).

One of the most effective ways to show students in grades 2–5 the power of verbs is to have them circle or underline verbs in a piece of writing. Start with a poor example like this on the overhead projector:

> I <u>have</u> a bike. It <u>is</u> red. I <u>like</u> to ride it. It <u>is</u> fun. My friend and I <u>like</u> to ride in the woods. It <u>is</u> really cool there. We <u>have</u> a good time. When it <u>is</u> time to go home I <u>have</u> to put my bike in the garage. That <u>is</u> where I keep it.

Underline the verbs with a colored pen. Now read them in a monotone voice (*have, is, like, is, like, is, have, is, have, is*). Ask the class if there is variety, excitement, or energy. They will see how dull the verbs are and how often the verbs *is* and *have* appear. When students are writing and you tell them to check their use of verbs, recognizing dull verbs and verbs used several times will be one thing they can do to see which ones need revising.

To help students find just the right verb, put the following animal names on the overhead and have them supply a verb showing a movement that best matches the animal:

Animal	Verb
rabbit	hop
squirrel	scamper
horse	gallop
cat	pounce
mouse	scurry
snake	slither
frog	leap
elephant	stomp
rooster	strut
chicken	scratch
deer	prance
bear	lumber
duck	waddle

The verb *to be* has eight forms: *is, am, are, was, were, be, been,* and *being*. While they need to be used on occasion, overuse results in weak sentences. To avoid excessive use of helping verbs (*was, were*), have students change the verb ending in the following examples:

Original statement: They *were running* to school.
Revision: They *ran* to school.

Original statement: We *were eating* lunch.
Revision: We *ate* lunch.

Original statement: Joyce *was drawing* a picture.
Revision: Joyce *drew* a picture.

Original statement: We *were playing* cards.
Revision: We *played* cards.

Original statement: My family *was going* to the zoo.
Revision: My family *went* to the zoo.

Original statement: He *was laughing* at the clown.
Revision: He *laughed* at the clown.

To help students learn to use strong, specific verbs, put the following sentences on the board or overhead projector and have students help you revise them using a more precise verb:

Original statement: We *ate* popcorn at the movies.
Revision: We *munched* popcorn at the movies. Or use *enjoyed, devoured*.

Original statement: Mike *fell* from the top of the stool.
Revision: Mike *slipped* from the top of the stool. Or use *stumbled*.

Original statement: We *looked* for our lost cat.
Revision: We *searched* for our lost cat. Or use *hunted*.

Original statement: The old car *made a lot of noise* as it sped by.
Revision: The old car *rumbled* as it sped by. Or use *backfired, rattled*.

Original statement: The toddler *got up* on the bed.
Revision: The toddler *climbed* on the bed. Or use *scrambled, crawled*.

| **Original statement:** | The boys *looked around* the campground. |
| **Revision:** | The boys *explored* the campground. Or use *surveyed, investigated*. |

Nouns

A precise name for a person, place, or thing can create a clearer image in the reader's mind than general ones. If the writer describes being chased by a dog, the reader doesn't know how big it is, or if it is playing or on the attack. But, if the writer describes a snarling Doberman with its teeth bared, the reader has a vivid picture. Teach students to look for general nouns by having them circle or underline them in a sample piece of writing. Then have them help you change them to more specific ones. An example follows:

Last weekend we went camping. Our <u>spot</u> *campsite* was under some big <u>trees</u>. *firs/cedars*. The first day there we went fishing and caught some <u>fish</u>. *trout*. Then we went for a <u>walk</u> *hike* up a <u>path</u> *trail* along a <u>little river</u>. *stream/brook*. The next <u>day</u> *morning* my mom cooked <u>food</u> *breakfast* over the fire. Then we went on another <u>walk</u>. *hike*. It was <u>a good trip</u>. *an adventure*.

To help students find just the right noun, put the following generic nouns on the board or overhead and have students change them to more specific ones:

General	**Specific**
noise	*bang, crash, thud, thunder, plop*
car	*convertible, Ford, Corvette, jalopy*
candy	*licorice, Snickers Bar, fudge*
furniture	*couch, bed, chair, table*
room	*kitchen, basement, bedroom*
clothes	*shirt, pants, skirt, blouse, sweater*
flower	*rose, daisy, sunflower*
dog	*Collie, mutt, Great Dane*
meal	*dinner, lunch, breakfast*
dish	*plate, bowl, platter*

Other Parts of Speech

Advertisers carefully choose not only verbs and nouns, but also adverbs, adjectives, and other parts of speech. They have to communicate well in limited space, and they have to convince readers that the product is necessary for them (voice). Teachers can point out specific words and images in ads. Following are examples from commercial catalogs and brochures:

- A <u>sophisticated</u> woven plaid <u>breathes</u> new life into tired furniture. (an ad for slip-covers)
- Our new <u>Executive</u> Chef has been <u>pleasing the pallets</u> of <u>discriminating diners</u> around the world for more than 40 years. (a restaurant has a new cook)
- <u>Revolutionary</u> mulching blade <u>installs</u> in a snap onto your existing mower blade. Tough, metal-nylon filaments are the <u>mulching</u> elements that <u>recirculate</u> and re-cut clippings into fine pieces. Clippings make a great fertilizer for thicker, <u>lusher</u> lawns. (ad for lawn mower blade)
- Sonic bark control collar <u>safely silences howling hounds</u>! (collar to keep dog from barking)
- Jackson Hole lies at the base of the <u>rugged</u> Grand Tetons, and offers the summer visitor an <u>endless</u> <u>array of activities</u>.... (from a summer travel brochure)

Notice the use of active verbs (*breathes, installs, recirculate*); descriptive adjectives (*sophisticated, executive, revolutionary, rugged, mulching, lusher, endless*); and alliteration (*pleasing the pallet, discriminating diners, safely silences, howling hounds, array of activities*).

Introducing Literary Devices

Literary devices are common elements found in literature that move the reader beyond the literal interpretation of a story to appreciate its colorful language, subtle understatement, or unique tone (Hall, 1994). Picture storybooks can effectively illustrate many of these elements that authors use. According to Fletcher and Portalupi (1998), these devices are easier to recognize in books than to use in your own writing. But when children are exposed to rich literature, they can learn, with teacher guidance, not only to recognize these devices, but to understand why an author chooses specific words and ultimately to begin to use them in their own writing.

Alliteration, the repetition of the initial sounds in neighboring words or stressed syllables, is a literary device often used by writers. Think about familiar phrases like *blushing bride, nervous Nellie, bouncing baby boy, leapin' lizards, rambling rose,* and *Rudolph the Red Nosed Reindeer*. These are all examples of alliteration. Alliteration is effective as long as the word choice fits the subject and audience and is not chosen just because it begins with a particular letter of the alphabet. If you are writing about a mean cat, *ferocious feline* might be a better choice; as is *playful pup* or *pooch* instead of fun-loving dog. As you read books to students, ask them what they notice about phrases like *snarled with a sneer* or *slithered and slunk with a smile* from *How the Grinch Stole Christmas* (1957) by Dr. Seuss. Ask them about *curly and crunchy and cheesy* or *storing school supplies* from Kevin Henkes's *Lilly's Purple Plastic Purse* (1996). Let students discover alliteration for themselves and then introduce them to the word. Other books to use as examples of alliteration are *Clara Caterpillar* (2001) and *Some Smug Slug* (1996) by Pamela Duncan Edwards.

A *simile* is a comparison between unlike objects. The words *like, as, such as*, and *than* are used in these comparisons. In *White Snow, Bright Snow* (1947), author Alvin Tresselt describes "automobiles like fat raisins buried in snowdrifts." Yet a *metaphor* compares two unlike things by literally declaring that they are the same. An example is "Winter has feet that walk through cracks" from Nancy White Carlstrom's *Goodbye Geese* (1991).

Hyperbole is an exaggeration not meant to be taken literally. Most children realize that there are a lot of cats, but not really a million of them, in Wanda Gág's *Millions of Cats* (1928).

Writers use *imagery* to provide mental pictures by using terms that appeal to the senses. In Ezra Jack Keats's *The Snowy Day* (1962), "a great big tall heaping mountain of snow falls down—plop!"

Inference allows for conclusions to be drawn by the reader based on limited clues present in the story. Lois Ehlert uses inference in both illustrations and text to let the reader know why the cat won't catch the birds in *Feathers for Lunch* (1990). An example of a clue is "The cat's bell goes jingle-jingle."

Irony is a contrast between expected outcomes and what actually happens. After chasing the cat for three days, Angus in *Angus and the Cat* (1931), by Marjorie Flack, actually misses the cat when it disappears.

A humorous but recognizable imitation of another literary work is called a *parody*. Tony Johnston uses parody in a western version of *The Princess and the Pea*. Instead of a pile of mattresses, the pea is beneath 50 saddle blankets on a horse in *The Cowboy and the Black-Eyed Pea* (1992).

Onomatopoeia uses words that imitate the sounds they represent, like *clunk, plop*, and *swish*. In *Sky Dogs* (1990), Jane Yolen describes the sound of walking on lawn as "grass beneath our feet sang swee-swash, swee-swash."

Students who are familiar with these devices are able to use them in their own writing. In fact, they often include them before the concept is formally introduced because they have seen and heard them in literature. I don't belabor or focus on definitions, but only point out or ask students what they notice about the words that authors choose. Following a brief discussion in which I name or identify the device that the student has shown me, I then suggest that students may want to occasionally use these devices in their writing.

Using a Thesaurus, or Not?

A thesaurus is a dictionary of synonyms that is intended to help writers and speakers in search of a better way to say what they want. Strictly speaking, however, there are no synonyms because by definition *synonyms* are words having the same meaning, and no two words are identical in meaning. Words assumed to be synonyms can refer to different objects, make varying observations about these objects, and stir different sorts of pictures and emotions in users of the language (Laird, 1985). Many teachers are reluctant to allow students unlimited use of a thesaurus. I must admit that I am one of them. Although I do believe they are useful at times, when students rely or depend on them too much, results can be disastrous. Take an overused word (also known as tombstone words, forbidden words, or trite words), look it up in a thesaurus, and make a list of the entries. Use this list to show students how the meaning can be changed. Take the word *ran*, as used in "The river *ran* through the canyon." Just a few examples are *gushed, trickled, flowed, raged, dribbled, roared, rushed, raced,* and *sped*. These would all work within the context of the sentence, but look at the difference between *gushed* and *trickled*. And what about *hurried, skittered, darted, galloped, cantered, trotted, ambled,* and *fled?* They won't work at all. Let's look at the first paragraph of "Grandma's Porch" and use the thesaurus to revise some of the verbs and nouns.

> Grandma's ~~porch~~ *portico* was made of big ~~red cement squares~~ *scarlet glue rectangles.* You went up three ~~steps~~ *rises* to get on it, and it had a black wrought-iron ~~railing~~ *balustrade* around it *so* you wouldn't ~~fall~~ *drop* off. There was a big ~~blue porch~~ *indigo portico* swing on one end of the porch with a white fringed ~~canopy~~ *covering.* I spent hours sitting there with Grandpa, ~~swinging~~ *fluctuating.* On the other end there were some ~~metal chairs~~ *element seats* with legs that were ~~curved~~ *flexed* in one piece. I loved to ~~rock~~ *sway* those *seats,* but that made big ~~scratch marks~~ *scrape brands* on the ~~porch~~ *portico* so I'd get in ~~trouble~~ *difficulty* for doing that.

Granted, this is an extreme example, but it does show what can happen when a thesaurus is used incorrectly. Incidentally, I used the first entry for each word that I changed.

Discouraging Jargon and Slang

A word of warning about the use of jargon and slang in writing. These are usually regional terms and can become outdated in a short period of time. I ask students what the word *keen* means. If I'm lucky, someone may know that it means "sharp." I then tell students that when I was in school, *keen* was an expression for something really good. I ask them to tell me the current word for "really good." Over the years I have heard *rad*, *bad*, *buff*, *cool*, *neat*, and so forth. I then tell them that if they use those words in their writing, someone reading it in a few years will have no idea what they meant. That usually solves the problem.

Practicing Precision

Semantic Gradient

In teaching students to use more precise words, you may find it helpful to work with them on a *semantic gradient*, a graphic display of the range of meaning between and around opposites (see Figure 16). Jack Cassidy, past president of the International Reading Association, explained semantic gradient for vocabulary study at a conference session I attended. He says the following example of semantic gradient works with third graders and above. Take two overused words like *good* and *bad*. Place them at each end of the gradient. Then introduce similar words and ask students where they fit. Notice that *outrageous* belongs in the middle because it is related to both words.

Cloze Procedures

Another activity to help students increase their word choice skills is the cloze procedure. In a cloze procedure, students are required to complete omitted portions of text by reading its remaining context. Copy a passage from a book, omitting some of the nouns and verbs. Have students fill in the blanks. Then

```
FIGURE 16. A Semantic Gradient

    ▲   Splendid

        Terrific

        Wonderful

        Excellent

        **Good**


        Outrageous


        **Bad**

        Terrible

        Horrid

        Horrific

    ▼   Abominable
```

check the original and compare. Were any of the original words a surprise? Which ones work best?

The following paragraph is excerpted from *Caleb & Kate* (1977) by William Steig. Have students fill in the blanks:

> Kate _____ to love her dog, very much indeed. But, though they gave each
> other _____, they were far from happy. Kate _____
> for her missing husband; she couldn't _____ why he'd left her.
> And how Caleb _____ he could speak and explain! He would
> _____ by her feet, _____ a bone, while she worked at
> her weaving. Often a tear would _____ from her _____, or
> she would _____through the window and _____, and Caleb would
> put his _____ in her lap and _____ her sad face. Kate would
> _____ fondly behind his ears, _____ his fur, and tell him
> how _____ she was to have such a _____ friend.

Original text:

Kate grew to love her dog, very much indeed. But, though they gave each other comfort, they were far from happy. Kate longed for her missing husband; she

125

couldn't understand why he'd left her. And how Caleb wished he could speak and explain! He would sprawl by her feet, gnawing a bone, while she worked at her weaving. Often a tear would hang from her lashes, or she would stare through the window and sigh, and Caleb would put his paws in her lap and lick her sad face. Kate would scratch fondly behind his ears, caress his fur, and tell him how lucky she was to have such a faithful friend.

Let's look at the persuasive letter from the last chapter. Here is how students helped revise it for word choice:

Dear Mom,

Before you say no, just <u>listen</u> to what I <u>have</u> to say. Let me begin by saying how lovely you <u>looked</u> this morning. Your new hairdo <u>is</u> most becoming and that outfit you <u>wore</u> makes you <u>look</u> even slimmer than you are.

I'<u>ve been</u> thinking that Nicky really <u>needs</u> a friend. I <u>read</u> recently in *Cat Fancy* that cats ~~need~~ *require* companionship just as much as people do. With you at work and me at school, what <u>does</u> ~~that~~ *our* poor ~~animal~~ *creature* <u>have</u> to do all day? I'm afraid <u>we're</u> not providing him with the kind of environment that <u>is</u> best for his well being.

My friend Jennifer ~~told me~~ *explained* about a shelter for cats that she and her mom ~~went to~~ *visited*. There <u>are</u> hundreds of cats who <u>don't</u> have a home. She <u>said</u> it <u>was</u> the most depressing place she's ever ~~been to~~ *seen*. What in the world ~~is going to~~ *will* happen to all those poor kitties? If we <u>adopted</u> a friend for Nicky, we <u>would</u> be saving one of those poor creatures from a life of misery, or even worse, no life at all. I <u>think</u> it's our duty to rescue one of those ~~cats~~ *felines*.

Now, there's something else I <u>want</u> you to think about. I <u>know</u> how upset you are about all the furniture Nicky ~~has~~ <u>wrecked</u> with those *lethal* claws of his. I also <u>read</u> that if a cat has a playmate and something to do all day, it won't bother scratching furniture. We <u>could</u> also get one of those cute scratching posts for both of the cats to play on. Think of all the money you'll save on furniture by just investing a little bit of money now on another cat and a scratching post.

Speaking of money, I'd be willing to contribute some of my allowance ~~to buy~~ *for* extra cat food. And of course I <u>will</u> feed and brush and do everything to take care of the cats. I <u>know</u> I haven't done much to take care of Nicky but I'll change. This <u>is</u> the new me!

Oh, one more thing. Since you <u>are</u> the sweetest, kindest mother in the whole world, when we <u>get</u> this cat I've decided to let you name it. Start thinking of a name because we <u>have</u> to act soon. I'm the luckiest girl in the world to have such a wonderful mother.

Love,
Becky

P.S. Let me know when we can go pick out a cat.

After underlining the verbs the following changes were made: *need* was replaced with *require* because *needs* was in the preceding sentence; *told me* was changed to *explained, went to* with *visited,* and *said* was changed to *told me* because they were weak and overused; *is going to* became *will, has been to* changed to *seen,* and *is going to* was replaced with *will* because they had helping verbs. General nouns were changed to more specific ones (*animal* to *creature, cats* to *felines*), *that* was replaced with *our, has* was deleted, *to buy* was replaced with *for,* and *lethal* was inserted before *claws.*

Using Books as Examples of Word Choice

Sharing literature is an ideal way to demonstrate how authors choose just the right words. Look for books with rich, colorful, and precise language. Verbs should be powerful, active, and full of energy. Choose books in which the author uses simple language with striking clarity or those which stretch the reader's knowledge of language with unusual expressions or specialized language (Spandel, 2001a). As you read, ask students what expressions they notice. Select books with words or phrases you'd like students to know. These should be challenging, without being too technical or difficult, and the meaning must be clear from context.

When focusing on the trait of word choice, look for books with lively language like *Night Noises* (1989) by Mem Fox and *Blow Me A Kiss, Miss Lilly* (1990) by Nancy White Carlstrom; or puns and alliteration like Dav Pilkey's *Kat Kong* (1993). Read *Tough Boris* (1994) by Mem Fox and *Where Once There Was a Wood* (1996) by Denise Fleming to show how only a few carefully chosen words can tell a story. Share alphabet books like *Antics!* (1992) by Cathi Hepworth and *Alphabatics* (1986) by Suse MacDonald.

To expose students to specialized vocabulary, read *The Glorious Flight* (1983) by Alice and Martin Provensen. For word play, read *Double Trouble in Walla Walla* (1997) by Andrew Clements and *Hey, Hay!* (1991) by Marvin Terban. And to reinforce parts of speech and expose children to rich vocabulary, share *Merry-Go-Round* (1990) or any books by Ruth Heller. At the end of this chapter is an annotated list of children's literature to use for word choice.

Assessing Word Choice

When evaluating a paper for word choice, look for lively language, active verbs, and descriptions that form images in your mind. Did the writer choose the best words to convey his message? Are there phrases that you want to remember or share with someone? Can you tell that the writer has revised until she found the most precise words to use or does it appear to be the first thing she wrote down? Spandel (2001b) defines a paper high in word choice as having "well-chosen words that convey the writer's message in a clear, precise, and highly readable way, taking readers to a new level of understanding" (p. 277).

If you don't feel comfortable circling or underlining verbs in a paper you are scoring, you will soon learn to "eyeball" the verbs to see if they are active and varied. Also, look for "$5 words" or words that are specific, descriptive, and fit the mood of the paper. If alliteration is used, does it complement the piece and is it more subtle than overdone? Are literary devices, if used, appropriate to the topic and tone of the text? Are all words used correctly, or is there evidence that a thesaurus was used? Is the piece free of jargon or slang, or if it fits the mood, is it kept to a minimum?

When I am scoring papers I usually read the paper once to see if it appears to be functional. I then try to highlight (or in some way note) great verbs, memorable words, and phrases. If there are five or more of these highlights, the paper is usually strong in word choice. You will now be scoring for four traits, so it will take a little longer to give a fair assessment. Each trait needs to be assessed separately. Sometimes one or more traits will jump out at you, but you will need to go back and reread or actually count words or phrases to determine a score for a specific trait. A paper can be high in one or more traits and low in others, which is one of the advantages of scoring each trait separately. If a student gets a low score on some traits and a high score on others, it is easier for the student to work on weaknesses, knowing that there are strengths as well. Self-esteem plays an important part in motivation and willingness to revise and correct. Students find it much easier to revise for one or two traits than to be told that a paper is unacceptable and that they have to start over.

As with all the traits, after presenting the trait, sharing lots of literature demonstrating the trait, and doing several related activities, it is essential that you share many sample papers and have students help you evaluate them. Sharing and evaluating are the only ways in which they will understand what you are looking for and what the scores mean.

Student Checklist for Word Choice

• Did I use words I love?
• Did I use specific, not general words?

- Did I use lively and different verbs?

- Will the reader understand my words?

- Do my words create pictures?

Evaluator Checklist for Word Choice

RATING: STRONG (5)

- Words are not only correct, but just right.

- The writer uses lively verbs and precise nouns.

- Words create vivid images.

- Phrasing is original, sometimes memorable.

- The writer is in control; language is natural.

Following is a student example from grade 5:

> Plum Lake, "My Home Away From Home" (Favorite Place)
> Fog covers the ground on a warm summer night. Our car goes bumpity bump along the gravel road leading to our cabin. Soon we are there. My family and I lounge on the porch gazing at the beautiful sunset that turns the lake a rich plum color. I know I am home.
>
> Our property is gorgeous. There are three cabins, two on a hill and one on the lake's shore. Each cabin has a screened in porch, and one has an outdoor porch too. There are lots of towering trees and we have a great view of Plum Lake.
>
> I guess I'd better tell you about the inside of our cabins. The cabins all have nice kitchens and a porch. Only two have bathrooms though. The log cabin has a beautiful view of the lake that takes my breath away.
>
> Once a year the residents of Plum Lake hold competitions. We call it Cottager's Weekend. There is a swim across part of the lake, a golf tournament at Plum Lake Golf Club, a tennis tournament, a party for the adults, and a sailboat race. It's a blast!
>
> Plum Lake has three islands and one peninsula which we call Cook's Point. Clear water splashing the shore and paths that lead in different directions. It's great for cookouts and exploring. What great times we've had there.
>
> On a scorching hot day Plum Lake is the place to be. The water is like a cold front on a hot day. We have a boat (that I love waterskiing behind) and a diving raft. My sister Laura and I also love playing in the water. "Pood" my aunt's sailboat is really fun too.

Sometimes at night, our family sits on the porch talking and looking out toward the lake. Some of us sit on the floor, the swing, the couch, or the chairs. We all manage to squeeze on the porch. (There are usually 10–20 people.) I think it's an important family time.

Plum Lake is like a second home to me. The first time I went I was only a month old. It's a place for me to be alone or with family and friends I only see once a year. I feel more comfortable there than at my own house. You don't hear about crime there every day either. Plum Lake is my absolute favorite place. It may not seem great to you, but Plum Lake will always be my home away from home.

The topic is defined with relevant details and events. I would score this 5 in ideas. The sequence is logical. There is a definite beginning and ending, although the ending is better than the beginning. I would score this a 4–5 in organization. The writing is honest and you know exactly how she feels about Plum Lake. I would score this 4–5 in voice. The word choice is strong in this piece. Verbs are lively and varied (*lounge, gazing, manage*). Modifiers and nouns are vivid (*bumpity bump, peninsula, scorching*). I have counted at least five "memorable moments" (*towering trees, takes my breath away, like a cold front on a hot day, more comfortable there than at my own house, my home away from home*). This is a 5 in word choice.

RATING: DEVELOPING (3)

- Most words are correct, but only functional.
- The paper has a few lively verbs and memorable moments.
- Some attempts at colorful language are overdone.
- Words tell what the writer wants to say but few create images.
- Strengths and weaknesses equal.

Following is a student example from grade 4:

Roller Coaster Crazy (Something I'll Never Forget)
My family went to Orlando last year. We had the best time. First we went to Warner Brothers. That's where we got soaking wet. First we went on a couple of rides where we ended up going into water. We were soaked. The best was the river adventure. We looked like drowned rats after that one. Then we went on the Dueling Dragons. That's two different roller coasters and you think you're going to run into each

other. We saved the best for last. The Incredible Hulk. Strapped in like astronauts, it had to be the wildest roller coaster ever!

The next day we explored MGM Studios. It was blazing hot. We could have used some of that water from the night before. The Rockin Roller Coaster is indoors. There's neat music playing and it goes really fast. The best ride there wasn't a roller coaster but on a thrill scale, it was definitely a 10! The haunted hotel is a creepy looking place and the line takes so long you have lots of time to be worried about the ride. You finally get to the elevator and go in and sit down and get strapped in. Who sits down in an elevator?

Anyway, you go up a long way then all of a sudden the doors open and you see the bright sunlight and BAM you drop straight down about a hundred miles an hour. Then you go up again and down, about five times. My dad's camera case kept flying up even though he had the strap around his arm. It was awesome.

Our last day was spent at Epcot. They don't have very many neat rides but there was one good one. You guessed it, a roller coaster. It was a test drive. At first it was kind of dull but then you came to a big door and just when you thought you were going to crash into it opened and you were outside going like a rocket on a track really fast. It was neat. So that was our trip to Orlando. I've never been on that many roller coasters in 3 days.

This topic could be narrowed more. More relevant details could be told about one of the parks or even one of the rides. There is more telling than showing. I would score this 2–3 in ideas. The sequence is easy to follow, and there is a beginning and end, but they are not strong. I would score this 3 in organization. The writer had a good time, but the voice doesn't show us how he felt when the elevator was dropping, or when the two roller coasters looked like they were going to crash. I would score this 2–3 in voice. For the most part, verbs are boring and terms are general. There are a few "memorable moments" (*drowned rats, strapped in like astronauts, a hundred miles an hour, thrill scale, going like a rocket*), but the writer missed many opportunities to use vivid language. I would score this 3–4 in word choice.

RATING: WEAK (1)

- The writer uses vague or general words and phrases.
- Vocabulary is limited and some words are used incorrectly.
- The piece is full of clichés and jargon.
- There is repetition and redundancy.
- Writer's message is unclear.

Following is a student example from grade 3:

> My Broken Arm (Something I'll Never Forget)
> My worst day ever was the day I broke my arm. I was playing on the bars at recess and I fell and landed on my right arm. It really hurt. I started to cry and then the playground teacher came over. She told me not to move it and helped me get up. I went to the nurse. She put a sling on it and called my mom.
>
> Then we went to the doctor. It still hurt really bad, really bad when she touched it. Then I had to have x-rays and it hurt when they made me hold still where they put it. It was broken, but not really bad. I didn't have to have a operation or anything. The only good thing was I got to choose the color of the cast. I got purple which is my favorite color.
>
> I had that cast for six weeks and sometimes it itched but it didn't really hurt anymore. I was scared when they took it off with a saw and my arm looked funny. Now it's better. That was my worst day.

The topic is defined but has mostly telling statements. I would score this 2–3 in ideas. The organization is adequate. The beginning and end tie together, but they are not strong. The sequence is easy to follow. I would score this 3 in organization. The voice is weak or not present. Other than "hurt really bad," we do not know how the writer feels. I would score this 1–2 in Voice. The word choice is also weak. The writer has not told us how if felt when he fell, or went to the doctor. Why was he scared when the cast was taken off? Passive verbs and no memorable moments. I would score this 1–2 in word choice.

Sample Lesson Plans

When introducing word choice I always do a brief introduction or review of verbs and nouns (see section on Gaining Precision). I then take a few days for the verb activities described earlier in this chapter and an additional one or two days for the noun activity (changing general to specific). Being able to identify weak verbs and general nouns and then change them to strong and specific ones enables students to evaluate and revise their own writing. The remainder of the time spent on word choice should be spent scoring and revising writing samples together and sharing literature as an example of word choice. This is the time to point out and discuss literary devices and their uses and to discover why authors chose just the right words to convey their message. Following are two lesson plans that I have used for the trait of word choice.

Sample Lesson Plan (Grades K–1)

1. Read *Muddigush* (1992) by Kimberley Knutson.

2. Ask students if they think all the words in the story are real words or made-up words.

3. Explain that sometimes authors make up words by putting other words together or by rhyming with words.

4. Read the book again, stopping after each page. Ask students to pick out the best words and write them under the correct column on a chart (real words/made-up words).

5. These are the words the children will most likely identify:

Real
- *rushing, snapping, hushing*
- *splashing, stomping*
- *slush, gush, icky, sticky*
- *sludgy, squelchy, slimy, mush*
- *churn, smack, foam, bubbles*
- *mudballs*
- *scoop, slime, puddle, juice*
- *shivery, quivery, bubbly, wiggly, smack, whack*
- *crust, crumbly, slicker, gurgles*

Made Up
- *skoosh, goosh*
- *goosh, muddigush*
- *mudge, smucky, squooshy, slooshy*
- *mashpies, mudlucious*
- *slurgles, snurgles*

6. Have students write sentences using one of the real words and one of the made-up words. Depending on age and ability, students may dictate a sentence or copy one that you have written for them.

7. Have students illustrate their sentence.

Sample Lesson Plan (Grades 3–5)

1. Put the following passage from *A Job for Wittilda* (1993) by Caralyn and Mark Buehner on the board or overhead, substituting *said* after each quotation:

    Mrs. Hatrack looked up from her magazine.

    "EEEEEEE!" she said.

"WITTILDA!" Aunt Bort said, "WHAT HAVE YOU DONE?"

"I think it's pretty," Wittilda said defensively.

"YOU'RE FIRED!" said Aunt Bort.

2. Ask students to think of words that might substitute for *said* in the passage. Cross out *said* and write the words students suggest. Have students list other words that can be used instead of *said*. Record them on a chart. Make a copy for students or have them copy them into their writing notebooks.

3. Now read the book. Ask students to listen for words that are used in place of *said*.

4. Make a list of all the words used in place of *said*: *worried, queried, decided, grunted, murmured, cautioned, exclaimed, screamed, thundered, shouted, told, muttered, cackled, barked, fluttered, whispered, exclaimed, agonized, shouted, asked, cried,* and *sang*.

5. Explain that *said* is often used, but sometimes another word might be better. Encourage them to use the list as a reference for their own writing. Remind them to look for words as they read that can substitute for *said* and to record them in their writing notebooks.

Conclusion

Word choice involves rich, colorful language. It is finding words that are not only functional, but will convey the message and the mood in just the right way. Because of the precision required, it may take several revisions to achieve the desired results. Writers must realize that specific verbs and nouns are often more effective than generic ones with modifiers.

For word choice, students should automatically think *strong verbs*. After participating in teacher-led activities to identify and use powerful words, students will be able to check and revise their own work. Exposing children to literature that is strong in word choice and that uses alliteration, playful language, puns, and builds vocabulary is a most effective way to demonstrate this trait. When students see the various devices that good authors use, they will be able to use them in their own writing. And, having gained precision in word choice, they will be ready to go on to the next trait, fluency and rhythm, which I discuss in chapter 8.

ANNOTATED LIST OF CHILDREN'S LITERATURE
TO USE FOR WORD CHOICE

Appelt, Kathi. (2002). *The alley cat's meow.* (Jon Goodell, Illus.). San Diego, CA: Harcourt.

> A spoof of musicals, Red (a dashing, smashing downtown kind of cat) meets Miss Ginger (a jazzy, snazzy uptown sort of gal) at a boogie-woogie juke joint called the Alley Cat's Meow and they dance the night away. The story is full of puns and rich vocabulary. (Grades K–5)

Birdseye, Tom. (2003). *Oh yeah!* (Ethan Long, Illus.). New York: Holiday House.

> Two boys spending the night in a backyard tent try to outdo each other telling scary stories. The book demonstrates good use of alliteration and modifiers. (Grades 1–4)

Clements, Andrew. (1996). *Frindle.* (Brian Selznick, Illus.). New York: Simon & Schuster.

> Because his teacher is a fanatic about learning new words, Nick invents one for a pen: *frindle.* When the joke gets old, Nick doesn't back down and things get out of hand. (Grades 3–5)

Dodds, Dayle Ann. (1996). *Sing, Sophie!* (Rosanne Litzinger, Illus.). Cambridge, MA: Candlewick.

> Sophie has a song in her heart, and it needs to come out, but it bothers everyone and everything. But when her baby brother is frightened by a thunderstorm, it is only Sophie's singing that will quiet him. The story includes great verbs and descriptive words such as *caterwauling, strummed, twirled,* and *dangled.* (Grades K–3)

Edwards, Pamela Duncan. (1995). *Four famished foxes and Fosdyke.* (Henry Cole, Illus.). New York: HarperCollins.

> A tale about four foolish foxes and their wiser brother, Fosdyke. This book is an excellent example of alliteration. Illustrations and context help define more unusual words. (Grades 1–4)

Edwards, Pamela Duncan. (1997). *Barefoot: Escape on the Underground Railroad.* (Henry Cole, Illus.). New York: HarperCollins.

Based on stories about the Underground Railroad, this book focuses on the Barefoot (slave) who is running from the Heavy Boots (plantation owner) until the animals help him escape. The author uses symbolism in her choice of words. There are also active verbs. (Grades 2–5)

Falwell, Cathryn. (1998). *Word wizard*. New York: Clarion.

When her alphabet cereal floats in milk, Dawn discovers that by switching letters around, she can be a word wizard! Described as an anagram adventure, with illustrations helping to define the words, this book is excellent for vocabulary development. (Grades 1–3)

Frasier, Debra. (2000). *Miss Alaineus: A vocabulary disaster*. San Diego, CA: Harcourt Brace.

Sage misunderstands one of the new vocabulary words, and the fun begins. She turns embarrassment into triumph when she realizes her mistake. This book is also an alphabet book, uses alliteration, and gives definitions of bold print vocabulary words. (Grades 2–5)

Harper, Charise Mericle. (2002). *When I grow up*. San Francisco: Chronicle.

The left-hand page shows a word (*generous, dependable, optimistic,* etc.) and the right-hand side uses text and illustrations to define it. (Grades K–2)

Henkes, Kevin. (1991). *Chrysanthemum*. New York: Greenwillow.

Chrysanthemum loves her name until she goes to school and is teased. Everything in this story relates to the theme. When she is happy she *blooms*, and when teased, she *wilts*. The reader knows why Henkes has chosen these verbs. (Grades K–2)

Johnston, Tony. (1998). *Bigfoot Cinderrrrrella*. (James Warhola, Illus.). New York: Putnam.

The author's choice of words to tell this version of a familiar tale all link to the old-growth forest and Bigfoot characters. The prince is looking for a bride, and it is the unlikely Rrrrrella, who catches his eye, but she wants nothing to do with him. Also a good example of alliteration. (Grades 2–5)

Leedy, Loreen, & Street, Pat. (2003). *There's a frog in my throat! 440 animal sayings a little bird told me*. New York: Holiday House.

The authors have taken familiar sayings about animals and explain their meaning. Literal illustrations add to the humor. Good for vocabulary, especially for English language learners. (Grades K–5)

McGeorge, Constance W. (1995). *Snow riders*. (Mary Whyte, Illus.). San Francisco: Chronicle.

Instead of building an ordinary snowman, two children build snow horses that magically come to life. Descriptive words, especially verbs, make this an excellent example of word choice. (Grades K–3)

Pilkey, Dav. (1993). *Dogzilla*. San Diego, CA: Harcourt Brace.

The mice of Mousopolis try to defend themselves against the dreadful Dogzilla. Full of puns, alliteration, and, as the author states, may be too goofy for grown-ups. (Grades K–5)

Ryan, Pam Muñoz. (1997). *A pinky is a baby mouse, and other baby animal names*. (Diane deGroat, Illus.). New York: Hyperion.

Rhyming riddles reveal unusual names for newborn animals. (Grades K–2)

Sathre, Vivian. (1995). *Mouse chase*. (Ward Schumaker, Illus.). San Diego, CA: Harcourt Brace.

Two word sentences (noun/verb) tell the story of the mouse's escape from the cat, but it is the choice of words that is exceptional. (Grades K–5)

Sharp, N.L. (2003). *The ring bear*. (Michael T. Hassler, Jr., Illus.). Crete, NE: Dageforde.

Robert is delighted when told he will be the "Ring Bear" at his aunt's wedding. When his misunderstanding is explained to him he declares, "If I can't be a bear, I'm not going to be in the wedding!" (Grades K–2)

Steig, William. (1990). *Shrek!* New York: Farrar Straus Giroux.

Lively language and challenging vocabulary words tell the story of the ugliest ogre in the forest. Steig is a master of word choice. Most children are surprised that this was a book before a movie. (Grades K–5)

Waite, Judy. (1998). *Mouse, look out!* (Norma Burgin, Illus.). New York: Dutton.

Rhyme, alliteration, and powerful nouns and verbs tell the story of a mouse who is hunted by a cat. (Grades K–2)

Walton, Rick. (2002). *Herd of cows! Flock of sheep! Quiet! I'm tired! I need my sleep!* (Julie Olson, Illus.). Layton, UT: Gibbs Smith.

When Farmer Bob's house floods and he floats down the river, groups of all kinds of animals try to save him. Verbs (*trudged, stirred, hollered, rooting*) and labels for groups of animals (*herd, drove, colony, pack, army*) make this an excellent example of word choice. (Grades K–2)

Wells, Rosemary. (1997). *McDuff moves in.* (Susan Jeffers, Illus.). New York: Hyperion.

Lively verbs and alliteration help tell the story about the little stray dog that finally found a home. (Grades K–2)

CHAPTER 8

Apprehending Fluency and Rhythm

Clarity. Clarity. Clarity. When you become hopelessly mired in a sentence, it is best to start fresh.

—WILLIAM STRUNK, JR., AND E.B. WHITE, *THE ELEMENTS OF STYLE*

Sentence fluency gives writing a sense of rhythm and style. Sentences are well constructed, begin in different ways, and vary in length. But, fluency is much more than grammatical correctness. It is the ability to express oneself freely and naturally. If a paper is easy and enjoyable to read aloud and you feel the rhythm as you read, it is strong in fluency. The "read aloud value" helps distinguish fluency in most writing. And, the clarity of the sentence is also important. Just as in word choice, where the longest word is not always best, neither is the longest or most complex sentence always the best choice. In *Words Fail Me* (1999), Patricia O'Connor writes, "I'll always take a plain sentence that's clear over a pretty one that's unintelligible" (p. 40). Spandel and Stiggins (1997) define sentence fluency as

> finely crafted construction combined with a sense of rhythm and grace. It is achieved through logic, creative phrasing, parallel construction, alliteration, absence of redundancy, variety in sentence length and structure, and a true effort to create language that literally cries out to be spoken aloud. (p. 56)

Poetry is particularly fluent, as are songs, rhymes, and pattern books (see chapter 2). Well-written prose can also have a poetic flow, whether it is fiction or nonfiction. Surround children with poetry, highly predictable and pattern books, and books where language seems to flow as you read aloud. Ask them to listen for the rhythm or, sometimes, to say the words back and hear the beat (Spandel, 2001b). Have them clap to the beat or chant a refrain as you read. Rhythm is not only pleasant sounding or soothing, it is often very important to the meaning of both the words and story. According to Saccardi (1996), "meaning is conveyed as much by the rhythm of the chosen words as by words themselves" (p. 29).

Although reading fluency and sentence fluency as it pertains to writing are different, I would argue that they are indeed related. The report of the National Reading Panel (NICHD, 2000) indicates that fluency should be a key component of effective reading instruction. Fluency is the ability to read a text quickly, accurately, and with proper expression. By reading orally to students, we model what fluent, meaningful reading is like (Rasinski & Padak, 2001). We also model the presence of fluency in writing. Many of the same techniques used to teach reading fluency can also be used in writing. Choral reading of the school pledge or motto, poems, and stories builds reading fluency and demonstrates phrasing in writing. Readers Theatre focuses on conveying the meaning of the script through reading voices. Reading dialogue aloud teaches students to infer the author's message with both intonation and feelings.

I think sentence fluency is the most difficult trait to teach. This trait seems to require more inherent talent than the others. For this reason, I urge you to share literature often and talk about the importance and power of fluency. By exposing students to poems, stories, and writing samples, they will be able to recognize good sentence fluency and apply it to their own writing. When you read *Slugs* (1983) by David Greenberg, students will hear the rhyme and alliteration, but most likely the humor will appeal to them more. When you read *The Reason I Like Chocolate* (1993) by Nikki Giovanni, they will notice that not all poetry rhymes, but it definitely has a rhythm and flow. And, when you read *When the Earth Wakes* (1998) by Ani Rucki, they will see how simple text and symbolic language can tell the story of the seasons in a lyrical way.

In addition to sharing literature, teachers can work with students in the following areas to help them learn to write with fluency: sentence beginnings, sentence length, sentence combining activities, and run-on sentences.

Sentence Beginnings

When I begin teaching the trait of fluency, I tell students to think *sentence beginnings*. Sentences should begin in different ways. Let's take the example we used to check the verbs in chapter 7. Because students previously underlined the verbs in this passage, we will circle the words that begin each sentence. You might also have students use different colored pencils or pens. You want them to check their work for both traits so they need to mark words in a different way.

I have a bike. It is red. I like to ride it. It is fun. My friend and I like to ride in the woods. It is really cool there. We have a good time. When it is time to go home I have to put my bike in the garage. That is where I keep it.

Now read them in a monotone voice (*I, It, I, It, My, It, We, When, That*). Ask the class if there is variety, excitement, or energy. Notice that the structure is nearly the same in all the sentences. Major revision will be needed. I tell students to be careful of overusing *I, the,* and *there.*

Now let's look at the third paragraph of "Grandma's Porch."

One January morning, Grandma and I looked out the picture window and saw snow. About six inches of white, fluffy stuff formed a big cloud on the porch. Grandma was the youngest of seven children and always said it wasn't fair that I had no brothers or sisters to play with. So, guess what we did? Dressed in our warmest clothes, we put on hats, mittens and boots and went out the back door. We walked around the yard, carefully tiptoeing up the edge of the porch steps. Plopping in the snow in front of the window, we made snow angels. Getting up carefully, we left the same way we came. When Grandpa got home from work we took him into the living room and had him look out the window. There were two perfect snow angels, one big and one little. Grandma and me.

I point out to the students that the sentence beginnings and structure are varied (*One, About, Grandma, So, Dressed, We, Plopping, Getting, When, There, Grandma*). Notice the fragment at the end of the paragraph. Fragments are acceptable if they are used effectively. But, I rarely point this out to students unless they notice and comment on it. I then explain that sometimes authors use fragments to emphasize or set a mood. *Quiet, Please* (1993) by Eve Merriam and *Welcome Back Sun* (1993) by Michael Emberley are good examples of simple and complex sentences, as well as fragments, used effectively.

Sentence Length

In addition to varied beginnings and structure, sentences should not always have the same number of words. Have students count the words in each sentence. If they are all about the same length, revision is needed. Using the sample about the bike, have students count the words in each sentence.

(I) have a bike.(4) (It) is red.(3) (I) like to ride it.(5) (It) is fun.(3) (My) friend and I like to ride in the woods.(10) (It) is really cool there.(5) (We) have a good time.(5) (When) it is time to go home I have to put my bike in the garage.(16) (That) is where I keep it.(6)

Most of the sentences contain 3–5 words. Point out that there needs to be more variety in sentence length. Indicate how some sentences should be combined. For example, the first four sentences could be combined to read: *My red bike is fun to ride* or *I like to ride my red bike*.

Now let's take a look at the paragraph from "Grandma's Porch" for sentence length:

(One) January morning, Grandma and I looked out the picture window and saw snow.(14) (About) six inches of white, fluffy stuff formed a big cloud on the porch.(14) (Grandma) was the youngest of seven children and always said it wasn't fair that I had no brothers or sisters to play with.(23) (So,) guess what we did?(5) (Dressed) in our warmest clothes, we put on hats, mittens and boots and went out the back door.(18) (We) walked around the yard, carefully tiptoeing up the edge of the porch steps.(14) Plopping in the snow in front of the window, we made snow angels.(13) (Getting) up carefully, we left the same way we came.(10) (When) Grandpa got home from work we took him into the living room and had him look out the window.(20) (There) were two perfect snow angels, one big and one little.(11) (Grandma) and me.(3)

Point out that sentence length is varied. Students need practice combining sentences so they will be able to revise their own work when necessary.

Combining Short, Choppy Sentences

Sentence combining is making one smoother, more detailed sentence out of two or more shorter sentences. In *Synthesis of Research on Teaching Writing* (1987), G. Hillocks, Jr., reviewed 20 years of research and found that the practice of building complex sentences from simpler ones has been shown to be effective in a large number of experimental studies. Sentence-combining activity positively impacts the quality of student writing (Routman, 1996). Short, choppy sentences can be combined by deleting unnecessary words, moving words around, or using adjectives in a series. They can also be joined together with conjunctions (*and, but, or, nor, for, so, yet*), subordinate conjunctions (*after, when, since, because, before*), and relative pronouns (*who, whose, which, that*). With younger children (grades K–2), I call these *connecting* words. Words and phrases can also show how sentences interrelate (*however, therefore, natural-*

142

ly, after a while, on the other hand, to be specific, for example, although, as it turned out).

In the following activity, you can show students how to combine sentences. Put the following sentences on the board or overhead projector:

I am going to the dentist.

Her name is Dr. Akins.

I am going tomorrow.

Have students help you combine these into one sentence.

Revision: Tomorrow I have an appointment with my dentist, Dr. Akins.

The class can continue to practice combining sentences with the following examples:

My dog loves to swim.

He loves to jump off the dock.

He loves to fetch the ball.

Revision: My dog loves to jump off the dock, retrieve the ball, and swim back to shore.

My mom is short.

She is blonde.

She is pretty.

Revision: My mom is short, blonde, and pretty.

The house is big.

It has three floors.

It has five bedrooms and three bathrooms.

Revision: The big house has three floors, including five bedrooms and three bathrooms.

Ted ran in the race.

Kathy and Sue ran in the race, too.

Revision: Ted, Kathy, and Sue ran in the race.

Dad slipped on the dock.

He fell in the water.

He got soaked.

Revision: Dad slipped on the dock, fell in the water, and got soaked.

My baby sister loves carrots.

She loves peaches, too.

But she hates peas.

Revision: My baby sister loves carrots and peaches, but hates peas.

I ate three artichoke hearts.

My mom doesn't like them.

My dad doesn't like them either.

Revision: I ate three artichoke hearts because my mom and dad don't like them.

Correcting Run-On Sentences

Run-on sentences occur when two or more sentences are joined, without punctuation or a connecting word. Often they can be fixed simply by adding punctuation or a connecting word. But other times, they should be rewritten as two separate sentences. This is especially true of sentences that are connected with the word *and*. Have students practice adding periods and capitals to revise the following run-on sentences.

Original statement:	We went to the mall and bought some stuff and then we ate at the food court and then my dad picked us up and took us home.
Revision:	We went to the mall, bought some stuff, and ate at the food court. Then dad picked us up and took us home.
Original statement:	John woke up late and got dressed in a hurry and had breakfast in a hurry and then he ran for the school bus and he was late so he missed it.
Revision:	John woke up late and hurried to get dressed and have breakfast. Although he ran to the bus stop, he still missed the bus.
Original statement:	I was scared when the fire alarm rang and it hurt my ears and I didn't know what it was at first and then I saw everyone lining up at the door so I went over there and then we went outside and it was cold and I didn't have a coat.

Revision: I didn't know what it was when I heard the fire alarm go off. Ears hurting, I saw the class line up at the door so I followed. It was cold outside because I didn't have my coat.

As with all activities, it is essential to have the class practice until they can perform the task independently. Then, they will know how to revise their own writing. And remember, a surefire technique to check for fluency is to read it aloud.

Revising for Sentence Fluency

Let's look at the persuasive letter from chapters 6 and 7. In the following example, strikethroughs and italics indicate where students helped to revise the letter for sentence fluency

~~Dear Mom~~ Dearest Mother,

Before you say no, just listen to what I have to say.(12) Let me begin by saying how lovely you looked this morning.(11) Your new hairdo is most becoming and that outfit you wore makes you look even slimmer than you are.(19)

I've been thinking that Nicky really needs a friend.(9) ~~I read recently~~ *Recently* I read in *Cat Fancy* that cats ~~need~~ require companionship ~~just~~ as much as people.(14) ~~do.~~ With you at work and me at school, what does that our poor ~~animal~~ creature have to do all day?(19) ~~I'm afraid~~ *Maybe* we're not providing him with the kind of environment that is best for his well being.(17)

My friend Jennifer ~~told me~~ explained about a shelter for cats ~~that~~ she and her mom ~~went to~~ visited.(14) ~~There are~~ *Hundreds* of cats ~~who~~ don't have ~~a home~~ homes!(6) She ~~said~~ told me it was the most depressing place she's ever ~~been to~~ seen.(12) What in the world ~~is going to~~ *will* happen to all those poor kitties?(11) If we adopted a friend for Nicky, we would be saving one of those poor creatures from a life of misery, or even worse, no life at all.(28) ~~I~~ Don't you think it's our duty to rescue one of those ~~cats~~ felines?(12)

Now, there's something else I want you to think about.(10) I know how upset you are about all the furniture Nicky ~~has~~ wrecked with those lethal claws of his.(18) ~~I also read that~~ *If* a cat has a playmate and something to do all day, it won't bother scratching furniture.(17) We could also get ~~one of those cute~~ a scratching post for both ~~of the~~ cats to play on.(13) Think of all the money you'll save ~~on furniture~~ by just investing a little bit ~~of money~~ now on another cat and a scratching post.(21)

Speaking of money, I'd be willing to contribute ~~some~~ a percentage of my allowance ~~to buy~~ for extra cat food.(17) ~~And~~ *Of* course I will ~~feed and brush and do everything to take care of~~ take full responsibility for the cats.(10) I know I haven't done much to take care of Nicky but I'll change.(14) This is the new me!(5)

145

    <u>Oh</u>, one more thing.(4) <u>Since</u> you (are) the sweetest, kindest mother in the whole world, when we (get) this cat I've decided to let you name it.(23) <u>Start</u> thinking of a name because we (have) to act soon.(11) <u>I'm</u> the luckiest girl in the world to have such a wonderful mother.(13)

Love,
Becky

P.S. Let me know when we can go pick out a cat.(12)

After underlining sentence beginnings, we decided that some needed changing. To eliminate *I* in some, *I read recently* was changed to *Recently I read* and *I'm afraid* was changed to *Maybe*. *I also read that* was eliminated, as were *And* and *There are*. Sentence length was varied but some unnecessary words and phrases (*that, just, do, who, one of those cute, of the, on furniture*, and *of money*) were removed. *Some* was replaced with *a percentage of* and *feed and brush and do everything to take care of* became *take full responsibility for* for clarity and flow. *Dear Mom* became *Dearest Mother* because the more formal address sounded better when read aloud and was intended to impress the mother.

Using Books as Examples of Fluency

The best way to teach fluency is to share examples through literature: "Read aloud regularly from text that is strikingly fluent" (Spandel, 2001b, p. 209). Mem Fox (1993) explains that literature she *heard*, rather than read, as a child resonates in her memory whenever she sits down to write. "Vocabulary and a sense of rhythm are almost impossible to teach.... So how are children expected to develop a sense of rhythm or a wide vocabulary? By being read to, alive, a lot!" (p. 68).

    When choosing books for fluency, find poetry or those that read like poetry. Share books like *Song of the Circus* (2002) by Lois Duncan, *Sun Song* (1995) by Jean Marzollo, and *My Mexico-Mexico mio* (1996) by Tony Johnston. Choose books with sentences that are highly varied in length and structure like *Mister Got To Go and Arnie* (2001) by Lois Simmie and *Canoe Days* (1999) by Gary Paulsen. Share books that read with a flow like *My Father's Boat* (1998) by Sherry Garland and *Ballpark* (1998) by Elisha Cooper. And read books with repeated rhythms, words, or refrains like *The Cat's Purr* (1985) by Ashley Bryan and *Up and Down on the Merry-Go-Round* (1988) by Bill Martin, Jr., and John Archambault. Above all, look for books that invite expressive interpretive reading. At the end of this chapter is an annotated list of children's literature to use for fluency.

Assessing Fluency

When evaluating a paper for fluency, look for well-constructed sentences, varying in length and structure. Read the paper aloud to see if there is a cadence, rhythm, or natural flow of words. If it flows and you can feel the rhythm, even if the punctuation is incorrect, give it a high score in fluency. "Fluency is rhythm, grace, smooth sentence structure, readability, variety, and logical sentence construction" (Spandel & Stiggins, 1997, p. 45). Spandel (2001b) describes a paper strong in fluency as one where sentences are strong, grammatical, clear, and direct. Text can be read quickly and without any confusion. Sentences begin with meaningful words (*then, therefore, in fact*) and vary in length, with most being concise.

Look at the beginning of each sentence. Do the same words and patterns appear frequently? Look at the length of each sentence. Do all sentences have approximately the same number of words? Are most sentences short and choppy or long and run-on? At first you may have to actually circle and count, but as you become more familiar with the traits you will be able to scan the piece for this information. If you are having difficulty scoring this trait, go back and actually count and highlight.

Remember to score each trait separately. By the time you get to sentence fluency, you and your students should have had ample experience with the first four traits, making it easier for you to score. Continue to discuss and point out all the traits as you add a new one so that they remain fresh in everyone's mind.

Student Checklist for Fluency

- Do my sentences begin in different ways?
- Are some sentences short and some long?
- Does it sound good when read aloud?
- Is there a rhythm or flow?
- Have I used only the words that I need?

Evaluator Checklist for Fluency

RATING: STRONG (5)

- Sentences vary in structure and length.
- Sentence beginnings are varied.

- The writing has rhythm, cadence, or flow.

- The piece is easy to read aloud.

- Sentences are grammatically correct.

Following is a student example from grade 3:

Seaside (Favorite Place)

Do you have a favorite place that you can go to even in your dreams? I do. It's Seaside, Oregon. My family has been there three times. The first time I was about five and my little sister was two. We stayed in this neat hotel, right on the beach. We had two rooms, with a bathroom in between. Annie and I had twin beds but she kept crawling out of hers. Finally my mom put the couch cushions around it so she wouldn't get hurt. The first day we rented bikes and pedaled up and down the boardwalk that separated the town from the ocean. My dad got a bike with a seat for Annie and I got my own, although it was smaller than his. Annie sang and laughed as we rode through the wind. She'd never been on a bike before and she loved it. We ate out for every meal. What a treat! I'll never forget that first trip to the seashore.

The second time we went to Seaside I was seven. This time we stayed in a motel farther down but it had a little kitchen and we could walk right to the beach. The surf was so inviting, but freezing cold. It was like sticking your big toe in ice cubes. After awhile, your feet get numb, so you don't notice the cold as much. The roar of the waves put us to sleep every night. And do you know that at night the foam on the waves glow in the dark? Dad says it's phosphorus. We rented bikes that time, too. Annie still had to ride on Dad's but she didn't love it this time. She howled because she couldn't have her own. The town has all sorts of neat shops that sell shells, boat stuff, and best of all, salt water taffy. Annie loves that the most. I like it, too, but the best part is that when Annie has her mouth full of taffy, she can't talk. There's even an arcade and bumper cars right down town. Annie threw a hissy fit because she was too little to go on the cars but Dad and I crashed into each other while Mom stuffed taffy into Annie's mouth.

The last time we went to Seaside was this year on spring break. No bikes this time, but roller blades! Not Annie, though. She pouted at first but lit up when she got white roller skates. Just like Tara Lapinsky, she said. I didn't have the heart to tell her they weren't really ice skates. This time we skipped the bumper cars and tried bumper boats. They were incredible. Mom and Annie were in one, but Dad and I got our own. We were only dry for about one second. Then, SPLASH! I plowed into Mom and Annie, soaking them. But then Dad torpedoed me. We were drenched, but laughing. Dad put towels on the seats before he would let us in the car. That's how wet we were. By the time we got back to the motel we were shivering. After all, it was only April and we weren't in Florida. A soak in the hot tub soon warmed us up.

Now, when I'm bored I close my eyes and imagine I am in Seaside, roller blading, bicycling, or just enjoying the beautiful ocean view. I can't wait until we go back.

The topic is defined with relevant details and events. There is more showing than telling, although there are some words that tell rather than show (*neat*; *incredible*). Perhaps the topic could be narrowed more to tell about only one of the trips. I would score this 4 in ideas. The paper has a definite beginning and end, with easy to follow sequencing. I would score this 4–5 in organization. The writing is honest, and you can tell how much the writer cares about this place. I would score it 4–5 in voice. The verbs are active and descriptive (*pedaled, howled, drenched, torpedoed*) and there are memorable moments (*stuffing taffy into Annie's mouth*; *sticking your big toe in ice cubes*). I would score this 5 in word choice. Sentence structure and length are varied, and they begin in different ways. It is easy to read aloud. I would score this 4–5 in sentence fluency.

RATING: DEVELOPING (3)

- Sentences are generally correct.
- Some sentences begin in the same way.
- The paper has some short, choppy sentences and run-on sentences.
- There may be rhythm, but then returns to functional.
- Parts are easy to read aloud.

Following is a student example from grade 4:

My First Plane Ride (Something I'll Never Forget)
Wow! I'm so excited I can hardly stand it. I'm finally going to fly on a plane. My grandma and grandpa live in Arizona and my mom said I could visit them for spring break. First came the packing. Mom took care of most of it but I made sure my favorite baseball shirt was in that suitcase. Who cares about underwear and socks? If you forget them you can always go to K-Mart and buy some more. We had a minor fight over the suitcase. Mom wanted me to use hers but it had blue and pink flowers on it. No way! So, my uncle loaned me his black one. It didn't have wheels like Mom's but it wasn't so girly.

When we got to the airport Mom had to fill out some papers and I had to have a tag tied to my coat. Just like the kindergartener's bus tag! But I got to go on the plane first and the stewardess had me sit in the front, by the window. Not the very front, that's called first class, where the rich people sit. Anyway, I got to go up in the cockpit and talk to the captain. He gave me a little pin with wings. Kind of baby-ish, but secretly I thought it was pretty neat. I was kind of scared when we took off. It was so noisy. But I acted cool. There was no one in the middle seat but a girl was in the next one. She was by herself too. She didn't talk to me so I didn't talk to her. At first I could see things on the ground and they looked real small. But then we got into clouds, then above them so there wasn't anything to see.

Then they came with food but it wasn't very much. I had a coke and a tiny bag of pretzels. But it didn't cost anything. Pretty soon I could see the ground but it was just flat. Almost two hours later we started going down. The noise changed and it felt kind of funny. My ears popped. There it was. Phoenix. It was bigger than I expected. I heard the wheels go down and we landed. It didn't take too long before we got off. It was hot. This is going to be fun. At the end of the ramp there was my grandma and grandpa. I made it.

The idea is developed and narrowed down to one incident. There is an equal amount of telling and showing. I would score this 3 in ideas. The organization is adequate. There is a beginning and ending, although the beginning is not particularly strong. The sequence is logical. I would score this 3–4 in organization. Although the writer sounds excited we don't know exactly how he feels. I would score this 3 in voice. The verbs are passive and there are no memorable moments. I would score this 2 in word choice. The piece is not very fluent. It sounds choppy when read aloud. Sentence construction is varied, as are the beginnings, but they are bland. I would score this 3 in sentence fluency.

RATING: WEAK (1)

- Sentence structure is irregular.

- Most sentences begin the same way.

- Most sentences are choppy or rambling.

- The paper has no rhythm or cadence.

- The piece is difficult to read aloud.

Following is a student example from grade 5:

My Flute (Most Prized Possession)
I got my flute for Christmas. I had to rent one before. It was kind of hard to play. The high notes were really hard. I was so excited when I got it. I almost cried. I kept saying "thank you". I still can't believe I got it. It's so shiny. It's a lot easier to play, too.

I really wanted it but I was surprised. I know my mom can't afford it. I don't know how she did it. I'm so happy. I got some clothes and a sleeping bag. I thought that was all. My mom said there was one more. I saw a skinny package. I grabbed it. I tore the paper off. There it was. I told my mom I love it.

I'm the only one in band with my own flute. I don't rub it in but its so neat. I know the others are jealous. I have the shiny one. They have the old rentals. I will practice so I can be first chair in high school.

The idea is narrowed down, but there is more telling than showing. I would score this 2–3 in ideas. The paper has a definite beginning and ending, but they are not tied together. The sequencing is not clear. I would score this 2 in organization. Although the writer appears very excited, there is nothing that shows true feelings. I would score this 2–3 in voice. Verbs are not active and there are no memorable moments. This is a 1–2 in word choice. This piece is difficult to read aloud because it is choppy and has no flow. Most sentences begin with *I* and *It's* and are of equal length. I would score this 1 in sentence fluency.

Sample Lesson Plans

For sentence fluency I usually take two to three days for the sentence beginning activities, using many writing samples (both good and bad). Then another three or four days on sentence length (sentence combining and run-on sentences). Because sentence fluency is the most difficult trait to teach, it is essential that a large part of instruction time is spent reading and analyzing literature as an example of fluency. If it flows, ask students how the author achieved that effect. Actually look at the beginnings of sentences and notice the length of sentences in the books you read. Have students practice reading aloud from different selections, noticing if some are easier to read than others because of the fluency. Following are two lesson plans that I have used for the trait of fluency.

Sample Lesson Plan (Grades K–2)

1. Read *Rich Cat, Poor Cat* (1963) by Bernard Waber. Ask students if they see a pattern in this book.
2. Explain that this story has a seesaw pattern, where the story goes back and forth. One page tells about rich cats, and the next describes Scat, the poor cat. This pattern continues until the end of the book where the pattern is broken and Scat becomes a rich cat.

3. Tell students that this pattern works best when comparing opposites. Ask students to think of things they do at home that they don't do at school (eat dinner, watch television, take a bath, play with toys, walk the dog). Record responses on the board or chart.

4. Now have them name things they do at school that they don't do at home (eat lunch, go to recess or gym, drink out of fountain, do math, line up). Record their replies on the board or chart.

5. For a class or individual book, have the first page begin: I/We eat dinner at home. The next page would be: I/We eat lunch at school. Continue with other responses.

6. The final page will break the pattern by telling about something that is done both at home and at school such as, But I/We read books at home and at school.

7. Have students write, or copy, and illustrate.

8. Other subjects to use with the pattern: seasons, days of the week, when I'm happy/sad, the good thing/bad thing about.

9. Other books to use that have a seesaw pattern: *Pierre* (1962) by Maurice Sendak or *Fortunately* by Remy Charlip.

Sample Lesson Plan (Grades 3–5)

1. Read *Dogteam* (1993) by Gary Paulsen.

2. Ask students if they notice that some sentences are short and some are long.

3. Explain that writers vary the length of sentences and sometimes add fragments to create an effect for the reader.

4. Reproduce several pages from the book and show on the overhead projector. Have students count the words in each sentence.

> Sometimes we run at night. (5)
>
> In the full moon when it is blue and white on the snow at the same time, so bright and clean and open you could read in the dark, we harness the dogs and run at night. (37)
>
> They tremble. (2)
>
> Some small songs of excitement when the harnesses are put on because they want to run, breathe to run, eat to run, live to run.... (25; note fragment)

5. Point out that on pages 8–13 the author uses fragments as titles or headings (e.g., "The dance." "Into the night." "A lake." "Wolves.")

6. Ask students if they notice any connection between the length of the sentences and the illustrations. (Most of the longer sentences are accompanied by illustrations of several dogs.)

7. Encourage students to apply this technique to their own writing.

8. Other books by Gary Paulsen that can be used as examples of varied sentence length are *Canoe Days* (1999), *The Tortilla Factory* (1995), and *Work Song* (1997).

Conclusion

Sentence fluency is the most difficult trait to teach. To be fluent, writers need a sense of rhythm. Exposing students to good literature where the writer uses patterns, rhymes, flow, smooth phrasing, and thoughtful sentence structure is the best way to familiarize students with this trait. Reading aloud allows the listener to hear the rhythm of the words and phrases and grasp the meaning that the author intends through expression. For younger students, innovations and choral reading of pattern books, books with rhythmic refrains, and poetry give them experience and practice with fluency.

For sentence fluency, students should automatically think *different beginnings* and *varied length*. They should also make sure that sentences begin in meaningful ways and try a variety of sentence forms. To become more fluent writers, students can also practice revising short, choppy sentences into longer, smoother ones and correcting the punctuation of run-on sentences. The final check for fluency should always be to read the piece aloud. When students have apprehended the subtle trait of fluency and rhythm, they are ready to move on to the trait of conventions. Teaching students how to edit for the conventions of spelling, punctuation, grammar, capitalization, and paragraphing—the topic of the next chapter—will further refine their writing skills.

**ANNOTATED LIST OF CHILDREN'S LITERATURE
TO USE FOR FLUENCY**

Aylesworth, Jim. (1992). *Old black fly*. (Stephen Gammell, Illus.). New York: Henry Holt.

This is an alphabet book with lots of rhythm. Comical illustrations and a surprise ending make this a favorite. (Grades K–2)

Bunting, Eve. (1994). *Flower garden*. (Kathryn Hewitt, Illus.). San Diego, CA: Harcourt Brace.

Bunting uses rhyme to tell the story of a special birthday surprise. (Grades K–2)

Cochran, Orin. (1988). *Cinderella chant*. (Terry Gallagher, Illus.). Steinbach, Manitoba: Derksen Printers.

This book retells the Cinderella tale in "rap" form. This poem can be chanted as a two-part or choral reading. (Grades 2–5)

Daly, Niki. (1999). *The boy on the beach*. New York: Margaret K. Elderry.

A small boy and his parents go to the beach on a hot summer day. Soon the boy runs off and finds a small, abandoned boat. He soon realizes he is lost, but all ends well. Although the text is prose, the author incorporates rhyming on some pages, as well as varied sentence length and occasional fragments. (Grades K–2)

Dr. Seuss (1990). *Oh, the places you'll go!* New York: Random House.

Deemed Dr. Seuss' graduation speech, this rhyming verse gives a boost to all as they start any new adventure. The book is great for promoting self-esteem. (Grades K–5)

Fleischman, Paul. (1988). *Joyful noise*. (Eric Beddows, Illus.). New York: Harper & Row.

This book has poems for two voices. It can also be used for choral reading by two groups. (Grades 4–5)

Frost, Robert. (1978). *Stopping by woods on a snowy evening*. (Susan Jeffers, Illus.). New York: Dutton.

This picture book is one of Frost's most famous poems. (Grades K–5)

Hoberman, Mary Ann. (1997). *The seven silly eaters*. (Marla Frazee, Illus.). San Diego, CA: Harcourt Brace.

Mrs. Peters has seven children, each with definite tastes and dislikes, requiring special meals. On their mother's birthday the children find a recipe that pleases everyone, including their mother. The story is told in rhyme. (Grades K–3)

Johnston, Tony. (1994). *Amber on the mountain*. (Robert Duncan, Illus.). New York: Dial.

Two young girls become friends on a lonely mountain, and Anna teaches Amber to read. But Anna moves away before she can teach her friend to write. Amber is "stubborn as our mule, Rockhead," so she teaches herself. All the traits are exemplified in this book, but it is the fluency that makes it so exceptional. (Grades K–5)

Joose, Barbara M. (1991). *Mama, do you love me?* (Barbara Lavallee, Illus.). San Francisco: Chronicle.

An Arctic setting and animals are part of this story of a little girl's quest for independence. The question-and-answer format makes it suitable for paired reading. (Grades 1–3)

Mannis, Celeste Davidson. (2002). *One leaf rides the wind: Counting in a Japanese garden*. (Susan Kathleen Hartung, Illus.). New York: Viking.

This counting book introduces haiku in an easy to read and understand format. Text on the bottom of each page explains something in each poem (bonsai, temple dogs, pagoda, Shinto, etc.). (Grades 2–5)

Moore, Clement C. (1995). *The night before Christmas*. (Ted Rand, Illus.). New York: North-South Books.

Beautiful illustrations enhance this classic Christmas poem and invite readers and listeners to join in. (Grades K–5)

Newman, Lesléa. (2001). *Cats, cats, cats!* (Erika Oller, Illus.). New York: Simon & Schuster.

Rhyming text describes Mrs. Brown's day as the cats lie around and nap. But when Mrs. Brown goes to bed, the cats have a party! (Grades K–2)

Paolilli, Paul, & Brewer, Dan. (2001). *Silver seeds: A book of nature poems*. (Steve Johnson & Lou Fancher, Illus.). New York: Viking.

Acrostic poems describe nature. (Grades 2–5)

Paulsen, Gary. (1993). *Dogteam*. (Ruth Wright Paulsen, Illus.). New York: Delacorte.

> Paulsen describes in prose the running of a dog team on a moonlit winter night. The variety in sentence length in this book is remarkable. (Grades 2–5)

Paulsen, Gary. (1997). *Worksong*. (Ruth Wright Paulsen, Illus.). San Diego, CA: Harcourt Brace.

> Lyrical text and elegant illustrations describe people at work: "It is keening noise and jolting sights, and hammers flashing in the light, and houses up and trees in sun, and trucks on one more nighttime run." (Grades 2–5)

Paxton, Tom. (1999). *The jungle baseball game*. (Karen Lee Schmidt, Illus.). New York: Morrow Junior Books.

> The whacky hippos play the magnificent monkeys in a baseball game. The monkeys are heavily favored, but the hippos find a way to win. Told in rhyme, this book also has a song with music and words on the end pages. (Grades K–3)

Polacco, Patricia. (1997). *In Enzo's splendid garden*. New York: Philomel.

> In a pattern similar to *The House That Jack Built*, Polacco introduces readers to her husband, Enzo. A boy drops a book, tripping the waiter in a restaurant, and the adventure begins. It doesn't take long before students begin chanting the refrain with you. (Grades 2–4)

Rylant, Cynthia. (1996). *The whales*. New York: Blue Sky Press.

> Simple, sparse, poetic text describes whales: "In the blackness of the Black Sea, the whales are thinking today." and "They are floating like feathers in the deep blue green." Different species of whales are labeled at the back of the book. (Grades K–2)

Thayer, Ernest Lawrence. (2000). *Casey at the bat: A ballad of the Republic sung in the year 1888*. (Christopher Bing, Illus.). Brooklyn, NY: Handprint Books.

> The first stanza of this famous poem is presented in picture book form. Collages of newspaper articles, tickets, programs, and baseball cards accompany the text. (Grades 2–5)

Van Laan, Nancy. (1990). *Possum come a-knockin'*. (George Booth, Illus.). New York: Knopf.

> This rollicking tale of a possum that comes a-knockin' on the door invites hand clapping and thigh slapping. (Grades K–3)

Yolen, Jane. (1998). *Welcome to the icehouse*. (Laura Regan, Illus.). New York: Putnam.

> Poetic text describes animals in the Arctic winter, through the seasons, until winter returns: "Beware, for behind stalks a lynx, now quick, now slow, now silent as snow." (Grades K–3)

CHAPTER 9

Editing for Conventions

Editing is easy. All you have to do is cross out
the wrong words.

—MARK TWAIN

The trait of *conventions* deals with spelling, punctuation, grammar, capitalization, and paragraphing. When I was in elementary school, conventions
were taught with an English book and skill sheets. Writing was assessed almost entirely on conventions. Many students and parents gauged the success or
failure of a paper by the number of red marks on it. Teacher comments related to
errors, very rarely having to do with content. In 1985 the National Council of
Teachers of English adopted a resolution affirming the position that the use of iso-
lated grammar and usage exercises not supported by theory and research is a de-
terrent to the improvement of students' speaking and writing, and that, in order to
improve both of these, class time at all levels must be devoted to opportunities for
meaningful listening, speaking, reading, and writing.

Fortunately, times have changed in most schools, and writing is taught as a
process, and it is the content, not the correctness, that is first assessed. Books
aren't published because they are spelled right. They are published because they
tell a story in a meaningful way, which appeals to the reader. According to
Routman (1996), "When correctness is valued above all else in writing, we get students who write correctly but who refuse to take risks or accept challenges" (p. 7).
Calkins (1999) states,

> The most important thing we can do for these students is to help them write freely
> and unselfconsciously. Our students need to realize that it is okay to make editori-
> al errors as they write; all of us do, and then we correct them as we edit. (p. 290)

Research quoted in *Becoming a Nation of Readers: The Report of the Commission
on Reading* (Anderson, Hiebert, Scott, & Wilkinson, 1985) suggests that the finer

points of writing, such as punctuation and subject–verb agreement, may be learned best while students are engaged in extended writing that has the purpose of communicating a message to an audience. Dahl and Farnan (1998) observe,

> Although explicit instruction on the conventions of writing may not be the central focus in classrooms that emphasize writing processes, many classroom writing programs address these issues in editing sessions and instructional minilessons. (p. 61)

Although I think conventions are vitally important, they are only one of the traits, one part of the writing process, and are best left until last to be addressed.

The trait of conventions requires editing. The first five traits require revision. This difference is important to remember. I tell students that *edit* is synonymous with *fix* and that *revise* is synonymous with *change*. We need to fix the spelling, capitalization, punctuation, and grammar. In many cases, paragraphing has simply been omitted and can be corrected. If paragraphing is a more serious problem, ideas and organization may require a major revision. A paper that is strong in the first five traits, but weak in conventions, can easily be fixed. A paper that is weak in three or more of the first five traits requires major revision. Change means erasing, crossing out, and sometimes starting over. Telling statements need to be changed to showing ones (ideas, voice); boring verbs need to be changed to active ones and ordinary words to precise ones (word choice); beginnings of sentences must be changed if they are all the same, and some must be changed by breaking them up or combining them if they are all about the same length (sentence fluency).

There is a big difference between revising and editing. I was fortunate to be able to see a chapter from the original manuscript of *Harry Potter* (1997) at the National Library of Scotland in Edinburgh. It was handwritten in longhand on notebook paper. Author J.K. Rowling had crossed out, added between lines, and written in the margins. She was changing things to make her manuscript better. I wish every child could see firsthand how real authors continually revise their work.

Another thing to remember about conventions is that it is the only trait that is truly grade-level specific. A third and a fifth grader can produce a paper that is high in the first five traits. Their papers are scored using the same criteria. But, a fifth grader would be expected to use more sophisticated spelling, punctuation, grammar, capitalization, and paragraphing skills than a third grader. Use your district- or grade-level objectives or guidelines as the standard when evaluating students' use of conventions.

Spelling

Invented spelling is a convenience to the writer. Conventional spelling is a convenience to the reader. For very young children, invented spelling should not only be accepted, it should be encouraged during the drafting and revision stages of writing. In *Early Literacy Instruction in Kindergarten* (2001), Lori Jamison Rog warns that a child who is writing creative pieces in invented spelling may suddenly discover that there is a right way to spell words and begin limiting her vocabulary choice to words she knows how to spell conventionally. Emergent writing can be left alone most of the time. But if it is to be published or displayed publicly, I make sure it is transcribed to conventional standards. For later grades, I always insist that conventions are correct before displaying or publishing.

By first grade there will be some words that have been taught, and they should be spelled correctly. If you have a spelling program, students should be expected to spell correctly words that have been taught previously. One of the best ways to teach spelling is to notice which words are consistently misspelled by students and teach those as spelling words. Individual spelling lists can also be compiled using this method. Another source of spelling words is "The 100 Most Common Words in English Writing" and "Spelling Demons—197 Words Frequently Misspelled by Elementary Students" in *The New Reading Teacher's Book of Lists* (Fry, Polk, & Fountoukidis, 1985) or "High Frequency Nouns" (Johns, 1975). Word walls in the classroom, personal dictionaries, writing notebooks, and favorite books can also be a source of correct spellings for familiar words. Students should be taught to utilize these resources.

Encourage students to find spelling errors in the world around them. I am amazed at how many errors are found on signs, posters, newspapers, and on television. Teach children to have a critical eye for spelling. It is hard to teach about something that "looks right," but that's the way most of us correct our spelling. Much practice is necessary to achieve this eye for correctness. On a road I travel frequently, a sign nailed to a tree says "Finnish Carpenter" and gives a phone number. I have always wondered if this person is a carpenter who does finishing work or if he is from Finland. One of my favorite neighborhood restaurants recently advertised in the local paper that they would now be open on Friday and Saturday evenings "for your dinning pleasure." Where was the proofreader? Spell-check did not pick it up. Is *dinning* a word blend of *dining* and *dinner*? Actually I looked it up because my spell-check accepted it, too. It is a form of *din*, a raucous noise. I have had two disasters with spelling on cakes that I have ordered. One was for a retirement party for a colleague. The cake read "Congradulations." We joked that the bakery worker must have been one of my colleague's former students. Another time, I ordered four cakes from a different bakery for a "Read Across America" celebration at school. All four cakes read, "Happy Birthday, Dr. Suess [instead of Seuss]." I was able to use a toothpick to rearrange the icing and correct the spelling. I share these things with students, emphasizing the need to be careful while checking spelling and proofreading.

A good way for teachers to give students practice in editing for spelling is to take a passage from a book, introduce spelling errors into it, and then have students find the errors. You may want to use a passage from a book that students are reading. That way they can check the book for the correct spellings. The following example passage is from *Double Fudge* (2002) by Judy Blume:

> Fudge has his ferst loos tooth. Bottom frunt. He's planning on collecting big-time form the tooth fairy. He's been wigling his loos tooth for weaks. He was still wigling it at our farewell diner with the Howies. Mom invited Olivia Osterman, to, so the three heroes cood have a reunion. But Mimi was more intrested in Uncle Feather than a reunion. She took off fore Fudge's room rite away. I was glad to sea Cousin Howie folloe him.

As in all examples, demonstrate and work together before expecting students to work in groups or independently. Ask if anyone notices a spelling error in the first sentence. When a student replies that *ferst* is misspelled, ask for the correct spelling. Correct the spelling and ask if there are any other words misspelled in the sentence. Continue in this manner until all corrections have been made.

Punctuation

The amount of research on punctuation learning is far smaller than the body of work on children's spelling (Dahl & Farnan, 1998). Young writers experiment with the use of commas, periods, and apostrophes, but children's understandings of their appropriate use are often unclear. By third grade, most students use periods and question marks correctly but have difficulty with commas and apostrophes. The misuse of the apostrophe in plurals is common and bothers me the most. I am amazed at how many adults are guilty of this error. There is a latte stand nearby that has a sign, "Kelly Latte's." I am assuming that Kelly is the owner or proprietor of the stand and the sign should read, "Kelly's Lattes." But, although it is unlikely, Kelly's last name could be "Latte." Because this type of error irritates me so much, I admit that I might overdo instruction on plurals and possessives.

By sharing samples of writing and having students help you edit, they will develop a "proofreader's eye," becoming better equipped to edit their own writing. One way to emphasize how punctuation aids the reader's understanding is to take a passage from a story or book and take out all punctuation. Then have students put in the punctuation. The following is an example I have used with students. It is a passage from *Ramona and Her Father* (1977) by Beverly Cleary:

> There was a strong smell of cat food in the kitchen What Ramona saw and what Beezus saw did not strike them as one bit funny Their jack-o-lantern the jack-o-lantern their father had worked so hard to carve no longer had a whole face Part of its forehead one ferocious eyebrow one eye and part of its nose were gone replaced by a jagged hole edged by little teeth marks Picky-picky was crouched in guilt under the kitchen table the nerve of that cat bad cat bad cat shrieked Ramona stamping her bare foot on the cold linoleum The old yellow cat fled to the dining room where he crouched under the table his eyes glittering out of the darkness.

Notice that I included capitals in this passage because I am only concerned with punctuation at this time. The same passage can be used omitting the capitals if capitalization is what you want to emphasize. Again, it is more effective to use a passage from a book that students are reading, allowing for correction using familiar text.

Capitals

For a minilesson on the use of capitals, you might start by asking students to list words that need capitals (names, titles, streets, towns, lakes, mountains, states, countries, sentence beginnings, and so on). Post this list in the classroom or have students copy and put it in their writing notebooks. Then share samples of writing with capitals omitted and have students help you edit them. Have students correct the following passage, from *A Letter to Mrs. Roosevelt* (1999) by C. Coco DeYoung, for capitalization:

> maple avenue was snuggled between twin hillsides. there were no wealthy people or fancy houses in my neighborhood. our house was painted brown and had three stories. my bedroom was directly above our front porch and had two huge windows that met in the corner. from the front window i could see all of maple avenue, from the brickyard to the acme bakery. the side window looked out onto rosa's front porch and, beyond that, st. anthony's church.

Editing Skills

Children need practice with editing skills. Show lots of sample writing (not their own work) and have them help you edit. You may have to rewrite the text so it includes the kinds of errors you are focusing on. Don't ask beginning editors to find a wide range of errors at first. Focus on one type of error at a time. Demonstrate, and then have the class work in groups or pairs, then independently. If students are still having difficulty, it's time for a minilesson. I must admit that occasionally I pull out the old English texts (most schools surplus them but keep a few) to use for a particular skill. The final step is to have students look at their own writing and edit for errors.

Don't do the editing for your students. Remember the red marks on the papers that many of us had as students? Think of the time it took for the teacher to mark those papers. Did the writer actually learn editing skills by looking at the red marks? Perhaps some did, but I doubt if it had an impact on the majority of the students. Occasionally, you may have to give a hint such as "I see several spelling errors" or "You need to use some commas," but your main objective is to teach students how to edit for themselves.

Many teachers use a program designed to teach editing skills called *Daily Oral Language* (Vail & Papenfuss, 1990). This program presents a short paragraph (to be put on the overhead projector) for students to edit for spelling, punctuation, and capitalization. It is often the first activity done in the morning and immediately gets the class focused. Although the program has a book for each grade level, teachers should be sure that they have taught all the skills presented before using the materials. You should only require students to make corrections on what has already been taught. Several basal reading series include grammar and spelling activities. These often include editing lessons similar to *Daily Oral Language*.

Derek Furr (2002) came up with a procedure called CAPS, an acronym for capitals, agreement, punctuation, and spelling. These four areas represented his students' fundamental weaknesses in grammar and mechanics. Demonstrating first, he required students to look at their own writing four times, once for each kind of error.

Proofreading symbols can vary. If you choose to use them, my advice is to have an agreement with the entire school to use the same symbols. Then, when students progress from one grade to the next, there will be no confusion.

Using Books as Examples of Conventions

All books go through an editing process before they are published, so the conventions should be correct. But to emphasize the trait, you can share books that use a wide range of conventions, use conventions in an unusual way, or have a different format than most. The main idea is to remind students that good writing requires a lot of revising and editing before it is ready for publication. If you have access to galleys, advance copies, or review copies of books, you can show students that sometimes additional editing is required before the final printing. You may also want to share books about the making of a book (see chapter 2) to emphasize the editing process. At the end of this chapter is a bibliography of books to use with conventions.

Assessing Conventions

When scoring papers keep in mind that conventions are grade-level specific. You know what your students should be able to do as far as capitalization, punctuation, grammar, spelling, and paragraphing are concerned. If you are in a situation where you are scoring papers from a different grade level or if you work with several grade levels, be sure you have a copy of your school or district scope and sequence, standards, or objectives. If in doubt, ask a teacher of the grade level you are scoring what the norm is for punctuation, spelling, and so on. A paper with many errors may be a 4 or 5 when written by a second or third grader if the errors are sophisticated in nature and have not been taught at that grade level. On the other hand, that same paper written by a fifth-grade student might be a 2 or 3 because those errors are in conventions that have been taught by grade 5.

Remember that the trait of conventions encompasses all five areas mentioned above. If punctuation is nonexistent, but the spelling, grammar, capitalization, and paragraphing are good, you can't score the piece low in conventions. This trait, with its many areas, is where rater bias sometimes comes in, and we must strive to avoid it. I am a good speller and I expect good spelling. It is hard for me to rate a paper 3 or 4 with numerous spelling errors, but that is what I have to do if the other conventions are strong. Look for what is done well. Then score lower for those areas that need work. If one or two areas are strong, the score will rarely be below a 2 or 3. In that case, comments are valuable to the student. Point out what is good and what still needs work. By assessing all five areas, you will know what minilessons some students (or the entire class) require.

And, as hard as it seems to accept, handwriting and neatness should not affect the score. This criterion is also difficult for me to accept. If you truly can't read the piece, then certainly you can ask the student to redo it. Tell the student that you want to be able to fairly evaluate it, but until it is legible you just can't. The same is true for the length of the piece. If a piece is only two or three sentences long (for grades 2 and above), it is too short to score for any of the traits. On some district assessments, I occasionally have had to write, "Too short to evaluate" on a paper. And last, does the paper have to be absolutely perfect to score a 5? No, but there should be very few errors.

Student Checklist for Conventions

- Have I checked my paper for mistakes?
- Did I use periods and question marks?
- Are my words spelled correctly?
- Do I have capitals in the right places?
- Did I use paragraphs?

Evaluator Checklist for Conventions

RATING: STRONG (5)

- Spelling and grammar are correct, even on harder words.
- Punctuation guides the reader.
- Capitals are used correctly.
- Paragraphing fits the organization.
- Text appears polished and edited, and it is easy to read.

Following is a student example from grade 3:

> Dog's (My Favorite Thing)
> Dog's are my favorite animals. They make wonderful pet's. If you live in an apartment or have a small house and yard, you should get a small dog. Some people like dog's with not much hair like Chiwawas or Dachsunds. They don't shed much, but you'll need to get them a sweater or coat when you take them outside if it's

cold. Some small dog's have lots of hair, like Lasa Apsos and Malteeze. If you have one of these you'll need to brush them every day to keep them looking good.

If you live in a house with a medium sized yard, you can have a little bit bigger dog like a cocker spaniel or a beagle. You will still need to brush them and take them for walks, though. They make eggselent pet's.

Big dog's like labs and Golden Retrevers or German Sheperds need room to run. You need a big yard, or even better a lake for the labs or retrevers. They love to swim. They can be in a house, too but you have to be careful. They can knock things over.

Now if you have acres and acres you can get a huge dog like a Saint Burnard or a Great Dane. They are as big as a small horse. They eat lots so you have to buy lot's of dog food. Also, you need a big van or a truck to take them places. My grandma has lots of property but she has to borrow my Dads truck to take her Great Dane to the vet. He won't fit in her little car.

So get a dog. They make the best pet's. But get one that fits your house and yard.

The topic is narrow and focused. There are relevant details and more showing than telling. I would score this 4–5 in ideas. The paper is organized and has a definite beginning and ending. The ending is strong. I would score this 4–5 in organization. The writer knows and cares a lot about dogs and is persuasive. You know what his position is. This is a 4–5 in voice. The verbs are not particularly active or exciting, but there are memorable moments (*love to swim, knock things over, big as a small horse*), and the writer uses names of dogs. I would score this paper 4 in word choice. Sentences are varied in length and construction, although many begin with *They*. It has a flow to it when read aloud. I would score this 4 in sentence fluency. Although the writer consistently confuses plurals and possessives (*dog's, pet's, dads*), the rest of the conventions are strong. Misspelled words (*Chihuahua; Bernard; Dachshunds; Lhasa Apso; Maltese; Retrievers; Shepherd, excellent*) are not words that the average third grader would know, and the writer usually capitalizes names of breeds of dogs. The writer has taken risks. Paragraphing is good and complements the organization. Even though the misuse of plurals and possessives personally irritates me, I would have to score this a 4 in conventions. I would then do a minilesson on plurals.

RATING: DEVELOPING (3)

• Spelling is correct on easy words.

• Minor problems exist in grammar, punctuation, and capitalization.

• Paragraphing is attempted.

- The paper has consistent errors.
- More editing needs to be done.

Following is a student example from grade 5:

> Disneyland (My Favorite Place)
> My family went to Disneyland last summer. We had a great time. It was hot but we didn't care.
>
> My sister and I went on all kinds of rides. We had fun. My mom and dad went on some too, but sometimes they just watched us. My favorite ride was the Materhorn. It felt good when we got splashed with water at the end. My sister liked the teacups. My dad liked Space Mountain and my mom liked the Pirates of the Carribean.
>
> They have good food at Disneyland. Some of it was expensive but we were on vacation. My favorite snack was the frozen bananas on a stick with choclate on them. My sister liked the choclate chip ice cream sandwiches. We ate dinner at the hotel.
>
> There are lots of neat store there, too. My mom got a silver pin of Mickey Mouse. Dad got a Mickey Mouse tie. My sister got a big stuffed Minnie Mouse and a Snow White music box. I got a Mickey Mouse shirt and a Star Wars backpack. I bought a key chain for my friend Jeff.
>
> One night we stayed late and saw the electric parade. There were lots of characters and everything was lit up. At the end there were really neat fireworks. It was a blast.
>
> I'm glad we went to Disneyland. It was lots of fun. I hope we go back soon.

The topic is not narrow or focused. There are only *telling* statements. The writer missed opportunities to tell relevant details about events. This is a 2 in ideas. The organization is adequate. There is a definite beginning and end, but they are not strong, although the sequence is easy to follow. I would score this 3 in organization. There is very little voice in this piece. We know the writer had a good time, but he uses general terms (*fun*, *neat*, *good*, and *great*) instead of specific examples. This is a 2 in voice. Verbs lack excitement (*was*, *were*). There are no memorable moments. I would score this 1–2 in word choice. Most sentences begin with *My* or *We*. They vary in length but not in structure. The piece is fairly easy to read aloud, but there is no rhythm. This is a 2–3 in sentence fluency. Most words are spelled correctly, but they are easy words. Paragraphing, punctuation, and grammar are correct, and there are very few errors in capitalization. However, there are no risks taken. This is a "safe" paper. For this reason, I would score this a 3 in conventions. This is the type of paper I would expect from a student who has not had experience with writing process, writing workshop, or the six traits.

RATING: WEAK (1)

- The paper has numerous spelling errors, even on easy words.
- Consistent errors occur in grammar, punctuation, and capitalization.
- Paragraphing is random or nonexistent.
- The paper is difficult to read because of errors.
- There is no evidence of editing.

Following is a student example from grade 4:

> Jay (Something I'll Never Forget)
> I will never forget my brother Jay. I was only three when Jay died. But just because your little dosen't mean you can't tell somethings wrong. He was just born. everybody was happy. Then my mom called my grandma's house where I was staying. My grandma started crying my grandpa wouldn't let me talk to my mom. About an hour later we started off to Sacred Heart Medical Center the hospital where my mom was. I remember walking up and down the hallways all day. We had been there for at least two days off and on until I was allowed to see him. I was a little bit scared to touch him at first because he had all of these gadgets and things stuck on him. But I got used to it. He got to come home for a little while about two weeks. I don't even remember when he died. Because I was braut to my other grandmas house. But I remember going to the cemetery and walking around until we found his spot by the pine trees and rearranging pinecones on his headstone. giving him flowers and going home. My brother was a perfect little person for the 44 days he was alive. And I hope he is haveing a good time in heaven.

The topic is narrow and focused. There is showing, rather than telling. This is a 5 in ideas. It is sequential and easy to follow. The lead is good and is tied to the ending. I would score this 4–5 in organization. The voice is exceptionally strong in this piece. There is insight (*just because you're little doesn't mean you can't tell something is wrong*) and you know exactly how the writer feels. This is a 5 in voice. The word choice is also strong, although the verbs *was* and *had* appear a little too frequently. There are memorable moments (*gadgets and things stuck on him, rearranging pinecones, a perfect little person for the 44 days he was alive*). This is a 4–5 in word choice. Sentences are varied in length and structure and begin in different ways, but there are a few fragments that do not work well. However, it is easy to read aloud. (I have read it aloud many times and still choke up!) This is a 4 in sentence fluency. There are misspelled words that a fourth grader should know (*braut*, *haveing*, and *dosen't*), but she correctly spells *gadgets* and *cemetery*. There is some misuse of possessives, but others are correct. Capitalization is generally correct, but occasionally the first word of a sentence is not capitalized. She knows to capitalize the name of the hospital, though. Most of the ending punctuation is correct but commas need to be used. There is no paragraphing. Because the errors are not consistent, it appears that more thorough editing is required. I would score this 2 in conventions. This is a paper I have used many times in presentations to illustrate how a piece can be strong in the first five traits and low in conventions. Editing could easily fix this paper. When I called the mother to get permission to use this piece, she was horrified that I would want to use it. She thought it was terrible, but she was only looking at the conventions. This student is a talented writer who needs to learn to edit.

Sample Lesson Plans

Unlike the first five traits, where approximately two weeks should be devoted to each trait, I believe that the components of conventions (spelling, punctuations, grammar, capitalization, and paragraphing) should be taught throughout the school day. When teachers begin the day with *Daily Oral Language* (Vail & Papenfuss, 1990) or a similar program, they are addressing editing in all five areas in about 10 minutes. Your spelling program is used to teach one part of conventions and since some reading programs include grammar lessons, they also can be used for instruction in conventions. During reading instruction, conventions should be discussed. "Why do you think the word is in bold type?" "Read the part that shows what Molly said." "Why are the words *Yellowstone Park* capitalized?" Social studies is also an ideal time to discuss capitalization because cities, states, provinces, and countries are always capitalized. Students are often required to write in response journals for math and science. Conventions can be reinforced during this time. And during read-alouds, discuss with students how the author used conventions to emphasize or illustrate a point.

I like to conduct minilessons at the beginning of the writing block because then students can immediately apply the lesson to their own writing. In first, second, and third grade I always include minilessons on punctuation, capitalization, plurals, and contractions, assuming that these young children all need a basic understanding of these skills, even if it is a review for some. By grades 4 and 5, actual student writing will indicate what skills need to be taught with minilessons.

Of course the writing of students in grades 1–3 will also inform you what skills need to be further emphasized.

Following are two lesson plans that I have used for the trait of conventions. The first sample is a minilesson on using commas. The second lesson is a review after all the traits have been taught, with an emphasis on editing for conventions as compared to the more complex revision of the other traits.

Sample Lesson Plan (Grades 1–2)

1. Read *Henry and Mudge in the Green Time* (1987a) by Cynthia Rylant.

2. Explain that writers use commas to separate phrases and things in a list. Readers should pause when they come to a comma.

3. On the overhead projector, write the first sentence from chapter 1, omitting the comma.

    In the summer Henry and his big dog Mudge liked to go on picnics.

4. Read it aloud, without pausing.

5. Now, put the comma after the word *summer* and read it again, pausing when you come to the comma.

6. Put the next two sentences on the overhead, omitting the commas.

    Henry packed the food.
    He packed jelly sandwiches pears and gingersnaps for himself.

7. Read the sentences without pausing.

8. Ask students how many things Henry packed (three). Explain that commas are used to separate words in a list. Ask students to tell you the first thing Henry packed (jelly sandwiches). Place a comma after *sandwiches*. Have them tell you the next thing (pears). Place a comma after *pears*. Now the three items are separated by commas.

9. Read the sentence, pausing at the commas.

10. Put the next sentence on the overhead.

    He packed dry dog food and popcorn for Mudge.

11. Ask students how many things Henry packed for Mudge (two). Explain that because there are only two items and they are separated by the word *and*, a comma is not needed.

12. Remind students that when they are writing, they need to use commas to separate phrases and words in a list.

Sample Lesson Plan (Grades 3–5)

1. Read *Amber on the Mountain* (1994) by Tony Johnston.

2. After reading, go back through the story and read the following phrases, asking the students to identify the strong trait they hear:

> Poked through the clouds like a needle stuck in down (ideas)
>
> The air made you giddy (ideas)
>
> Skedaddled before winter came (word choice)
>
> Sky was streaked with morning (word choice)
>
> Hopping around crazy as a doodlebug (word choice)
>
> Twirled through the grass (word choice)
>
> Learning to read was like walking up a wall (voice)
>
> Amber stiffened up mulish as could be (word choice)
>
> Watched her friend down the mountain till she melted into blue mountain mist (sentence fluency)
>
> Glowed with happiness (voice)
>
> You're peltering me with words, thick as spring rain. I feel drenched (word choice)
>
> My letters are lopsided as a herd of one-horned cows (word choice)
>
> Huddled under a quilt (word choice)
>
> Clouds like grey geese flocked in the sky and rain glazed the land (sentence fluency)
>
> Tongue curled like a lizard stalking a bug (word choice)
>
> Squeezed her pencil nearly to splinters (word choice)

3. Copy Amber's letter from the next-to-last page and put on the overhead projector.

> Dear Anna,
> I am a rockhead to. I fixed my mind on riting. I teached myself to rite sos I can rite you. I hop you faint to the flor.
>
> Love from yer frend Amber

4. Have students help you score Amber's letter for the traits.

> **Ideas:** Does Amber know what she wants to say? It is focused?
>
> **Score:** 4–5
>
> **Organization:** Does Amber know the format for a letter?
>
> **Score:** 5
>
> **Voice:** Do you know how Amber feels?
>
> **Score:** 4–5
>
> **Word Choice:** Are the verbs active? (*fixed, teached, hope*) Are there memorable moments? (*faint to the floor*)
>
> **Score:** 5
>
> **Sentence Fluency:** Sentence beginnings? (all the same) Actually, this piece is too short to adequately score for fluency.
>
> **Conventions:** Errors in spelling and grammar. Capitalization is correct. Most punctuation is correct (no comma in closing).
>
> **Score:** Most will say it is a 1–2. However, because Amber has never been to school, and the trait of conventions is grade-level specific, there may be a strong argument here in favor of a higher score.

5. Ask students if the conventions can be easily fixed. (yes) Stress that the content is good, most traits are strong, and errors in the conventions will need only a little editing.
6. Remind students that they should focus on content and the first five traits, then carefully edit for conventions.

Conclusion

The trait of conventions encompasses five areas: spelling, punctuation, grammar, capitalization, and paragraphing. This trait has been presented last because it deals with the mechanics of writing, rather than the content. The conventions require editing rather than revision like the first five traits. Because conventions are grade-level specific, students should only be expected to be proficient on what has been previously taught at their grade level. In evaluating work, teachers and students should remember to assess the five areas separately. If only one or two of the areas within this trait are weak or not present, it may affect the score; but if the other areas are strong, the score will not be low.

Although perfection is not expected, the rater should look for density of errors. The conventions should not keep the rater from focusing on the other traits. To be strong in conventions, the writer must take a certain amount of risk, and the piece should require very little additional editing to make it ready for public display.

This chapter completes my discussion of the six-trait model from a literature-based perspective. In chapter 10, I close with some final thoughts on opportunities for students to read and write.

ANNOTATED LIST OF CHILDREN'S LITERATURE TO USE FOR CONVENTIONS

Arnold, Katya. (1998). *MEOW!* New York: Holiday House.

"MEOW!" Something wakes the puppy. He searches for the sound and meets animals that make different sounds. Sound words have hyphens, capital letters, and get larger as the sound increases. Quotation marks are also used. (Grades K–2)

Baer, Gene. (1989). *THUMP, THUMP, Rat-a-Tat-Tat.* (Lois Ehlert, Illus.). New York: Harper & Row.

Rat-a-tat-tat, Rat-a-tat-tat. THUMP, THUMP, THUMP, THUMP. A parade goes by. The sounds are characterized by using hyphens and capitals with large, bold print. (Grades K–1)

Cameron, Polly. (1961). *"I can't" said the ant*. New York: Putnam.

This classic story introduces and reinforces the use of quotation marks. (Grades 1–3)

Carlson, Nancy L. (1988). *I Like Me!* New York: Viking Kestral.

A positive reinforcement for self-image, this book uses commas and exclamation points. (Grades K–2)

Ehlert, Lois. (1995). *Snowballs*. San Diego, CA: Harcourt Brace.

The cover and first few pages are in conventional book format. But when the snowmen are made, the reader must turn the book because text and illustrations are from top to bottom. When the snowmen melt, the format goes back to traditional left to right. (Grades K–5)

Maestro, Betsy, & Maestro, Giulio. (1992). *All Aboard Overnight*. (Giulio Maestro, Illus.). New York: Clarion.

> A book of compound words, with compounds in bold print. At the beginning of the book is a list of compounds not in the text but appearing in the illustrations. The reader is challenged to find them. (Grades 2–4)

Martin, Bill, Jr. (1994). *The Wizard*. (Alex Schaefer, Illus.). San Diego, CA: Harcourt Brace.

> One and two words per page describe the spell the wizard and his assistants are casting, but the letters in the words take on some of the characteristics of the spell. (Grades K–3)

Merriam, Eve. (1992). *Fighting Words*. (David Small, Illus.). New York: William Morrow.

> Leda and Dale hate each other and decide to have a fight. As they start out, the names they call each other are in bold print and, as the fighting continues, the words get louder, thus bigger! As they become hoarse from yelling, they begin to lose their voices, and the words become smaller and are no longer in bold print. (Grades K–5)

Monrad, Jean. (1986). *How Many Kisses Good Night?* (Eloise Wilkin, Illus.). New York: Random House. (Original work published 1949)

> This book of questions emphasizes the question mark. (Grades K–2)

Richardson, Bill. (2002). *Sally Dog Little*. (Celine Malepart, Illus.). Toronto, ON: Annick Press.

> Sally Dog barks at two mysterious intruders, only she can see, so her family becomes annoyed with the noise. Was it all a dream? The dialogue uses quotation marks, and some words are in larger bold print, indicating loudness. (Grades K–3)

Stevens, Janet. (1995). *Tops & Bottoms*. San Diego, CA: Harcourt Brace.

> A trickster tale based on European and American South folk tales, this book opens from bottom to top, rather than left to right. (Grades K–5)

ANNOTATED LIST OF GRAMMAR BOOKS FOR TEACHERS

Because many of us can't always remember rules or find examples when we need them, I have listed a few books on grammar that I have found helpful. These books offer tips you can use in the classroom.

Fine, Edith H., & Josephson, Judith P. (1998). *Nitty-gritty grammar: A not-so-serious guide to clear communication.* Berkeley, CA: Ten Speed Press.

> This book explains grammar, giving good and bad examples. My favorite chapter is "Punctuation Pointers." Punctuation is compared to traffic signals: Period is a stop sign, comma a flashing yellow light, semicolon a flashing red light, colon an arrow or road sign, and parentheses and dashes are a detour.

Maizels, Jennie, & Petty, Kate. (1996). *The amazing pop-up grammar book.* New York: Dutton.

> Although classified as a children's book, it is hard to share with a class because details are small and it is truly a pop-up book. For a minilesson, you can share one or two pages on adverbs, pronouns, adjectives, and other parts of speech.

Summerhays, Joe. (2002). *Spot on punctuation.* Salt Lake City, UT: Metra Publishing.

> Summerhays Productions has a series of five little books on punctuation, one each covering commas, question marks, periods, exclamation points, and quotation marks.

Terban, Marvin. (1993). *Checking your grammar.* New York: Scholastic.

> This is a handy guide intended for students ages 9–12. I find this helpful when planning minilessons on noun-verb agreement, punctuation, and spelling.

CHAPTER 10

Some Final Thoughts

The writing classroom is based on a foundation of literature.

—Ralph Fletcher

Writers grow in their ability by being immersed in opportunities to read and write. The development of children's writing is best achieved through substantial time devoted to writing, multiple opportunities to write during the school day, and focused instruction. According to Goldberg (1986), "Basically, if you want to become a good writer, you need to do three things: Read a lot, listen well and deeply, and write a lot" (p. 53). I would suggest that if you want your students to become good writers, you need to do three things: Read to them, write for and with them, and give them time to write.

In 1984 the Commission on Reading reported that the single most important activity for building the knowledge required for eventual success in reading is reading aloud to children (Anderson et al., 1984). Although the research on reading aloud to children and its effect on their writing proficiency is not as explicit or abundant as the reading aloud–reading connection, it is evident that the connection between literature and writing is a strong one. I believe that listening to and reading good literature is an essential ingredient of good writing instruction. I would also argue that reading aloud is one of the most important things you can do to help your students become better writers.

Both Mem Fox (1993) and Regie Routman (1996) stress the importance of teachers writing and sharing with students throughout the writing lesson. This is a new and difficult challenge for many, but it is essential. Taking time to write is a major problem for many teachers. The school day is not long enough to include all the subjects we used to teach. Educators are faced with the dilemma of reducing time in one area to make room for new demands. Teachers need to find creative ways to provide big blocks of time for writing.

Read a Lot

Teachers need to read widely to know what to write about and how to write effectively. Likewise, "The writing you get out of your students can only be as good as the classroom literature that surrounds and sustains it" (Fletcher & Portalupi, 1998, p. 10). Talk about how authors write. Provide a variety of genres for students to enjoy and learn from. Books can give us ideas for topics, patterns, techniques, and devices used to create a story or report. Students learn to be better writers from what they read. They need to read like writers, engaging with the author. To read like a writer requires that students see the need to learn from the author, which is dependent on whether they see themselves as writers (Smith, 1983). Students should be taught to listen to or read the book like a writer. Writers read differently than other people. After the initial reading, you know what the book is *about*, but now read it again and look closely for *how* the writer wrote it. Discuss any writing traits that are particularly strong in the book. "Unless children are conscious of an author's technique when they read, it is hard to imagine that they will deliberately borrow these techniques when they write" (Calkins, 1994, p. 283).

I am deeply disturbed when a teacher tells me that there isn't time to read aloud. Routman (1996) advises that "no matter what the grade level, real aloud every day" (p. 83). We must find the time. Many of my colleagues read to their class during lunch or recess. This type of reading is pleasure reading, which is important. But, much of reading aloud can be instruction. There are good books that can be used to cover all subject areas. They are often more current and interesting to students than outdated textbooks. When you share books to illustrate writing traits, you are using them for instruction. Reading aloud is not an extra or frivolous activity that can be dropped. It needs to be an essential part of the curriculum. Whether I am teaching a class to young children or to adults, I always include at least one read-aloud during the presentation. It is something I will never give up.

Teachers as Writers

Students must have writing models if they are to become writers, and teachers must be those models. "If you are not a writer, you will not understand the difficulties of writing. If you are not a writer, you will not know the fears and hopes of the writers you teach" (Fox, 1993, p. 163). Would you take piano lessons from someone who does not play the piano? Of course not. Teachers need to write in order to be the best teachers of writing. Share letters or notes you have written for a specific purpose. Write a shared story with the class after an assembly or field trip or demonstrate writing a letter to parents telling about a special class project. Shared writing and class innovations of pattern books are not just "cute" or superfluous activities. Recently, my daughter's beloved cat died. Wanting to help her and her husband deal with their loss, I wrote "Ode to Buddy," loosely based on *The Tenth Good Thing About Barney* (1971) by Judith Viorst, listing 10 attributes and events about their cat's life.

Routman (1994) cautions, "Until we demonstrate and value the craft ourselves, many students will fail to take writing seriously or to see writing as a tool for thinking and learning" (p. 194). Do real writing. Let students see you think aloud, revise, and edit. "Writing makes us better teachers. When our students see how we struggle, organize, think, reread, revise, edit, and get ideas with and through our own writing, they are supported in their writing" (Routman, 1996, p. 183). That is why I write on the overhead projector during instruction on the traits and have students help me revise my own writing. "When teachers share both their writing processes and their writing products with their students, they do the one thing nonwriters need most: They *demystify* writing" (Tomason & York, 2000, p. 5).

I know there is much resistance to the idea of teachers sharing their writing. For most of my teaching career, I did not write or share my writing with anyone, especially in the classroom. Only a handful of states require courses in writing for certification for elementary teachers. Pre- and in-service teacher professional development rarely offers teachers an opportunity to see themselves as writers—to experience the power and satisfaction of writing as a means of learning and self-expression (National Commission on Writing for America's Families, Schools, and Colleges, 2003). Sharing one's writing can be like revealing one's soul. It is risky business. It can be embarrassing and threatening. But how can we expect our students to write if we don't write? We must be models ourselves and also give our students writing models through literature.

Time to Write

Learning how to present one's thoughts on paper requires time. In 1985, the Commission on Reading reported that in one study in grades 1, 3, and 5, only 15% of the school day was spent in any kind of writing activity (Anderson et al., 1985). According to data from the National Assessment of Educational Progress

(National Assessment Governing Board, 1998), at the elementary school level practically all students (97%) report spending 3 hours a week or less on writing assignments, which amounts to about 15% of the time they spend watching television. Donald Graves (1994) says, "If students are not engaged in writing at least 4 days out of 5, and for a period of 35 to 40 minutes, beginning in first grade, they will have little opportunity to learn to think through the medium of writing" (p. 104).

The National Commission on Writing for America's Families, Schools, and Colleges (2003) offered three recommendations concerning time spent on writing in elementary classrooms:

- The amount of time most students spend writing should be at least doubled. This time can be found through assignments at home and by encouraging more writing during the school day in curriculum areas not traditionally associated with it.

- Writing should take place across the curriculum. Students should be encouraged to write more in mathematics, science, and social studies.

- There should be more use of out-of-school time for writing. Students should be expected to produce written work as part of their normal homework assignments. Just 15 minutes of writing four nights a week would add 33 percent to the amount of time the average elementary student spends writing. (p. 28)

Teachers must find ways to set aside big blocks of time for writing. Think back to when you were in school or college and had a paper to write. If you only had 15 to 20 minutes per day, would you have been able to write a thoughtful, comprehensive paper? When we leave writing and then come back to it, it takes a certain amount of time to recall what we were doing yesterday, get started again, and once we get going it is time to put it away. That is not constructive and often wastes more time than it saves. Writing this book has increased my understanding of the importance of blocks of time in the writing process. I have been very frustrated when interrupted during a writing session by a phone call, appointment, or the need to fix dinner. Writers need time to think, organize, reflect, review, and to write. In the classroom, I prefer big blocks (of at least 1 hour) on consecutive days for 3 to 4 days at a time, rather than 15 to 20 minutes daily.

Walmsley and Walp (1990) suggest combining reading, writing, and content area instruction through the use of themes. Rather than simply adding content to the literacy curriculum, teachers need to rethink their curricula to take advantage of the many opportunities to combine different aspects of language arts and content areas. Social studies and science are both areas where writing can be taught along with content. Opportunities to write have been found to contribute to knowledge of how written and oral language are related and to growth in phonics, spelling, vocabulary development, and reading comprehension (Tierney & Leys, 1986). Routman (1996) concurs, stating that the only way to find time is to integrate the curriculum by stopping the artificial separations between reading and writing. Writing is one of the best tools for learning any material because it activates thinking (Zemelman, Daniels, & Hyde, 1998).

All of the leading advocates of writing cited in this book believe that allocating big blocks of time for writing in the classroom is essential if children are to become proficient writers. Fortunately, more and more educators, administrators, and policymakers are also becoming aware of the importance of writing and of taking time for actual writing in elementary classrooms. In a report of a study on Exemplary Reading Programs in Illinois Public Schools, time was considered an important consideration in writing ability, and a pattern of variability was found (North Central Regional Educational Laboratory, 2004). In some classrooms, children did fewer than one extended writing activity each week, while in others the average was eight. Schools with higher achievement levels in writing had more teachers offering longer blocks of time for writing. Research conducted by the Center for Performance Assessment identified what they called 90/90/90 schools, where more than 90% of students qualified for free and reduced lunch, were from ethnic minorities, and were meeting or achieving high academic standards (Reeves, 2000). One of the characteristics common to the 90/90/90 schools was that they all had a strong emphasis on writing and devoted the great majority of the school day to reading, writing, and math. The report of the National Commission on Writing for America's Families, Schools, and Colleges (2003) stresses that writing is an essential skill, but has been shortchanged in the past, and has not received the full attention it deserves. The commission calls for a writing revolution, stating that writing must now be put squarely at the center of the school agenda.

So, read to your students. Immerse them in all forms of writing, genres, and literature. Share your writing and favorite books with them. Demonstrate the writing process and point out and discuss writing traits with them. Be creative and find ways to offer uninterrupted writing time for your class. And most of all, enjoy. Your enthusiasm and love for literature and literacy will be contagious.

References

Anderson, R.C, Hiebert, E.H., Scott, J.A., & Wilkinson, I.A.G. (1984). *Becoming a nation of readers: The report of the commission on reading.* Washington, DC: National Institute of Education.

Aronie, N. (1998). *Writing from the heart: Tapping the power of your inner voice.* New York: Hyperion.

Atwell, N. (1987). *In the middle: Writing, reading, and learning with adolescents.* Upper Montclair, NJ: Boynton/Cook.

Calkins, L.M. (1994). *The art of teaching writing.* Portsmouth, NH: Heinemann.

Cullinan, B., & Weiss, M.J. (Eds.). (1980). *Books I read when I was young: The favorite books of famous people.* Commission on Literature of the National Council of Teachers of English. New York: Avon.

Dahl, K.L., & Farnan, N. (1998). *Children's writing. Perspectives from research.* Newark, DE: International Reading Association; Chicago: National Reading Conference.

Donovan, C., & Smolkin, L. (2002). Children's genre knowledge: An examination of K–5 students' performance on multiple tasks providing differing levels of scaffolding. *Reading Research Quarterly, 37*, 428–465.

Eckhoff, B. (1983). *How reading affects children's writing. Language Arts, 60*(5), 607–616.

Fletcher, R. (1993). *What a writer needs.* Portsmouth, NH: Heinemann.

Fletcher, R. (1996). *A writer's notebook: Unlocking the writer within you.* New York: Avon.

Fletcher, R., & Portalupi, J. (1998). *Craft lessons: Teaching writing K–8.* Portland, ME: Stenhouse.

Fletcher, R., & Portalupi, J. (2001). *Nonfiction craft lessons: Teaching information writing K–8.* Portland, ME: Stenhouse.

Fox, M. (1993). *Radical reflections: Passionate opinions on teaching, learning, and living.* San Diego, CA: Harcourt.

Frank, M. (1995). *If you're trying to teach kids how to write...you've gotta have this book!* Nashville, TN: Incentive Publications.

Fry, E.B., Polk, J.K., & Fountoukidis, D. (1985). *The new reading teacher's book of lists.* Englewood Cliffs, NJ: Prentice Hall.

Furr, D. (2002). Struggling readers get hooked on writing. *The Reading Teacher, 56*, 518–525.

Goldberg, N. (1986). *Writing down the bones: Freeing the writer within.* Boston: Shambhala.

Graves, D.H. (1994). *A fresh look at writing.* Portsmouth, NH: Heinemann.

Graves, D.H. (2003). *Writing: Teachers and children at work.* Portsmouth, NH: Heinemann. (Original work published 1983)

Hall, S. (1994). *Using picture storybooks to teach literary devices: Recommended books for children and young adults.* Phoenix, AZ: Oryx.

Harrington, S.L. (1994). An author's storyboard technique as a prewriting strategy. *The Reading Teacher, 48*, 283–285.

Harste, J.C., Short, K.G., & Burke, C.L. (1988). *Creating classrooms for authors: The reading-writing connection.* Portsmouth, NH: Heinemann.

Harwayne, S. (2000). *Lifetime guarantees: Toward ambitious literacy teaching*. Portsmouth, NH: Heinemann.

Heard, G. (1995). *Writing toward home: Tales and lessons to find your way*. Portsmouth, NH: Heinemann.

Heffernan, L. (2004). *Critical literacy and writer's workshop: Bringing purpose and passion to student writing*. Newark, DE: International Reading Association.

Hillocks, G., Jr. (1987). Synthesis of research on teaching writing. *Educational Leadership, 44*(8), 71–76, 80–82.

Holdaway, D. (2000). Affinities and contradictions: The dynamics of social or acquisition learning. *Literacy Teaching and Learning: An International Journal of Early Reading and Writing, 5*(1), 7–25.

Johns, J.L. (1975). Dolch list of common nouns—A comparison. *The Reading Teacher, 28*, 538–540.

Kamberelis, G. (1999). Genre development and learning: Children writing stories, science reports, and poems. *Research in the Teaching of English, 33*(4), 403–460.

Korkeamaki, R.-L., Tiainen, O., & Dreher, M.J. (1998). Helping Finnish second graders make sense of their reading and writing in their science project. In T. Shanahan & F.V. Rodriguez-Brown (Eds.), *National Reading Conference yearbook 47* (pp. 334–344). Chicago: National Reading Conference.

Laird, C.G. (1985). *Webster's new world thesaurus* (Rev. ed.). New York: Simon & Schuster.

Lancia, P.J. (1997). Literary borrowing: The effects of literature in children's writing. *The Reading Teacher, 50*, 470–475.

Lane, B. (1996). Quality in writing. *The Writing Teacher, 9*(3), 3–8.

Lane, B. (1999). *Reviser's toolbox*. Shoreham, VT: Discover Writing Press.

Le Guin, U.K. (1998). *Steering the craft: Exercises and discussions on story writing for the lone navigator or the mutinous crew*. Portland, OR: Eighth Mountain.

Murray, D.M. (1984). *Write to learn*. New York: Holt, Rinehart and Winston.

Murray, D.M. (1985). *A writer teaches writing* (2nd ed.). Boston: Houghton Mifflin.

National Assessment Governing Board. (1998). *Writing framework and specifications for the 1998 National Assessment of Educational Progress*. Washington, DC: U.S. Department of Education. Retrieved August 10, 2004, from http://www.nagb.org/pubs/writing.pdf

National Commission on Writing for America's Families, Schools, and Colleges. (2003). *The neglected "R": The need for a writing revolution*. New York: College Entrance Examination Board. (ERIC Document Reproduction Service No. ED475856) Retrieved August 10, 2004, from http://www.writingcommission.org/prod_downloads/writingcom/neglectedr.pdf.

National Council of Teachers of English. (1985). *Resolution on grammar exercises to teach speaking and writing*. Urbana, IL: Author.

National Institute of Child Health and Human Development. (2000). *Report of the National Reading Panel. Teaching children to read: An evidence-based assessment of the scientific research literature on reading and its implications for reading instruction* (NIH Publication No. 00-4769). Washington, DC: U.S. Government Printing Office.

North Central Regional Educational Laboratory. (2004). *Exemplary reading programs in Illinois Public Schools*. [Report prepared for the Illinois State Department of Education.] Oak Brook, IL: Author. Retrieved August 10, 2004, from http://www.ncrel.org/sdrs/areas/isbe/titlepg.htm.

O'Conner, P. (1999). *Words fail me: What everyone who writes should know about writing.* San Diego, CA: Harcourt Brace.

Ogle, D.M. (1986). K-W-L: A teaching model that develops active reading of expository text, *The Reading Teacher, 39,* 564–570.

Olswanger, A. (2002). From hocus pocus to the Newbery: The writing life of Sid Fleischman. In *Children's Writer's & Illustrator's Market* (p. 83). Cincinnati, OH: Writer's Digest Books.

Peck, R. (2002). *Invitations to the world: Teaching and writing for the young.* New York: Dial.

Poindexter, C.C., & Oliver, I.R. (1998/1999). Navigating the writing process: Strategies for young children. *The Reading Teacher, 52,* 420–423.

Pope, A., & Michael, M. (Eds.). (2002). *2003 children's writer's & illustrator's market.* Cincinnati, OH: F & W Publications.

Rasinski, T.V. & Padak, N.D. (2001). *From phonics to fluency: Effective teaching of decoding and reading fluency in the elementary school.* New York: Longman.

Reeves, D. (2000). *Accountability in action: A blueprint for learning organizations.* Denver, CO: Advanced Learning Press.

Rog, L.J. (2001). *Early literacy instruction in kindergarten.* Newark, DE: International Reading Association.

Routman, R. (1994). *Invitations: Changing as teachers and learners, K–12.* Portsmouth, NH: Heinemann.

Routman, R. (1996). *Literacy at the crossroads: Crucial talk about reading, writing, and other teaching dilemmas.* Portsmouth, NH: Heinemann.

Routman, R. (2003). *Reading essentials: The specifics you need to teach reading well.* Portsmouth, NH: Heinemann.

Saccardi, M.C. (1996). More predictable books: Gateways to a lifetime of reading. *The Reading Teacher, 49,* 668–670.

Serafini, F., & Giorgis, C. (2003). *Reading aloud and beyond: Fostering the intellectual life with older readers.* Portsmouth, NH: Heinemann.

Sloan, M.S. (1996). Encouraging young students to use interesting words in their writing. *The Reading Teacher, 50,* 268–269.

Smith, F. (1983). Reading like a writer. *Language Arts, 60*(5), 558–567.

Smith-D'Arezzo, W.M., & Kennedy, B.J. (2004). Seeing double: Piecing writing together with cross-age partners. *Journal of Adolescent & Adult Literacy, 47,* 390–401.

Spandel, V. (2001a). *Books, lessons, ideas for teaching the six-traits: Writing in the elementary and middle grades.* Wilmington, MA: Great Source Education Group.

Spandel, V. (2001b). *Creating writers: Through 6-trait writing assessment and instruction* (3rd ed.). New York: Longman.

Spandel, V., & Culham, R. (1995). *Six trait writing for assessment and instruction.* Portland, OR: Northwest Regional Educational Laboratory.

Spandel, V., & Stiggins, R.J. (1997). *Creating writers: Linking writing assessment and instruction* (2nd ed.). New York: Longman.

Strickland, K., & Strickland, J. (1998). *Reflections on assessment: Its purposes, methods & effects on learning.* Portsmouth, NH: Boynton/Cook.

Thomason, T., & York, C. (2000). *Write on target: Preparing young writers to succeed on state writing achievement tests.* Norwood, MA: Christopher-Gordon.

Tierney, R.J., & Leys, M. (1986). What is the value of connecting reading and writing? In B. Peterson (Ed.), *Convergences: Transactions in reading and writing* (pp. 15–29). Urbana, IL: National Council of Teachers of English. (ERIC Document Reproduction Service No. ED265568)

Tierney, R.J., & Pearson, P.D. (1983). Toward a composing model of reading. *Language Arts, 60*(5), 568–580.

Vail, N., & Papenfuss, J. (1990). *Daily oral language.* Evanston, IL: McDougal Littel.

Walmsley, S.A., & Walp, T. (1990). Integrating literature and composing into the language arts curriculum: Philosophy and practice. *The Elementary School Journal, 90*(3), 251–274.

Zemelman, S., Daniels, H., & Hyde, A. (1998). *Best practice: New standards for teaching and learning in America's schools.* Portsmouth, NH: Heinemann.

LITERATURE CITED

Adler, D.A. (1998). *A picture book of Amelia Earhart.* (Jeff Fisher, Illus.). New York: Holiday House.

Andrews-Goebel, N. (2002). *The pot that Juan built.* (David Diaz, Illus.). New York: Lee & Low.

Arnold, C. (1991). *A guide dog puppy grows up.* (Richard Hewett, Photog.). San Diego, CA: Harcourt Brace.

Auch, M.J. (1995). *Hen Lake.* New York: Holiday House.

Base, G. (1988). *The eleventh hour.* New York: Harry N. Abrams.

Baylor, B. (1992). *One small blue bead.* (Ronald Himler, Illus.). New York: Scribner.

Birdseye.T. (1988). *Airmail to the moon.* (Steven Gammel, Illus.). New York: Holiday House.

Blume, J. (2002). *Double Fudge.* New York: Dutton.

Bradby, M. (1995). *More than anything else.* (Chris K. Soentpiet, Illus.). New York: Orchard Books.

Brett, J. (1989). *The mitten.* New York: Putnam.

Brown, M. (1996). *Arthur writes a story.* New York: Little, Brown.

Brown, M.W. (1949). *The important book.* (Leonard Weisgard, Illus.). New York: Harper.

Bryan, A. (1985). *The cat's purr.* New York: Atheneum.

Buehner, C., & Buehner, M. (1993). *A job for Wittilda.* New York: Dial.

Bunting, E. (1990). *The wall.* (Ronald Himler, Illus.). New York: Clarion.

Bunting, E. (1991). *Fly away home.* (Ronald Himler, Illus.). New York: Clarion.

Bunting, E. (1994). *Smoky night.* (David Diaz, Illus.). San Diego, CA: Harcourt Brace.

Bunting, E. (1995). *Once upon a time.* Katonah, NY: Richard C. Owen.

Bunting, E. (2001). *Jin Woo.* (Chris Soentpiet, Illus.). New York: Clarion.

Bunting, E. (2002). *One candle.* (K. Wendy Popp, Illus.). New York: Joanna Cotler Books.

Canizares, S., & Chessen, B. (1998). *From egg to robin.* New York: Scholastic.

Carlstrom, N.W. (1990). *Blow me a kiss, Miss Lilly.* (Amy Schwartz, Illus.). New York: Harper & Row.

Carlstrom, N.W. (1991). *Goodbye, geese.* (Ed Young, Illus.). New York: Philomel.

Celsi, T. (1990). *The fourth little pig.* (Doug Cushman, Illus.). Milwaukee, WI: Raintree.

Charlip, R. (1964). *Fortunately.* New York: Parents' Magazine Press.

Cherry, L. (1990). *The great kapok tree: A tale of the Amazon rain forest.* San Diego, CA: Harcourt Brace.

Cleary, B. (1977). *Ramona and her father.* (Alan Tiegreen, Illus.). New York: William Morrow.

Cleary, B.P. (1999). *A mink, a fink, a skating rink: What is a noun?* (Jenya Prosmitsky, Illus.). Minneapolis, MN: Carolrhoda.

Cleary, B.P. (2000). *Hairy, scary, ordinary: What is an adjective?* (Jenya Prosmitsky, Illus.). Minneapolis, MN: Carolrhoda.

Cleary, B.P. (2001). *To root, to toot, to parachute: What is a verb?* (Jenya Prosmitsky, Illus.). Minneapolis, MN: Carolrhoda.

Clements, A. (1997). *Double trouble in Walla Walla.* (Sal Murdocca, Illus.). Brookfield, CT: Millbrook.

Cole, H. (1995). *Jack's garden.* New York: Greenwillow.

Cole, J. (1991). *My puppy is born.* (Margaret Miller, Photog.). New York: Morrow. (Original work published 1973)

Cooper, E. (1998). *Ballpark.* New York: Greenwillow.

Day, A. (1993). *Carl goes to daycare.* New York: Farrar Straus Giroux.

de Paola, T. (1978). *The popcorn book.* New York: Holiday House.

De Young, C. (1999). *A letter to Mrs. Roosevelt.* New York: Delacorte.

deGroat, D. (1998). *Trick or treat, smell my feet.* New York: Morrow Junior Books.

DiCamillo, K.(2000). *Because of Winn-Dixie.* Cambridge, MA: Candlewick.

Dr. Seuss (1957). *How the Grinch stole Christmas.* New York: Random House.

Duncan, L. (2002). *Song of the circus.* (Meg Cundiff, Illus.). New York: Philomel.

Duke, K. (1983). *The guinea pig ABC.* New York: E.P. Dutton.

Edwards, P.D. (1995). *Four famished foxes and Fosdyke.* (Henry Cole, Illus.). New York: HarperCollins.

Edwards, P.D. (1996). *Some smug slug.* (Henry Cole, Illus.). New York: HarperCollins.

Edwards, P.D. (2001). *Clara caterpillar.* (Henry Cole, Illus.). New York: HarperCollins.

Egan, T. (1995). *Chestnut cove.* Boston: Houghton Mifflin.

Ehlert, L. (1990). *Feathers for lunch.* San Diego, CA: Harcourt Brace.

Elting, M., & Flosom, M. (1980). *Q is for duck: An alphabet guessing game.* (Jack Kent, Illus.). New York: Clarion.

Emberley, M. (1993). *Welcome back, sun.* Boston: Little, Brown.

Flack, M. (1931). *Angus and the cat.* Garden City, NY: Doubleday, Doran.

Fleming, D. (1992). *Lunch.* New York: Henry Holt.

Fleming, D. (1996). *Where once there was a wood.* New York: Henry Holt.

Fox, M. (1989). *Night noises.* (Terry Denton, Illus.). San Diego, CA: Harcourt Brace.

Fox, M. (1994). *Tough Boris.* (Kathryn Brown, Illus.). San Diego, CA: Harcourt Brace.

Fox, M. (1997). *Whoever you are.* (Leslie Staub, Illus.). San Diego, CA: Harcourt Brace.

Gág, W. (1928). *Millions of cats.* New York: Coward-McCann.

Gantos, J. (1976). *Rotten Ralph.* (Nicole Rubel, Illus.). Boston: Houghton Mifflin.

Gantos, J. (1978). *Worse than rotten, Ralph.* (Nicole Rubel, Illus.). Boston: Houghton Mifflin.

Garland, S. (1998). *My father's boat.* (Ted Rand, Illus.). New York: Scholastic.

Gelman, R.G. (1992). *More spaghetti, I say!* (Mort Gerberg, Illus.). New York: Scholastic.

Gibbons, G. (1991). *From seed to plant.* New York: Scholastic.

Gibbons, G. (1993). *Pirates: Robbers of the high seas.* Boston: Little, Brown.

Gibbons, G. (2002). *The berry book.* New York: Holiday House.

Giovanni, N. (1993). The reason I like chocolate. In W. Hudson (Ed.), *Pass it on: African-American poetry for children* (p. 11). (Floyd Cooper, Illus.). New York: Scholastic.

Granowsky, A. (1993a). *Cinderella/That awful Cinderella.* (Barbara Kiwak & Rhonda Childress, Illus.). Austin, TX: Steck-Vaughn.

Granowsky, A. (1993b). *Rumpelstiltskin/A deal is a deal.* (Linda Graves & Tom Newbury, Illus.). Austin, TX: Steck-Vaughn.

Granowsky, A. (1996a). *Henny Penny/Brainy bird saves the day.* (Mike Krone & Eva Vagreti Cockrille, Illus.). Austin, TX: Steck-Vaughn.

Granowsky, A. (1996b). *The little red hen/Help yourself, little red hen.* (Wendy Edelson & Jane Manning, Illus.). Austin, TX: Steck-Vaughn.

Graves, K. (2001). *Pet boy.* San Francisco: Chronicle Books.

Gray, L.M. (1993a). *Dear Willie Rudd.* (Peter M. Fiore, Illus.). New York: Simon & Schuster.

Gray, L.M. (1993b). *Miss Tizzy.* (Jada Rowland, Illus.). New York: Simon & Schuster.

Greenberg, D. (1983). *Slugs.* (Victoria Chess, Illus.). Boston: Little, Brown.

Grimes, N. (1998). *Talkin' 'bout Bess. The story of aviator Elizabeth Coleman.* (Joseph Lorusso, Illus.). New York: Orchard.

Harrison, T. (1992). *O Canada.* Toronto: Kids Can Press.

Harwayne, S. (Ed.). (2002). *Messages to ground zero.* Portsmouth, NH: Heinemann.

Heller, R. (1990). *Merry-go-round: A book about nouns.* New York: Grosset & Dunlap.

Henkes, K. (1991). *Chrysanthemum.* New York: Greenwillow.

Henkes, K. (1996). *Lilly's purple plastic purse.* New York: Greenwillow.

Hepworth, C. (1992). *Antics! An alphabetical anthology.* New York: Putnam.

Herold, M.R. (1995). *A very important day.* (Catherine Stock, Illus.). New York: William Morris.

Hest, A. (1995). *The private notebook of Katie Roberts, age 11.* Cambridge, MA: Candlewick Press.

Hoffman. M. (1995). *Boundless Grace.* (Caroline Black, Illus.). New York: Dial.

Holm, J.L. (2002). *Boston Jane: Wilderness days.* New York: HarperCollins.

Hopkinson, D. (2003). *Girl Wonder.* (Terry Widener, Illus.). New York: Atheneum.

Houston, G. (1992). *My great-aunt Arizona.* (Susan Condie Lamb, Illus.). New York: HarperCollins.

Johnston, T. (1992). *The cowboy and the black-eyed pea.* (Warren Ludwig, Illus.). New York: Putnam.

Johnston, T. (1994). *Amber on the mountain.* (Robert Duncan, Illus.). New York: Dial.

Johnston, T. (1996). *My Mexico—Mexico mio.* (F. John Sierra, Illus.). New York: Putnam.

Keats, E.J. (1962). *The snowy day.* New York: Viking.

Killilea, M. (1992). *Newf.* (Ian Schoenherr, Illus.). New York: Philomel.

Kimmel, E.A. (1990). *Nanny goat and the seven little kids.* (Janet Stevens, Illus.). New York: Holiday House.

King-Smith, D. (1994). *I love Guinea Pigs.* (Anita Jeram, Illus.). Cambridge, MA: Candlewick Press.

Knutson, K. (1992). *Muddigush.* New York: Macmillan.

Lasky, K. (1993). *The tantrum.* (Bobette McCarthy, Illus.). New York: Macmillan.

Lasky, K. (1997). *Pond year.* (Mike Bostock, Illus.). Cambridge, MA: Candlewick.

Leemis, R. (1993). *Smart dog.* (Chris L. Demarest, Illus.). Honesdale, PA: Caroline House.

Lester, H. (1997). *Author.* Boston: Houghton Mifflin.

Little, J., & DeVries, M. (1991). *Once upon a golden apple.* (Phoebe Gilman, Illus.). New York: Viking.

Lobel, A. (1990). *Alison's zinnia.* New York: Greenwillow.

Lobel, A. (1994). *Away from home.* New York: Greenwillow.

MacDonald, B.B. (1947). *Mrs. Piggle-Wiggle.* (Hilary Knight, Illus.). Philadelphia: Lippincott.

MacDonald, S. (1986). *Alphabatics.* New York: Bradbury.

MacLachlan, P. (1985). *Sarah, plain and tall.* New York: Harper & Row.

MacLachlan, P. (1994). *All the places to love.* (Mike Wimmer, Illus.). New York: HarperCollins.

Martin, B., Jr. (1983). *Brown bear, brown bear, what do you see?* (Eric Carle, Illus.). New York: Henry Holt. (Original work published 1967)

Martin, B., Jr., & Archambault, J. (1988). *Up and down on the merry-go-round.* (Ted Rand, Illus.). New York: Henry Holt.

Martin, J.R. (1993). *Now everybody really hates me.* (Roz Chast, Illus.). New York: HarperCollins.

Marzollo, J. (1995). *Sun song.* (Laura Regan, Illus.). New York: HarperCollins.

McBratney, S. (1995). *Guess how much I love you.* (Anita Jeram, Illus.). Cambridge, MA: Candlewick.

McCully, E.A. (1993). *The amazing Felix.* New York: Putnam.

Melmed, L.K. (1993). *I love you as much—.* (Henri Sorensen, Illus.). New York: Lothrop, Lee & Shepard.

Merriam, E. (1993). *Quiet, please.* (Sheila Hamanaka, Illus.). New York: Simon & Schuster.

Mikaelsen, B. (1995). *Stranded.* New York: Hyperion.

Miller, S.S. (1997). *Three stories you can read to your cat.* (True Kelley, Illus.). Boston: Houghton Mifflin.

Milstein, L. (1993). *Amanda's perfect hair.* (Susan Meddaugh, Illus.). New York: Tambourine Books.

Mora, P. (1997). *Tomás and the library lady.* (Raúl Colón, Illus.). New York: Knopf.

Munsch, R. (1985). *Thomas' snowsuit.* (Michael Martchenko, Illus.). Toronto: Annick Press.

Munsch, R. (1986). *Love you forever.* (Sheila McGraw, Illus.). Scarborough, ON: Firefly.

Nixon, J.L. (1999). *If you were a writer.* (Bruce Degan, Illus.). New York: Macmillan.

O'Callahan, J. (1992). *Tulips.* (Deborah Santini, Illus.). Saxonville, MA: Picture Book Studio.

Okimoto, J.D. (1990). *Blumpoe the grumpoe meets Arnold the cat.* (Howie Schneider, Illus.). Boston: Little, Brown.

Pallotta, J. (1986). *The icky bug alphabet book.* (Ralph Masiello, Illus.). Watertown, MA: Charlesbridge.

Pallotta, J. (1988). *The flower alphabet book.* (Leslie Evans, Illus.). Watertown, MA: Charlesbridge.

Park, B. (1995). *Mick Harte was here.* New York: Knopf.

Paulsen, G. (1993). *Dogteam.* (Ruth Wright Paulsen, Illus.). New York: Delacorte.

Paulsen, G. (1995). *The tortilla factory.* (Ruth Wright Paulsen, Illus.). San Diego, CA: Harcourt Brace.

Paulsen, G. (1997). *Worksong.* (Ruth Wright Paulsen, Illus.). San Diego, CA: Harcourt Brace.

Paulsen, G. (1999). *Canoe days.* (Ruth Wright Paulsen, Illus.). New York: Doubleday.

Peck, R. (1981). *Close enough to touch.* New York: Delacorte.

Peck, R. (2000). *A year down yonder.* New York: Dial.

Peck, R. (2001). *Fair weather.* New York: Dial.

Peters, C. (1995). *Food to eat.* New York: Houghton Mifflin.

Pilkey, D. (1993). *Kat Kong.* San Diego, CA: Harcourt Brace.

Polacco, P. (1998). *Thank you, Mr. Falker.* New York: Philomel.

Polacco, P. (2001). *Mr. Lincoln's way.* New York: Philomel.

Potter, B. (1907). *The tale of Tom Kitten.* London: F. Warne.

Potter, B. (1909). *The tale of the flopsy bunnies.* London: F. Warne.

Price, M. (1993). *The reindeer Christmas.* (Atsuko Morozumi, Illus.). San Diego, CA: Harcourt Brace.

Provensen, A., & Provenson, M. (1983). *The glorious flight: Across the Channel with Louis Blériot.* New York: Viking.

Rand, G. (1994). *The cabin key.* (Ted Rand, Illus.). San Diego, CA: Harcourt Brace.

Rathmann, P. (1995). *Officer Buckle and Gloria*. New York: Putnam.

Rockwell, A. (1998). *One bean*. (Megan Halsey, Illus.). New York: Walker & Company.

Ross, J., & Myers, P. (Eds.). (1996). *Dear Oklahoma City, get well soon: America's children reach out to the people of Oklahoma*. New York: Walker & Company.

Rowling, J. (1997). *Harry Potter and the sorcerer's stone*. New York: Scholastic.

Rucki, A. (1998). *When the earth wakes*. New York: Scholastic.

Ryan, P.M. (1996). *The flag we love*. (Ralph Masiello, Illus.). Watertown, MA: Charlesbridge.

Rylant, C. (1982). *When I was young in the mountains*. (Diane Goode, Illus.). New York: Dutton.

Rylant, C. (1987a). *Henry and Mudge in the green time*. (Suçie Stevenson, Illus.). New York: Macmillan.

Rylant, C. (1987b). *Henry and Mudge: The first book*. (Suçie Stevenson, Illus.). New York: Macmillan.

Rylant, C. (1992). *An angel for Solomon Singer*. (Peter Catalanotto, Illus.). New York: Orchard Books.

Rylant, C. (1999). *The cookie-store cat*. New York: Blue Sky Press.

Say, A. (1993). *Grandfather's journey*. Boston: Houghton Mifflin.

Scieszka, J. (1989). *The true story of the 3 little pigs!* (Lane Smith, Illus.). New York: Viking Kestral.

Sendak, M. (1962). *Pierre*. New York: Harper & Row.

Shannon, D. (1995). *The amazing Christmas extravaganza*. New York: Blue Sky Press.

Shelby, A. (1995). *Homeplace*. (Wendy Anderson Halperin, Illus.). New York: Orchard Books.

Simmie, L. (2001). *Mister Got to Go and Arnie*. (Cynthia Nugent, Illus.). Vancouver, BC: Raincoast Books.

Steig, W. (1977). *Caleb & Kate*. New York: Farrar Straus Giroux.

Stevens, J. (1995). *Tops & bottoms*. San Diego, CA: Harcourt Brace.

Terban, M. (1991). *Hey, Hay! A wagonful of funny homonym riddles*. (Kevin Hawkes, Illus.). New York: Clarion.

Tresselt, A. (1947). *White snow, bright snow*. (Roger Duvoisin, Illus.). New York: Lothrop, Lee & Shepard.

Tsuchiya, Y. (1988). *Faithful elephants: A true story of animals, people, and war*. (Ted Lewin, Illus.). Boston: Houghton Mifflin.

Van Allsburg, C. (1985). *Polar express*. Boston: Houghton Mifflin.

Viorst, J. (1968). *Sunday morning; a story*. (Hilary Knight, Illus.). New York: Atheneum.

Viorst, J. (1971). *The tenth good thing about Barney*. (Erik Blegvad, Illus.). New York: Atheneum.

Waber, B. (1963). *Rich cat, poor cat*. Boston: Houghton Mifflin.

Wells, R. (1994). *Lucy comes to stay*. New York: Dial.

West, P. (1987). The army of Emperor Qin. In *Scott Foresman Reading: An American tradition* (pp. 184–191). Glenview, IL: Scott Foresman.

Wiesner, D. (2001). *The Three Pigs*. New York: Clarion.

Wild, M. (1994). *Toby*. (Noela Young, Illus.). New York: Ticknor & Fields.

Wilder, L.I. (1932). *Little house in the big woods*. (Garth Williams, Illus.). New York: Harper & Brothers.

Wojciechowski, S. (1995). *The Christmas miracle of Jonathan Toomey*. (P.J. Lynch, Illus.). Cambridge, MA: Candlewick.

Woodson, J. (2001). *The other side*. (E.B. Lewis, Illus.). New York: Putnam.

Yolen, J. (1990). *Sky dogs*. (Barry Moser, Illus.). San Diego, CA: Harcourt Brace.

Index

Note: Page numbers followed by *f* indicate figures.

D

E

M

N

P

S

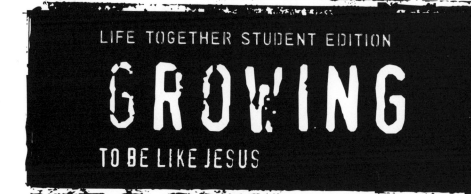

LIFE TOGETHER STUDENT EDITION

GROWING

TO BE LIKE JESUS

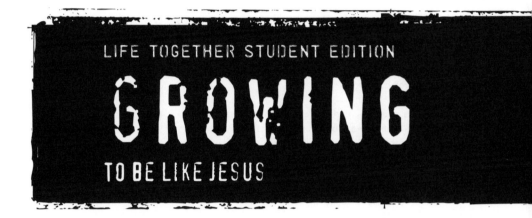

LIFE TOGETHER STUDENT EDITION

GROWING

TO BE LIKE JESUS

6 small group sessions
on fellowship

Doug Fields &
Brett Eastman

lifetogether
student edition

Youth Specialties

ZONDERVAN™

WWW.ZONDERVAN.COM

GROWING to Be Like Jesus: 6 Small Group Sessions on Discipleship

Copyright© 2003 by Doug Fields and Lifetogether™

Youth Specialties Books,300 South Pierce Street, El Cajon CA 92020, are published by Zondervan, 5300 Patterson Avenue Southeast, Grand Rapids MI 49530

Library of Congress Cataloging-in-Publication Data

Fields, Doug, 1962-   .
   Growing to be like Jesus : 6 small group sessions on discipleship /by
Doug Fields and Brett Eastman.
          p. cm.
Summary: Provides exercises, readings, and other materials for a
six-week spiritual journey toward becoming a better follower of Jesus
through such activities as daily prayer, Bible study, and perseverance
in the face of trials.
   ISBN 0-310-25335-7 (pbk.)
   1. Christian life--Juvenile literature. 2.   Christian
teenagers--Religious life--Juvenile literature. [1. Christian life. 2.
Teenagers--Religious life.] I. Eastman, Brett, 1959- II. Title.
   BV4531.3.F542 2003
   248.8'3--dc21

                                              2003005872

Unless otherwise indicted, all Scripture quotations are taken from the Holy Bible: New International Version (North American Edition). Copyright © 1973, 1978, 1984 by International Bible Society. Used by permission of Zondervan.

Concept and portions of this curriculum are from Doing Life Together (Zondervan, 2002), used by per-mission from Brett & Dee Eastman, Karen Lee-Thorpe and Denise & Todd Wendorff.

Editorial and Art Direction: Rick Marschall
Production Coordinator: Nicole Davis
Edited: Vicki Newby
Cover and interior design: Tyler Mattson, NomadicMedia.net
Interior layouts, design management, production: Mark Rayburn, RayburnDesign.com
Proofreading: Vicki Newby and Linnea Lagerquist
Design Assistance: Katherine Spencer
Production Assistance: Roni Meek, Amy Aecovalle
Author photos: Brian Wiertzema and Art Zipple

Printed in the United States of America

05 06 07 08 09 / DC / 12 11 10

ACKNOWLEDGMENTS

I'm thankful to the adult volunteers at Saddleback Church who are great small group leaders and to the students who are growing spiritually because they're connected to other believers. Good things are happening, and I'm so proud of you!

I'm thankful to the team at www.simplyyouthministry.com for working so hard to help create these types of resources that assist youth ministers and students throughout the world.

Gratitude for help on this project goes to Dennis Beckner, Kathleen Hamer, Erica Hamer, and especially Matt McGill who read every word of each book in the series and has made a big difference in my life and the books I write. What a joy to do life together with friends!

—DF

CONTENTS

Welcome to a relational journey!

My prayer is that this book, a few friends, and a loving adult leader will take you on a journey that will revolutionize your life. The following six sessions were designed to help you grow as a Christian in the context of a caring, spiritual community. This community is a group of people committed to doing life together, at least for a season of your life. Spiritual community is formed when each small group member focuses on Jesus and the others in the group.

Creating spiritual community isn't easy. It requires trust, confidentiality, honesty, care, and commitment to meet regularly with your group. These are rare qualities in today's world. Any two or three people can meet together and call it a group, but it takes something special from you to create a community in which you can be known, be loved, be cared for, and feel safe enough to reveal thoughts, doubts, and struggles and still to be yourself. You may be tempted to show up at the small group session and sit, smile, and be nice, but never speak from your heart or say anything that would challenge another group member's thinking. This type of superficial participation prevents true spiritual community.

Most relationships never get beneath the relational surface. This LIFETOGETHER series is designed to push you to think, to talk, and to open your heart. You'll be challenged to expose some of your fears, hurts, and habits. As you do this, you'll find healing, experience spiritual growth, and build lasting, genuine friendships. Since God uses people to impact people you'll most likely become a richer, deeper, more vibrant person as you experience LIFETOGETHER with others. If you go through this book (and the 5 other books in this series) you will become a deeper and stronger follower of Jesus Christ. Get ready for something big to happen in your life!

WHAT YOU'LL FIND IN EACH SESSION

For each session, the group time contains five sections, one for each of the primary biblical purposes: fellowship, discipleship, ministry, evangelism, and worship. The five purposes can each stand alone, but when they're fused together, they make a greater impact on you and your world than the five of them might if approached separately. Think about it like this: If you play baseball or softball, you might be an outstanding hitter, but you also need to be able to catch, throw, run, and slide. You need more than one skill to make an impact for your team. In the same way, the five purposes individually are good, but when you put them all together, you're a balanced player who makes a huge impact.

The material in this book (and the other LIFETOGETHER books) is built around God's Word. You'll find a lot of blank spaces and journaling pages where you can write down your thoughts about God's work in your life as you explore and live out God's purposes.

Here's a closer look at what you'll find in these five sections:

FELLOWSHIP: CONNECTING Your Heart to Others'
[goal: to have students share about their lives and listen attentively to others]

These questions give you and the members of your small group a chance to share from your own lives, to get to know one another better, and to offer initial thoughts on the session theme. The picture for this section is a heart because you're opening up your heart so others can connect with you on a deeper level.

DISCIPLESHIP: GROWING to Be Like Jesus
[goal: to explore God's Word, learn biblical knowledge, and make personal applications]

This is the time to explore the Bible, gain biblical knowledge, and discuss how God's Word can make a difference in your life. The picture for this section is a brain because you're opening your mind to learn God's Word and ways.

You'll find lots of questions in this section; more than you can discuss during your group time. Your leader will choose the questions your group will discuss. You can respond to the other questions on your own during the week, which is a great way to get more Bible study. (See **At Home This Week** on page 29.)

MINISTRY: SERVING Others in Love
[goal: to recognize and take opportunities to serve others]

During each small group session, you'll have an opportunity to discuss how to meet needs by serving others. As you grow spiritually, you'll begin to recognize—and take—opportunities to serve others. As your heart expands, so will your opportunities to serve. Here, the picture is a foot because you're moving your feet to meet the needs of others.

EVANGELISM: SHARING Your Story and God's Story
[goal: to consider how the truths from this lesson might be applied to our relationships with unbelievers]

It's too easy for a small group to become a clique and only care about one another. That's not God's plan for us. He wants us to reach out to people with the good news. Each session will give you an opportunity to discuss your relationships with unbelievers and consider ways to reach out to them. The picture for this section is a mouth because you're opening your mouth to have spiritual conversations with unbelievers.

WORSHIP: SURRENDERING Your Life to Honor God
[goal: to focus on God's presence]

Each small group session ends with a time of prayer. You'll be challenged to slow down and turn your focus toward God's love, his goodness, and his presence in your life. You'll spend time talking to God, listening in silence, and giving your heart to him. Surrender is giving up what you want so God can give you what he wants. The picture for this section is a body, which represents you surrendering your entire life to God.

AT HOME THIS WEEK

At the end of each session, you'll find reminders of ways you can help yourself grow spiritually until your small group meets again. You're free to vary the options you choose from week to week. You'll find more information about each of these options near the end of the first session.

Daily Bible Readings

Page 106 contains a list of Bible passages to help you continue to take God's Word deeper in your life.

Memory Verses

On page 110 you'll find six Bible verses to memorize, one related to the topic of each session.

Journaling

You're offered several options to trigger your thoughts, including a question or two related to the topic of the session. Journaling is a great way to reflect on what you've been learning or to evaluate it.

Wrap It Up

Each session contains a lot of discussion questions, too many for one small group meeting. So you can think through your answers to the extra questions during the week.

LEARN A LITTLE MORE

You might want to learn a little more (hey, great title for a subsection!) about terms and phrases in the Bible passage. You'll find helpful information here.

FOR FURTHER STUDY

One of the best ways to understand Bible passages is by reading other verses on the same topic. You'll find suggestions here.

BEING IN A SMALL GROUP

You probably have enough casual or superficial friendships and don't need to waste your time cultivating more. To benefit the most from your small group time and to build great relationships, here are some ideas to help you:

Prepare to participate

Interaction is a key to a good small group. Talking too little will make it hard for others to get to know you. Everyone has something to contribute—yes, even you! But participating doesn't mean dominating, so be careful to not monopolize the conversation! Most groups typically have one conversation hog, and if you don't know who it is in your small group, then it might be you. Here's a tip: you don't have to answer every question and comment on every point. The bottom line is to find a balance between the two extremes.

Be consistent

Healthy relationships take time to grow. Quality time is great, but a great *quantity* of time is probably better. Plan to show up every week (or whenever your group plans to meet), even when you don't feel like it. With only six sessions per book, if you miss just two meetings you'll have missed 33 percent of the small group times for this book. When you make a commitment to your small group a high priority, you're sure to build meaningful relationships.

Practice honesty and confidentiality

Strong relationships are only as solid as the trust they are built upon. Although it may be difficult, take a risk and be honest with your answers. God wants you to be known by others! Then respect the risks others are taking and offer them the same love, grace, and forgiveness God does. Make confidentiality a nonnegotiable value for your small group. Nothing kills community like gossip.

Come prepared

You can always arrive prepared by praying ahead of time. Ask God to give you the courage to be honest and the discipline to be respectful of others.

You aren't required to do any preparation in the workbook before you arrive (unless you're the leader—and then it's just a few minutes). But you may want to work through the **Growing** questions before your group time. Talk about this idea with your leader. If your group is going to, don't view the preparation as homework but as an opportunity to learn more about yourself and God to prepare yourself to go deeper.

Congratulations...

...on making a commitment to go through this material with your small group! Life change is within reach when people are united through the same commitment. Your participation in a small group can have a lasting and powerful impact on your life. Our prayer is that the questions and activities in this book help you grow closer to the other group members, and more importantly, to grow closer to God.

Doug Fields & Brett Eastman

Doug and Brett were part of the same small group for several years. Brett was the pastor of small groups at Saddleback Church where Doug is the pastor to students. Brett and a team of friends wrote Doing LifeTogether, a group study for adults. Everyone loved it so much that they asked Doug to revise it for students. So even though Brett and Doug both had a hand in this book, it's written as though Doug were sitting with you in your small group. For more on Doug and Brett see page 144.

FOR SMALL GROUP LEADERS

As the leader, prepare yourself by reading through the lesson and thinking about how you might lead it. The questions are a guide for you to help students grow spiritually. Think through which questions are best for your group. No curriculum author knows your students better than you. This small amount of preparation will help you manage the time you'll have together.

How to Go through Each Lesson

This book was written to be more like a guidebook than a workbook. In most workbooks, you're supposed to answer every question and fill in all the blanks. In this book, there are lots of questions and plenty of space.

Rule number one is that there are no rules about how you must go through the material. Every small group is unique and will figure out its own style and system. (The exception is when the lead youth worker establishes a guideline for all the groups to follow. In that case, respect your leader and conform your group to the leader's guidelines).

If you need a standard to get you started until you navigate your own way, this is how we used the material for a 60-minute session.

Intro (4 minutes)
Begin each session with one student reading the **Small Group Covenant** (see page 90). This becomes a constant reminder of why you're doing what you're doing. Then have another student read the opening paragraphs of the session you'll be discussing. Allow different students to take turns reading these two opening pieces.

Connecting (10 minutes)
This section can take 45 minutes if you're not careful to manage the time. You'll need to lead to keep this segment short. Consider giving students a specific amount of time and hold them to it. It's always better to leave students wanting more time for an activity than to leave them tired and bored.

Growing (25 minutes)
Read God's Word and work through the questions you think will be best for your group. This section will usually have more questions than you are able to discuss. Before the small group begins, take time to read through the questions to choose the best ones for your group. You may want to add questions of your own.

Serving and Sharing (10 minutes)
We typically choose one of these two sections to skip if pressed for time. If you decide to skip one or the other, group members can finish the section on their own during the week. Don't feel guilty about passing over a section. One of the strengths of this material is the built-in, intentional repetition. You'll have other opportunities to discuss that biblical purpose.

Surrendering (10 minutes)
We always want to end the lesson with a focus on God and a specific time of prayer. You'll be given several options, but you can always default to your group's comfort level to finish your time.

Closing Challenge (1 minute)
We encourage the students to pick one option from the **At Home This Week** section

that they'll do on their own. The more often students are able to take the initiative and develop the habit of spending time with God, the healthier they will be in their spiritual journey. We've found that students have plenty of unanswered questions that they want to go back and consider on their own.

Keep in Mind

- The main goal of this book isn't to have group members answer every question. The goal is **spiritual growth.**
- Make whatever adjustments you think are necessary.
- It's your small group, it's your time, and the questions will always be there. Use them, ignore them, or assign them to be answered during the week.
- Don't feel the pressure to have everyone answer every question.
- Questions are a great way to get students connecting to one another and God's Word.

Suggestions for Existing Small Groups

If your small group has been meeting for a while and you've already established comfortable relationships, you can jump right into the material. Make sure you take the following actions, even if you're a well-established group:

- Read through the **Small Group Covenant** on page 90 and make additions or adjustments.
- Read the **Prayer Request Guidelines** together (on page 128). You can maximize the group's time by following these guidelines.
- Consider whether you're going to assign the material to be completed (or at least thought through) before each meeting.
- Familiarize yourself with all the **At Home This Week** options that follow each lesson. They are detailed near the end of Session 1 (page 29) and summarized after the other five lessons.

Although handling business like this can seem cumbersome or unnecessary to an existing group, these foundational steps can save you from headaches later because you took the time to create an environment conducive to establishing deep relationships.

Suggestions for New Small Groups

If your group is meeting together for the first time, jumping right into the first lesson may not be your best option. You might want to have a meeting before you begin going through the book so you can get to know each other. To prepare for the first gathering, read and follow the **Suggestions for Existing Groups.**

When you get together with your group members, spend time getting to know one another by using ice-breaker questions. Several are listed here. Pick one or two that will work best for your group. Or you may have ice breakers of your own that you'd like to use. The goal is to break ground in order to plant the seeds of healthy relationships.

Ice Breakers

1. What's your name, school, grade, and favorite class in school? (Picking your least favorite class is too easy.)

2. Tell the group a brief (basic) history of your family. What's your family life like? How many brothers and sisters do you have? Which family members are you closest to?

3. What's one thing about yourself that you really like?

4. Everyone has little personality quirks—strange and unique habits that other people usually laugh about. What are yours?

5. Why did you choose to be a part of this small group?

6. What do you hope to get out of this small group? How do you expect it to help you?

7. In your opinion, what do you think it will take to make our small group work?

Great resources are available to help you!

Companion DVDs are available for the LifeTogether small group books. These DVDs contain teaching segments you can use to supplement each session by playing them before your small group discussion begins or just prior to the Growing to Be Like Jesus discussion. Some of my favorite youth ministry communicators in the world are included on these DVDs. (See page 140.)

In addition to the teaching segments on the DVDs, we've added small group leader tips that are unique to each session. Brett and I give you specific small group pointers and ideas that will help you lead each session. If you spend five to 10 minutes watching the leadership tips and then spend another 10 to 15 minutes reading through each session in advance, you'll be fully equipped to lead students through the material. The DVDs aren't required, but they're a great supplement to the small group material.

In addition, you can find free, helpful tips for leading small groups on our Web site, www.simplyyouthministry.com/lifetogether. These tips are general, so any small group leader may benefit from them. I encourage you to take advantage of these resources!

What GROWING TO BE LIKE JESUS is all about

Growing to Be Like Jesus teaches about discipleship. You have questions about God and how Scripture applies to your situation and how Jesus can make a difference in daily life. This book deals with these questions (and others, such as, How can we make a difference for Jesus?) Here, woven through the sessions, are new and fun ways to match your brain's work with your heart's desire to follow Christ and care for others.

You're ready to get started!

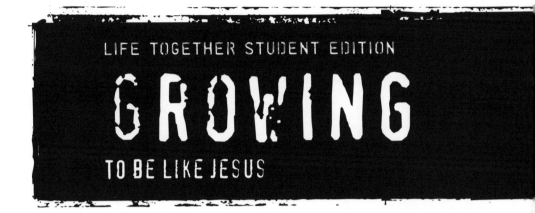

LIFE TOGETHER STUDENT EDITION

GROWING

TO BE LIKE JESUS

SPIRITUAL GROWTH ISN'T EASY

I'd like to have big muscles, but it won't ever happen. Big muscles require working out, and I'm not motivated to put my body through the pain to get the muscular gain. Too much sweat. Too much time in the gym. I'd rather eat.

Building muscles doesn't fit with my lifestyle. If I could get muscles from watching television or reading magazines by the pool, I'd be a ripped body builder. I like stuff that's easy and arrives quickly. My favorites are fast food, just-add-water recipes, and ads claiming instant success. I was raised on all of the slogans that told me I could get what I want right away. Quick, fast, and speedy are key words. Unfortunately, these slogans undermine the perseverance it takes to get big muscles.

Bodybuilding and spiritual growth have some principles in common. As you dig into this series of Bible study on spiritual growth, I'm sorry to tell you that there's no just-add-water routine for growing deeper in Christ. You may love fast food, but there's no such thing as a quick diet of Jesus. I know some people who have fast-food faith, but typically their faith doesn't last or make a difference in the world. If you're going to grow and be a follower of Jesus, you'll have to invest time and discipline. Sorry. Spiritual growth requires something from you. (But it's worth it!)

As you discuss how to grow spiritually, you'll discover that friends in your small group help you grow. They'll help you become more like Jesus, so don't take your friends for granted. Invite them into your life to help you grow in Christ. And you help them. It's a great adventure—though it's not easy or fast. This book and your small group are all about helping you develop spiritual muscles.

FELLOWSHIP: CONNECTING Your Heart to Others'
[goal: to have students share about their lives and listen attentively to others]

Strong friendships are key to growing deeper in Christ. We need the support. One way to strengthen friendships is to open up and reveal who we are when we take off our masks. Each time you're together with the members of this small group, be prepared to share a bit about your life—your inner life. Take a risk and share something personal. (But don't forget everyone needs a chance to talk, so don't go on for too long!)

1. Describe a time when you felt a close connection with God, what some would call a spiritual high. What happened? What was the result?

2. Describe your current relationship with God.

3. If you haven't discussed the **Small Group Covenant** on page 90, take time to read it together and discuss it now. Make commitments to one another so that your group time will reflect those values. You may want to have one person read the covenant to the group before you begin each lesson as a reminder.

Use the **Small Group Roster** (page 92) to record the names and contact information of the small group members.

DISCIPLESHIP: GROWING to Be Like Jesus
[goal: to explore God's Word, learn biblical knowledge, and make personal applications]

Growing spiritually begins with Jesus, the central focus of a maturing faith. When Christians find themselves spiritually stagnant, usually they've lost their focus on Jesus. The verses you're about to discuss are filled with challenges to keep you focused and running the Christian race without giving up. You don't see them here, but just before these three verses in Hebrews is a list of spiritual survivors, champions, heroes of the faith. Chapter 11 is a hall-of-fame list of people who followed God faithfully, people such as Abraham, Joseph, and Moses. We're told they were rewarded (**commended** in NIV) for their faith.

Wouldn't it be great to live a life of faith and be listed among the faithful who lived their lives focusing on God? In order to focus on God you need to clear the hurdles that will slow you down, fix your eyes on Jesus, and not give up when life gets tough.

> ¹Therefore, since we are surrounded by such a great cloud of witnesses, let us throw off everything that hinders and the sin that so easily entangles, and let us run with perseverance the race marked out for us. ²Let us fix our eyes on Jesus, the author and perfecter of our faith, who for the joy set before him endured the cross, scorning its shame, and sat down at the right hand of the throne of God. ³Consider him who endured such opposition from sinful men, so that you will not grow weary and lose heart.
>
> —Hebrews 12:1-3

Terms that look like this are described in **Learn a Little More** near the end of the session.

Why should "such a great cloud of witnesses" inspire you to be more faithful?

Voice of Martyrs

What currently hinders or entangles your spiritual life?
Do you find that these hindrances are a regular or continual problem, or are you facing them for the first time?

6 According to this text, what are some ways you can keep free from the things that hinder and entangle us?

7 Why is perseverance a vital connection to faith?

8 How do you fit together these two truths: salvation is a free gift from God and we have to give our best effort to run the race?

Haven't that about it
Don't trust God.
want to do my thing
why don't trust God?

9 Why are we called to run the race "marked out for us?" It's your life. Why don't you get to determine the race you run?

Why might Jesus be called the <u>author</u> and <u>perfecter</u> of our faith? **10**

He paid for it
sent H.S. to guide into truth
washing of regeneration

According to this passage, why did Jesus
endure the cross? *joy set before him* **11**

12 What was the joy that was set before Jesus?
What does that joy mean for us? How do we access that same joy?

– seeing people freed
relationship
fellowship

On a practical level, what does it mean for you to fix your
eyes on Jesus? For the last two weeks, how have you done
with this challenge? **13**

Describe a time when you were discouraged spiritually. What happened? **14**
What was it like? What was the cause? *– misperceptions of God*
– misunderstanding of Word
– eyes on people

How does thinking about Jesus help to keep you from **15**
growing weary and losing heart? *– what he endured → victory*

This passage is all about the long haul. What are some practical habits you might begin developing to help you become a strong believer when you graduate? (If you'll be graduating soon, then think about remaining strong for the next two years.)

faith goal
action goal

MINISTRY: SERVING Others in Love
[goal: to recognize and take opportunities to serve others]

One of the goals of a healthy small group is to provide support to one another. When you support one another, you serve one another. That's what ministry is—serving.

Ministry doesn't always include traveling to foreign countries or helping the homeless. Often ministry happens with those closest to you. Ministry opportunities can happen inside and outside of your small group. One of the ways you'll serve those in your small group is to help them grow spiritually and cheer them on in their growth efforts.

Over the next five lessons, you can have a ministry to the others in your small group by encouraging and challenging one another to develop regular habits that promote spiritual growth.

Pair up with a person next to you and answer the following question:
Which one or two of the following activities would you like to focus on during this season of your spiritual journey? Why? Consider circling one or two that would be new to you.

Prayer	Personal time with God
Bible study	Accountability with another Christian
Confession	Tithing
Solitude/silence	Journaling

Which of the activities listed in the previous question have become regular habits for you?

Make it a goal to encourage one another's spiritual growth between sessions of your small group. Call or e-mail one another to ask about progress on these activities that can be life-changing. One result of doing this is that you'll grow stronger in your walk with God when you experience life together with another Christian friend.

EVANGELISM: SHARING Your Story and God's Story

[goal: to consider how the truths from this lesson might be applied to our relationships with unbelievers]

Fortunately, you're not running the Christian race alone! We have more fun and motivation to run the Christian life when we run with others who are supportive and cheer us on.

How does your spiritual growth relate to your ability to make an impact in the lives of the unbelievers you know?

Describe a time when you allowed your life to be entangled with sin. (You don't have to give all the gruesome details.) How did it damage your credibility with a non–Christian?

Who is one person you know who isn't in the Christian race? Write this person's name down and pray for them during the week.

At the beginning of small groups such as this one, you should decide whether your group is open to inviting friends to join. If your group is open, list who you would like to invite and make plans for talking with them. Your small group leader or your leadership team may have already determined the group is closed at this time. If so, a good group respects and follows that decision. You may be able to invite friends to join you in the next LIFETOGETHER book.

Read **How to Keep Your Small Group from Becoming a Clique** (page 94) when you're at home.

WORSHIP: SURRENDERING Your Life to Honor God
[goal: to focus on God's presence]

The writer of Hebrews described the Christian life as a race. Any race that requires endurance always has a break station where people can rest and be refreshed.

Each time your small group gets together, when you get to this point in the session, be refreshed through a time of prayer to focus on God's presence. He loves you so much, and this break is an opportunity to take the focus off yourself, express your love back to him, and surrender your plans to his plans. You'll find that you can do this in a variety of ways.

22 Have members of the group share one specific way the others in the group can pray for them. Write down the prayer requests. (See the **Prayer Request Log** on page 132.)

You'll find three prayer resources in the back of this book. By reading and discussing them, you'll find your group prayer time more rewarding.

- **Praying in Your Small Group** (page 126). Read this article on your own before the next session.
- **Prayer Request Guidelines** (page 128). Read and discuss these guidelines as a group.
- **Prayer Options** (page 130). Refer to this list for ideas to give your prayer time variety.

23 Spend some time thanking God for the people in your group and be sure to praise him for the unique qualities each person has. All the group's qualities combine to make everyone a stronger follower of Christ.

24 Before your group breaks, read **At Home This Week** together. (If everyone in the group has already done this in another LIFETOGETHER book, you can skip the introduction if you'd like.)

AT HOME THIS WEEK

Each week, you'll have at least four options to help you grow and learn on your own—which means you'll have more to contribute when you return to the group.

Daily Bible Readings

On page 104 you'll find **Daily Bible Readings**, a chart of Bible passages that correspond with the lessons—five for each week. If you choose this option, read one passage each day. Highlight it in your Bible, reflect on it, journal about it, or repeat it out loud as a prayer. You're free to interact with the Bible verses any way you want, just be sure to read God's love letter—the Bible. You'll find helpful tips in **How to Study the Bible** (page 107).

Memory Verses

Memorizing Bible verses is an important habit to develop as you learn to grow spiritually on your own. **Memory Verses** (page 110) lists six verses—one per week—for you to memorize if you want to plant God's Word in your heart. Memorizing verses (and making them stick for more than a few minutes) isn't easy, but the benefits are undeniable. You'll have God's Word with you wherever you go.

Journaling

Use SCRIBBLE pages, 115-125

You'll find blank pages for journaling beginning on page 115. At the end of each session, you'll find several options and a question to get your thoughts going—but you aren't limited to the ideas in this book. Use these pages to reflect, to write a letter to God, to note what you're learning, to compose a prayer, to ask a question, to draw a picture of your praise, to record your thoughts. For more suggestions about journaling, turn to **Journaling: Snapshot of Your Heart** (page 112).

This week, choose one or more questions to reflect on.

- *How would you describe your spiritual journey?*
- *Where are you now spiritually?*
- *Where do you want to be spiritually?*

Wrap It Up

Write out your answers to the session questions your group didn't have time to discuss. You can use SCRIBBLE journaling pages starting on page 115.

This week share with the others in your group which option seems most appealing to try during the coming week. During other weeks, take time to share with the group what you did **At Home This Week.**

LEARN A LITTLE MORE

Everything that hinders and the sin that so easily entangles

We're experts at rationalizing and compromising. We quickly steer away from activities we consider sinful, yet we often participate in others that produce the same results...sin. Someone may choose to not drink alcohol but has no problem with talking badly about an acquaintance. Someone else won't ditch class, but cheats "just a little" on an exam after a busy evening at church and inadequate study.

This passage is clear. When we stop to take an inventory of our personal lives, if there is anything hindering us, whether we consider it to be sin or not, it should be discarded ruthlessly. Jesus taught this same thing: "If your right eye causes you to sin, gouge it out and throw it away" (Matthew 5:29).

Perseverance

Endurance. The commitment to remain under some kind of pressure rather than trying to escape it. In James 1:3 you see that endurance produces proven character. Responding to difficulties with persistent faith, not scrambling to get out from under hardships, is what produces proven character.

Jesus, the author and perfecter of our faith

This phrase is easily misunderstood. Hebrews 11:39-40 provides us with the context we need:

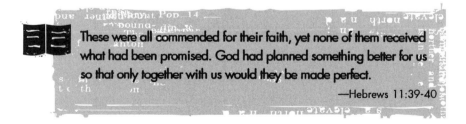

These were all commended for their faith, yet none of them received what had been promised. God had planned something better for us so that only together with us would they be made perfect.

—Hebrews 11:39-40

The men and women listed in Chapter 11 were faithful, but they never got to see the whole picture. They understood God's love, trusted in him, and lived in obedience. They received God's blessings, but they never experienced that which had been promised—Jesus, the Savior of the world. Peter explains that, even though the prophets of the Old Testament talked about Jesus, they never had full understanding about God's ultimate promise (1 Peter 1:10-12).

The life and teachings of Jesus provide everything we need to have the kind of faith that God desires. Jesus perfected our faith, meaning he completed it. We know that the law can never save us (Romans 3:20; Galatians 3:16; Hebrews 9:17; Romans 10:4). Instead we are saved by faith through the death and resurrection of Jesus.

The joy set before him

Jesus looked forward to the joy of returning to his Father and the joy of seeing us freed from slavery to sin and restored to our Father. We endure the race because of the great reward ahead of us, the joy of the Father's embrace.

FOR FURTHER STUDY

Leviticus 19:9-18
Deuteronomy 6:4-5; 10:12-13
Proverbs 4:23
1 John 3:16-18
1 John 4:7-12, 20-21

NOTES

THE POWER OF THE HOLY SPIRIT

I knew was in trouble when my daughter told me she would only play soccer if I became the coach. I knew nothing about soccer. I grew up playing football, basketball, and baseball. I occasionally saw soccer on television as a child, but no one played it where I came from. Technically, I was a soccer idiot leading a bunch of 10-year-old-girls. During the first practice I remember saying, "Okay girls, we're going to kick the ball...uh...in that direction."

A seasoned soccer veteran had a daughter on the team. After the first practice this kind dad pulled me aside. "You've never done this before, have you?"

"You could tell?"

He laughed. I quickly bestowed the title assistant coach on him and gave him total responsibility for everything I was assigned to do. Now I was the one laughing.

During the entire season, he coached me on how to be a coach. I watched him, followed him, and said what he told me to say. Parents saw me as the coach because I was doing what he told me to do. I set aside my way of coaching and trusted him to guide me. We had a great time, I learned a lot, and we actually won some games—a successful season!

When I think of the Holy Spirit, I think of this friend, not because my friend was perfect or invisible, but because he was a great guide. He prompted me and influenced me to do things I would never have thought to do on my own. The Holy Spirit is a great guide. He prompts me and influences me to do things I would never think to do on my own.

The role of the Holy Spirit is to guide, lead, and empower you to live the Christian life. If you have a relationship with God, the Holy Spirit will guide, lead, and empower you. Your role is to listen to the promptings of the Holy Spirit and follow his lead.

Your discussion today will be good, but you'll still probably leave with some unanswered questions. Not a problem. Having questions is all part of spiritual growth, and it's why you're meeting in a small group.

FELLOWSHIP: CONNECTING Your Heart to Others'

To grow spiritually, God's Spirit must do some work in your life. You won't become spiritually mature on your own; the Holy Spirit has an important role to play.

 Has there ever been a time when you've been aware of the Holy Spirit's presence? If so, briefly describe your experience. If not, share one question you have about the Holy Spirit.

Share what you know about the Holy Spirit's role in the lives of believers. Don't worry if you don't know much. One of the reasons we meet together is to learn from one another!

DISCIPLESHIP: GROWING to Be Like Jesus

The Bible contains word pictures of the Holy Spirit that help us understand who he is and how he works. Here are four:

- He is like wind blowing among us, acting powerfully, even though he is unseen (John 3:8).
- He is like fire in his power and brilliance (Acts 2:1-4).
- He gushes up from within a believer like a spring of water (John 7:37-39), giving life and refreshment.
- He is pure and sacred, making us holy temples where he dwells (1 Corinthians 3:16).

Wind, water, fire—all images of something powerful, uncontrollable, and beautiful.

When you put your faith in Jesus, the Holy Spirit takes up residence within you. He promises to change your character, produce fruit in your life, and give you new strength when you rely on him. He's an amazing presence that most Christians don't understand and a power that most don't rely on.

¹⁶So I advise you to live according to your new life in the Holy Spirit. Then you won't be doing what your sinful nature craves. ¹⁷The old sinful nature loves to do evil, which is just opposite from what the Holy Spirit wants. And the Spirit gives us desires that are opposite from what the sinful nature desires. **These two forces** are constantly fighting each other, and your choices are never free from this conflict. ¹⁸But when you are directed by the Holy Spirit, you are no longer subject to the law.

¹⁹When you follow the desires of your sinful nature, your lives will produce these evil results: sexual immorality, impure thoughts, eagerness for lustful pleasure, ²⁰idolatry, participation in demonic activities, hostility, quarreling, jealousy, outbursts of anger, selfish ambition, divisions, the feeling that everyone is wrong except those in your own little group, ²¹envy, drunkenness, wild parties, and other kinds of sin. Let me tell you again, as I have before, that anyone living that sort of life will not inherit the Kingdom of God.

²²But when the Holy Spirit controls our lives, he will produce this kind of fruit in us: love, joy, peace, patience, kindness, goodness, faithfulness, ²³gentleness, and self-control. Here there is no conflict with the law. ²⁴Those who belong to Christ Jesus have nailed the **passions and desires** of their sinful nature to his cross and crucified them there. ²⁵If we are living now by the Holy Spirit, let us follow the Holy Spirit's leading in every part of our lives.

—Galatians 5:16-25 **NLT**

How is a list of do's (verses 22–23) and don'ts (verses 19–21) helpful for living by the Spirit?

When you consider your life, do you face the kind of conflict described in this passage? If so, what is your conflict like? If not, why do you think you're not experiencing the tension between the two forces?

5 What do you think the last sentence in verse 21 means? Look closely at the text. What's the difference between sometimes doing these things and habitually doing these things?

6 Reread verses 22–25. What are one or two areas where you feel strong? Explain why you think so.

7 What's one area, positive or negative, from this passage you can focus on during the coming week? What practical changes can you make in that area?

8 What reason do you find in verses 22–25 that explain why we no longer have to live according to the sinful nature?

9 Respond to these two statements:

 If I make up my mind not to sin, then I will lead a good life.

 Now that I know the right things to do, I will always do them.

10 How can you live by the Holy Spirit as the last verse urges us to do? How would you follow the Holy Spirit's leading?

Turn to the **Spiritual Health Assessment** (on pages 97–105). Take a few minutes to rate yourself in the **Growing to Be Like Jesus** section. (You don't have to share your scores with the group.)

If you've never taken the Spiritual Health Assessment, consider taking the time to complete the remaining four areas later this week.

MINISTRY: SERVING Others in Love

It's an awesome sight when people allow the Holy Spirit's power to influence their lives. Dreams are born. Goals are designed. Hearts surrender. Prayers like this are common: "God, fill me with your Holy Spirit and use me to help others." A Spirit-filled follower of Jesus becomes an amazing part of the church and a local youth ministry.

Imagine you come upon Ephesians 3:20 one day: "Now glory be to God! By his mighty power at work within us, he is able to accomplish infinitely more than we would ever dare to ask or hope" (NLT). You understand in a new way that God can do anything. You're confident that you're filled with the Holy Spirit. You realize you're at a point in your life that has no restrictions, so you can serve God in any way and anywhere. Where and how would you want to serve God?

What is stopping you from pursuing your dream?

EVANGELISM: SHARING Your Story and God's Story

God wants everyone to be saved (1 Timothy 2:4), so when we keep in step with the Holy Spirit, eventually he'll give us opportunities to share our faith with others.

14 Describe the last time you felt the Holy Spirit leading you to have a spiritual conversation with an unbeliever. What happened? Did you take the opportunity or pass it up?

15 Why does the Holy Spirit usually work through people like us rather than communicating directly with unbelievers?

WORSHIP: SURRENDERING Your Life to Honor God

16 Break into pairs and briefly share a goal you want to pursue that will help you grow in your relationship with God and better understand the Holy Spirit. Here are some possibilities:

- I will spend 15 minutes a day reading the Bible.
- I will spend 15 minutes three times this week in solitude, focusing on God.
- At least twice this week, I'll journal my prayers.
- I will read a commentary to learn more about the power and role of the Holy Spirit.
- I will search the New Testament for more Bible verses on the Holy Spirit.

Write your goal here:

For the rest of the weeks your group is working through this book, let this person be your spiritual partner. Whenever your group breaks into pairs again, get together with your spiritual partner.

It's a normal part of group life to have a closer connection with some people than with others. If you find this to be the case and you'd like to spend more time throughout the week talking about life and challenging one another spiritually, consider using the **Accountability Questions** on page 96.

GROWING to Be Like Jesus

Stay with your spiritual partner for prayer. Take a few minutes to share prayer requests you might have. Pray for your requests and for the Holy Spirit's power to help you grow. If you're new to prayer, you may prefer to pray silently. The focus of this closing time isn't to master a prayer or to pray as well as another person does. The focus is on God. End your time together praising him.

AT HOME THIS WEEK

Daily Bible Readings
Check out the scriptures on page 106.

Memory Verses
Try memorizing a verse from page 110.

Journaling
Use **SCRIBBLE** pages, page 115-125
- Write whatever is on your mind.
- Read your journal entry from last week and write a reflection on it.
- Respond to this question: **How might I develop the habit of recognizing the presence and activity of the Holy Spirit in my life?**

Wrap It Up
Write out your answers to session questions your group didn't have time to discuss.

LEARN A LITTLE MORE

These two forces
If you've been a believer for more than a day, you know what it's like to face challenging temptations. Our lives are a continual struggle between living by the Spirit and living according to our old nature. I love the way one translation says it: "Your choices are never free from this conflict" (Galatians 5:17 NLT).

As long as we have the desire to live God's way while we're in this imperfect world, we're going to face difficult battles. Paul describes his own struggle: "I don't understand myself at all, for I really want to do what is right, but I don't do it. Instead, I do the very thing I hate" (Romans 7:15 NLT).

I often get the chance to talk with Christians in the midst of difficult struggles. As they wrestle with tough and crazy issues, I'm not usually worried—in fact I'm encouraged. What saddens me is the absence of the conflict Paul describes in many Christians. The conflict between our competing desires can often be displaced, and compromise becomes deeply rooted in the place of conflict. Complacent Christians no longer face conflict because they simply give in.

Passions and desires

Galatians 5:16-25 is a difficult passage. We can hardly read it without feeling challenged in some way. Living according to the Holy Spirit isn't simply a matter of the will, of strengthening our resolve. We can't just choose to live a perfect life on our own. A spiritual force is at work in us—our old nature. But we can defeat it along with its unhealthy passions and desires. We have the hope of our salvation and the help of the Holy Spirit.

We have a duty to look deeply within and to do it often. Our selfishness can take over at any time, so we need to continually be on the look out for it. We aren't at the mercy of uncontrollable passions and desires when we team up with the Holy Spirit and draw from his power. Then victory is ours!

FOR FURTHER STUDY

Luke 11:9-13
Acts 1:8
Ephesians 4:29-32; 5:15-18
1 John 1:9

NOTES

NOTES

HANGING OUT WITH GOD

You wake up in the morning, smack the reset button on your alarm clock, sleep a little longer, slink to the shower, throw on some clothes, grab your backpack, get a ride to school, meet up with some friends, sit through classes, start your homework, attend a sports event or work at your job, IM with your friends, fall into bed, wake up the next morning, and start the process all over again. Does this routine sound familiar?

Life easily falls into a predictable schedule. When life becomes routine, you may find it difficult to add new practices into your schedule. Finding time for something else may appear unrealistic—especially if you're not sure it will be fun. I mean, if you were told to make space in your schedule for God, you might think it's an odd request and a troublesome task. One more thing to do. And doing something with someone you can't see—well, that's just weird.

At church you probably hear messages about having daily devotions with God, and you feel guilty because you're not consistent at it. I understand that guilt feeling, and I know Christians who feel the same. I also know that as soon as a friend mentions going to a movie my typical reply is, "Sure! When?" I've learned that if something is important, I can usually find time for it. I hate to admit that sports, movies, television, and eating always seem like more fun than spending time with God.

Christians use a variety of terms for spending time with God. Here are a few:

Devotions   Devotional time   Quiet time

    Alone time   Hanging out with God

They all mean essentially the same thing. At the core is Bible reading and prayer, but many other elements can be included: Scripture memory, Bible study, meditation, contemplation, singing or playing an instrument, silence, fasting, and so on.

One of the goals of growing deeper in Christ is to learn to set time aside to be with God, to hang out with him. Since the Holy Spirit resides in you (remember last lesson?), you don't have to drive anywhere to be with God. You can hang out with him wherever you are and learn to make that time an important and regular part of your day.

So for the next hour or two that you're with your small group, forget about how bad you are at having quiet times. Forget the guilt you feel when you miss a day, and instead focus on new habits that might help you recognize God's presence. Learn to hang out with him like you would a best friend.

 # FELLOWSHIP: CONNECTING Your Heart to Others'

A typical barrier to having devotions is finding chunks of time to get by yourself and be quiet. In a world where we are surrounded by noise and options to keep us busy, it's tough to be alone and quiet.

What's your favorite thing to do with your best friend? What do you typically do when you're just hanging out together?

How might I be able to help a friend develop a regular habit of spending time with God—without sounding preachy?

In a usual week, approximately how much time do you spend alone just hanging with God without distractions?

DISCIPLESHIP: GROWING to Be Like Jesus

Every Christian I know struggles on some level with devotional time. It's a difficult habit to learn and to maintain. In the beginning, the rewards can't always be seen immediately, so we have a hard time realizing its true value. Over time, we become distracted, forgetting just how valuable time with the Creator is.

If you plan to take your faith seriously for the rest of your life, establishing this habit may be a struggle. It's been a struggle since the days of Jesus. When you look at the event that took place at Martha's house you may feel better about yourself and gain some insight into what's really important.

> [38]As Jesus and his disciples were on their way, he came to a village where a woman named Martha opened her home to him. [39]She had a sister called Mary, who sat at the Lord's feet listening to what he said. [40]But Martha was distracted by all the preparations that had to be made. She came to him and asked, "Lord, don't you care that my sister has left me to do the work by myself? Tell her to help me!"
>
> [41]"Martha, Martha," the Lord answered, "you are worried and upset about many things, [42]but only one thing is needed. Mary has chosen what is better, and it will not be taken away from her."
>
> —Luke 10:38-42

Why wasn't Martha commended for being a good servant? She was working hard to prepare the house and a meal for Jesus and his twelve disciples.

What compelled Mary to sit and listen to Jesus?

6 If hanging with Jesus and doing housework are both good things in their proper times, how do you know when is the right time to do each one?

7 What was Martha's biggest problem, according to Jesus?
🔲 Do you struggle with these issues yourself?

8 If you read the text carefully, you see that Mary started off doing housework with Martha ("Don't you care that my sister has left me..."). How was Mary able to change her focus?

9 Take the next five or ten minutes to experience personal time with God. Find a space away from others (as much as possible). Here are a few ideas about what you may want to do.
🔲 Talk quietly with God.
🔲 Focus your thoughts on God's character.
🔲 Quiet your thoughts as much as possible to give the Holy Spirit an opportunity to impress a truth, observation, or command on your heart.
🔲 Read Matthew 6:25–34 and respond to these questions:
   Who are you, Lord? You are a God who...
   What do you want me to do? You want me to...

10 When your group reassembles share from your experience. Feelings? Thoughts? Observations? What seemed natural? Comfortable? Forced? Too long? Too short? Weird? Refreshing?

Write down one goal for spending more time hanging out with God this week. When? Where? What might you do?

MINISTRY: SERVING Others in Love

Martha seemed to have difficulty managing ministry and personal devotion. Every Christian who spends life involved in ministry (that's all of us!) will face this same tension.

What's easier for you—doing ministry or spending personal time with God? Which is more important?

What does the following verse imply about the tension between worship and ministry?

Jesus answered, "It is written: 'Worship the Lord your God and serve him only. ' "

—Luke 4:8

How can you recognize when your involvement in ministry is at the expense of your spiritual life?

EVANGELISM: SHARING Your Story and God's Story

What's easier for you—doing ministry or spending personal time with God? Which is more important?

Mary was willing to change her plans to make the most of the opportunity in her situation. Do you make the most of your opportunities to share your faith with others?
- Are you so busy rushing from activity to activity that you have difficulty taking opportunities when they arise? If so, how might you change that?

WORSHIP: SURRENDERING Your Life to Honor God

Pair up with your spiritual partner from the last session (or another member if necessary). Choose one of the following ideas to do together before you close in prayer.

- Describe the quality of your daily devotional times with God.
- Share about something you've recently learned during your alone times.
- Discuss how well you did on the goal you set during the last small group session.
- Recite the memory verse you learned from the last meeting.
- Ask for accountability for your alone times this week. What will accountability look like?
- Share about one new idea you learned during this small group lesson.

Depending on what the leader or group decides, choose one of the **Prayer Options** on page 130 for the two of you or bring everyone together and close in a group prayer.

AT HOME THIS WEEK

Daily Bible Readings
Check out the scriptures on page 106.

Memory Verses
Try memorizing a verse from page 110.

Journaling
Use **SCRIBBLE** pages, page 115-125

- Write whatever is on your mind.
- Read your journal entry from last week and write a reflection on it.
- If you don't regularly have time when you hang out with God, respond to this question: *What's one activity (or nonactivity!) I do during the day that seems like a waste of time? Is it a waste? If yes, why?*
- If you regularly spend time with God, respond to this question: *How might I be able to help a friend develop a regular habit of spending time with God-without sounding preachy?*

Wrap It Up
Write out your answers to session questions your group didn't have time to discuss.

LEARN A LITTLE MORE

Martha...Mary
These sisters were Jesus' close friends. Their brother was Lazarus, whom Jesus later raised from the dead (John 11:43). You can find out more about this family in John 11:1-6; 12:1-8; and Matthew 27:61. We find Martha serving and Mary sitting at the Lord's feet on other occasions.

Sat at the Lord's feet
Sitting at the rabbi's feet while he was teaching was the typical position at the time Jesus lived. For a first-century teacher to accept a woman as a disciple was highly unusual.

What he said

Jesus spoke God's words to the disciples, the actual words of God. When we spend time reading the Bible, we're listening to Jesus' words, much as Mary did.

Mary has chosen what is better

This passage doesn't teach that we shouldn't be responsible for household, yard, family, or ministry duties so we can spend time with Jesus. We do need to be discerning about choosing the right activity at the right time. We shouldn't get so caught up in our daily responsibilities that we miss the times we ought to be sitting at Jesus' feet.

FOR FURTHER STUDY

Matthew 14:23
Mark 6:31
Isaiah 55:1-3
2 Timothy 3:16-17

NOTES

NOTES

If you are watching the LIFETOGETHER DVD, you may use this page to take notes.

NOTES

Live by the spirit so I won't gratify the sinful nature.

This means I need to focus on what God is trying to do in me to perfect me rather than focusing on what is happening. It means not focusing on what I shouldn't do but focusing on what he wants me to do. God I know I need you I need to make decisions to ensure my time with you

NOTES

If you are watching the LIFETOGETHER DVD, you may use this page to take notes.

PRAYER AND GOD'S PRESENCE

When we try to make new friends or we're hanging around people we don't know well, we usually feel tense or guarded. We're typically polite but reserved, a natural process. It takes time to feel comfortable with others and to be ourselves.

A more comfortable situation is when we're with a best friend. That's when we can be ourselves. Conversation is natural. We don't have to be entertaining, talkative, or even in a good mood. Being together is enough, at least some of the time. Being together is what friends do. Sometimes we take turns talking and listening. Our times together aren't always the same, aren't always perfect.

Spending time with our best friend is what this lesson is all about—learning to enjoy the presence of God and talking to him through prayer. As you continue to grow in your relationship with God, a time will come—maybe it already has—when you feel comfortable just being with God, just being who you really are. Prayer will be natural, comfortable, flowing, and a natural outflow of your day-to-day life.

When you first begin spending time with God, you may feel stiff and formal in your prayers. You may be stressed about making time, finding a place, figuring out where to read in your Bible, and having a full list of other things to do. The more you hang out with God, recognize his presence, and talk with him, the more normal, informal, and life-changing the time will become.

You don't have to go to church to pray. You can talk with God while you're waiting in the lunch line, walking between classes, sitting on the car bumper waiting for your parent—anywhere.

Imagine walking through the school parking lot after school. Your mom yelled at you before you left for school in the morning, you experienced conflict with one of your teachers, and one of your friends is mad at you. You're thinking about what a difficult day it's been, when you suddenly think, At least God loves me. You offer a silent prayer, "Thanks, God, for loving me today. I love you too. I need your strength today." Simple words can immediately change your focus and bring you into his presence.

You might miss out on going to a church Bible study, but you don't have to miss out on talking with God throughout the day. He's there! He's present! He's waiting for you to recognize his presence, call on him in need, talk to him about your fears, invite him to guide you, and hang out with him. That's what's about to happen within your small group. Talk with one another about God's presence. Help each other grow spiritually and remember that God is in your midst.

 # FELLOWSHIP: CONNECTING Your Heart to Others'

Simply put, prayer is conversing with God. It's one spiritual habit that immediately brings you into God's presence.

 1 What are some of the essential elements of a quality conversation? Write down the answers everyone gives.

interesting topic
interactive

2 Look at the list you just created and circle the ideas about conversation that are also true about prayer.

3 Rate your current prayer life on a scale of 1 (What prayer life?) to 10 (I'm in constant prayer). Explain your thinking.

 # DISCIPLESHIP: GROWING to Be Like Jesus

One day Jesus' disciples asked him, "Lord, teach us to pray" (Luke 11:1). What a relief to know I'm not the only one who needs coaching on prayer. Jesus gave the disciples an outline for prayer that we now know as the Lord's Prayer. Many Christians pray the Lord's Prayer word for word every day. As you study this prayer, you'll find the Lord's Prayer also provides helpful guidelines for prayer.

5And when you pray, do not be like the hypocrites, for they love to pray standing in the **synagogues** and on the street corners to be seen by men. I tell you the truth, they have received their reward in full. 6But when you pray, go into your room, close the door and pray to your Father, who is unseen. Then your Father, who sees what is done in secret, will reward you.

7And when you pray, do not keep on babbling like **pagans**, for they think they will be heard because of their many words. 8Do not be like them, for your Father knows what you need before you ask him.

9This, then, is how you should pray:

"Our Father in heaven,
hallowed be your name,
10your kingdom come,
your will be done
on earth as it is in heaven.
11Give us today our daily bread.
12Forgive us our debts,
as we also have forgiven our debtors.
13And lead us not into temptation,
but deliver us from the evil one."

—Matthew 6:5-13

Why would Jesus call the people who love to be recognized for their prayer lives hypocrites? Why aren't they setting a good example of devotion for others to follow?

How have the hypocrites (verse 5) received their reward in full? What does Jesus mean?

Why would Jesus encourage a prayer life that functions behind closed doors?

ck Strongs

What does "babbling like the pagans" mean in verse 7? He makes a scathing comment about their many words. Was Jesus limiting the number of words you should use in a prayer?

According to the example Jesus gave, what attitude ought you have toward God? What are some specific clues from the text that imply this attitude?

Why should you pray for God's will to be done on earth if God is all-powerful and always in control?

He waits for us das 4

What does it mean to ask God for your daily bread?

my needs

What is the connection between forgiveness and spiritual maturity?

Notice the pronouns in the Lord's Prayer—**our**, **us**, **we**. Why might Jesus have used those words instead of **I**, **me**, and **mine**? 12

Reread the Lord's Prayer (verses 9–13). What's your general response to this prayer? 13
- How does it challenge you?
- Why might it be helpful to begin your prayers by focusing on the Father's greatness?

14 If God knows what you need before you ask it, then why should you pray?

 relationship is key   Matt 7:7

Respond to this statement: I'd never be tempted if I prayed often enough and asked God for his help. 15
- What do you like about this comment (or agree with)?
- What do you dislike (or disagree with)?

18 What's the biggest hurdle that keeps you from a stronger prayer life?

17 Does Jesus' teaching mean you shouldn't pray in a public restaurant before eating? Discuss the pros and cons of that idea.

Public prayer - Corporate prayer

18 Rewrite the Lord's Prayer phrase by phrase in your own words. For example, "Forgive us our debts" might be written as, "I need your forgiveness, because I've made so many mistakes." The point is to personalize this prayer and explore its meaning, not to make it better.

MINISTRY: SERVING Others in Love

Prayer seems so personal, so intimate. It's part of your spiritual connection with God. But prayer is also a way to minister to other people. When you pray for others, you provide comfort, encouragement, hope, peace, and friendship.

Jas 5

19 With your group, make a list of five or more ways any of you can serve other people through prayer.

20 Look at the list and circle the one idea that you can do this week.

21 Share the idea you circled with your spiritual partner and ask for accountability throughout the week. Be sure to share your results next week with your friend.

EVANGELISM: SHARING Your Story and God's Story

22 When you're praying for a lost friend, what exactly are you praying for?

23 Discuss the strong connection between prayer and evangelism.

24 After your discussion, turn to **Prayer and Evangelism** on page 87. Spend five minutes writing about what you learned.

WORSHIP: SURRENDERING Your Life to Honor God

Listening is an important part of good communication, but we often do all the talking, especially when it comes to communication with God. Today as you end your time together, spend a few minutes in silence. During the silence simply close your eyes, sit quietly but comfortably, and try to subdue your own thoughts (admittedly it takes practice!). Listen for the thoughts that God might be whispering to you.

If your group members aren't familiar with extended silence, a few minutes may feel like an hour. Start with brief periods of silence. With a little practice, everyone will get more comfortable with silence and can handle longer periods.

Turn to **Personalizing the Lord's Prayer** (page 86). Take time to personalize the prayer using the prompts you'll find there. If you have to finish rather quickly during the group's meeting time, you may want to return to it later in the week during devotions. Use a blank journal page to complete a more thoughtful version.

The leader can now close by praying, "God, we want our prayers to..." Then each person finishes the sentence with a descriptive answer, such as the following examples:

- be genuine
- be a true reflection of what's in our hearts
- be heard
- be answered

Say whatever comes to mind at the moment. There are no right or wrong responses. Allow this time of prayer to help you focus on talking to God as a regular part of your daily life.

AT HOME THIS WEEK

Daily Bible Readings
Check out the scriptures on page 106.

Memory Verses
Try memorizing a verse from page 110.

Journaling
Use **SCRIBBLE** pages, page 115-125
- Write whatever is on your mind.
- Read your journal entry from last week and write a reflection on it.
- Respond to this question: *What would help me feel more comfortable talking to God?*

Wrap It Up
Write out your answers to session questions your group didn't have time to discuss.

LEARN A LITTLE MORE

Synagogues
The synagogue was—and still is—a place for Jews to assemble together for worship, prayer, and instruction in the Law of Moses. The main meeting is on the Sabbath (which is Saturday to Jews).

Originally the only place of worship for the Jews was at the temple in Jerusalem. During their captivity by the Babylonians and exile, synagogues arose as new places of worship, an alternative to the temple, which was out of reach.

One of the primary differences between worship at the temple and at the synagogue was participation. At the temple the priests played the active role. At the synagogue everyone is involved.

During the time of Jesus, the synagogue was the center of the community for many cities and villages.

Pagans
A pagan was typically a person who worshiped several gods. Pagans usually prayed to remind the gods of the sacrifices they had offered and the good works they had done, so they could experience blessing and good fortune as a result.

While Jesus condemned the babbling of the pagans, he didn't disapprove of repetition. He himself would pray three times in the Garden of Gethsemane, "saying the same words again" (Matthew 26:44.) His concern was about meaningless words and minds disconnected from them.

Hallowed

This term means holy or sacred, though it isn't used much in modern English. Praying for God's name to be holy is to pray that people recognize God as set apart. He's above and beyond and greater than anything else.

FOR FURTHER STUDY

Philippians 4:6-7
Mark 1:35
2 Chronicles 7:14
1 Thessalonians 5:17
Jude 20

- Stye-school - obstacles
- Bryce - bored
- friends - arranged marriage
-

NOTES

NOTES

DEVELOPING AN APPETITE FOR GOD'S WORD

Once upon a time the majority of the students in my church didn't read their Bibles. Many of the kids who grew up in church could spit out Bible answers during a small group Bible study, but having the correct answers couldn't mask the fact that they weren't reading the Bible on a regular basis. I didn't even have to ask them because I know that when students are reading the Bible, they'll have questions. They'll have a lot of questions. (I still have questions, and I've studied the Bible for over 20 years.) When you're reading you're learning, and when you're learning you're asking more questions.

I found it easy to tell my students they should read the Bible and to explain the benefit of spending time in God's Word. The challenge was making the task of reading (and reading something that was written thousands of years ago) seem attractive.

As a result, I helped create *The One Minute Bible for Students*. It contains 365 one-minute Bible readings. Almost anyone will read for one minute. I put it into my students' hands and challenged them to give God's Word one minute a day. I didn't care when or where they read—in bed, at school, in the car, in the bathroom, while stretching, anywhere. I just wanted them to read it!

Guess what? Within a week they were asking questions, learning and discovering the beauty and relevance of God's Word. Once they discovered a simple way to begin absorbing God's love letter, they had an entirely different attitude than before. With the attitude change came an appetite. They were hungry for God's Word, which became a central part of their spiritual journeys and growth. They learned to feed themselves and grow on their own. This habit brought God's voice to them daily.

As your small group meets to discuss God's Word, be honest about your struggles to make God's Word a regular part of your life. You'll be amazed what genuine sharing will do to help you develop an appetite for God's Word.

FELLOWSHIP: CONNECTING Your Heart to Others'

My own kids have no problem picking up a Bible and searching for God's direction. The Bible has been part of their lives since early childhood. They understand God's Word is the foundation of life. But some of their friends aren't as interested in making life choices based on a book that was written so long ago. This makes perfect sense. They weren't raised in homes where the Bible was read and used. The range of diverse experiences might be similar in your small group. (But you can only find out for sure if everyone is honest!)

1 Describe how important the Bible is in your home.

2 What do you think of the Bible? What place does it have in your life right now? (Again, the more honest you are about your own thoughts and the more respectful you are of the spiritual journeys of others, the better your small group will be—and the more you'll grow spiritually.)

DISCIPLESHIP: GROWING to Be Like Jesus

Learning how to read the Bible well is tough. It's thousands of years old, written in Hebrew and Greek, and made up of 66 individual books. To get better at it will take some practice. Understanding a basic three-step approach to studying the Bible will help too.

Observation: Just the facts

Begin with prayer to prepare your heart to learn. Then read through the passage (anywhere from a chapter to a part of a chapter to a few verses) and take notice of the basic facts. In fact, read it several times—slowly. Ask the basic questions: Who? What? When? Where? Why? How? Take notice of details, but don't get too caught up with them. For nearly every passage of the Bible, discovering the main points is relatively straightforward.

In this step, you're trying to discern what the author wanted his original readers to know. This is a crucial first step. Do your best to discover all of the basic, on-the-surface facts. Let the text speak for itself; don't read between the lines. Be aware of your personal assumptions, so you don't place them on the text.

Always keep a list of things that don't make sense, so you can ask someone what each one means.

Understanding: Nothing but the Truth

Once you've done a thorough job of figuring out the original meaning, it's time for you to figure out the timeless truths the passage teaches. Ask yourself this question: What is it about this passage that is always true, no matter what? Essentially you're looking for the eternal truths, the principles that never change.

The question is simple; the answers are tough!

Application: What's the point?

The final stage of studying the Bible is to take the truth and consider it in the context of your personal life. Many people consider this the practical side of Bible study because God's Word helps you change your practices. James says it like this: "Do not merely listen to the word, and so deceive yourselves. Do what it says" (1:22). Once you understand the passage in its original context and discover its eternal significance, you then consider how it impacts your life.

People can know a lot of Bible facts (observation) but not live a life that honors God (application). Some people believe that knowing God's Word is just as good as doing it. That's unfortunate.

The format of this session will be a little different than usual. Instead of studying the Bible together, you'll spend some time having a personal Bible study, so you can put these three actions into practice. Take the next few minutes to study this important passage from Philippians:

³Do nothing out of selfish ambition or vain conceit, but in humility consider others better than yourselves. ⁴Each of you should look not only to your own interests, but also to the interests of others.

⁵Your attitude should be the same as that of Christ Jesus:

⁶Who, being in very nature God,
did not consider equality with God something to be grasped, ⁷but made himself nothing,
taking the very nature of a servant,
being made in human likeness.
⁸And being found in appearance as a man,
he humbled himself
and became obedient to death—even death on a cross!
⁹Therefore God exalted him to the highest place
and gave him the name that is above every name,
¹⁰that at the name of Jesus every knee should bow,
in heaven and on earth and under the earth,
¹¹and every tongue confess that Jesus Christ is Lord,
to the glory of God the Father.

—Philippians 2:3-11

Observation: Just the Facts

3 Who is involved here? (sample answers below)
Yourselves, you, your—the Philippians (verses 3-5)
Paul, the author
Christ Jesus (verses 5, 11)
God the Father (verse 11)

4 What does Paul say about each of these people?

5 When do events happen?

6 Where do events take place?

Why do people act as they do? 7

How do people relate or respond to each other? 8

What doesn't make sense? List your questions here: 9

Understanding: Nothing but the Truth

10 What are the eternal truths this passage is communicating?

11 Are there any Bible verses or passages that contradict your answers to the previous questions?

Application: What's the point?

12 Based on your study of this passage, what does this mean for your life? How should you be different?

13 After you're finished (or when your leader calls your group back together), share the ideas you've learned or been reminded of or about your struggles.

MINISTRY: SERVING Others in Love

All Scripture is God-breathed and is useful for teaching, rebuking, correcting and training in righteousness, so that the man of God may be thoroughly equipped for every good work.

—2 Timothy 3:16-17

14 Read 2 Timothy 3:16-17. How can knowing God's Word help you be a more effective minister to others and equipped for every good work?

15 Can people serve others in love without the Bible being a significant part of their daily life? Explain your answer.

EVANGELISM: SHARING Your Story and God's Story

Look back at Philippians 2:3-5. You probably noticed that Paul makes a request for an unusual type of attitude. He's asking the Philippians to be servants.

16 Give examples of how servanthood can help in your evangelistic efforts.

17 If you only had one hour to give to God, would it be better to spend that hour studying the Bible or telling others about the good news in the Bible? For the sake of discussion, choose only one—the Bible or evangelism?

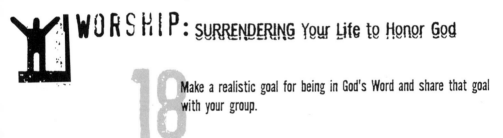

WORSHIP: SURRENDERING Your Life to Honor God

18 Make a realistic goal for being in God's Word and share that goal with your group.

Focus on God's Word as you close your time together. Turn to **Praying the Scriptures** (page 88) and assign each person one of the verses from the list to read. While one person is reading, the rest of the group closes their eyes to focus on God's Word. **19**

20 After all the verses have been read, move into a time of prayer. Thank God for one another, pray for the strength to complete the Bible goals you made earlier, and thank God for giving his Word to guide you.

AT HOME THIS WEEK

Daily Bible Readings
Check out the scriptures on page 106.

Memory Verses
Try memorizing a verse from page 110.

Journaling
Use **SCRIBBLE** pages, page 115-125
- Write whatever is on your mind.
- Read your journal entry from last week and write a reflection on it.
- Respond to these questions:
    What do I think about God's Word?
    Am I happy with the amount of time I spend in God's Word?
    With the quality?

Wrap It Up
Write out your answers to session questions your group didn't have time to discuss.

LEARN A LITTLE MORE

Here are extra ideas to take the three steps—observation, understanding, and application—a little further. These are more advanced ideas, so if they seem difficult, come back to them in a year or two. (Keep this book on your bookshelf.)

Observation: Just the Facts
1. Read the passage several times, read it once or twice out loud.

2. Check out the context—the verses before and after your passage. Take note of anything that impacts the meaning of your passage.

3. Give your passage a title.

4. Jot down a basic or detailed outline of the passage to help you notice the development of the ideas.

Understanding: Nothing but the Truth

1. Here are more questions you can ask about your text. (Not every question will apply to every text.)

TYPE	QUESTIONS
Introduction	What is the introductory sentence or paragraph?
Interrogation	Who? What? When? Where? Why? How?
Comparison	What elements or points are similar?
Contrast	What elements or points are different?
Interchange	Are there alternating elements?
Unifying theme	What theme dominates these verses?
Continuity	How does the theme relate to the entire context (surrounding chapters or the entire book)?
Cause and effect	Does one action or statement cause another?
Definition	How are key terms defined within the immediate text?
Progression	How are ideas or themes developed?
Repetition	What ideas or phrases are repeated?
Summary	What verse summarizes the entire passage?

2. What are the key words or phrases in the passage? Research the other verses in the Bible that contain the same key words.

Application: What's the point?

1. Think about the lessons you've learned from studying this passage. How do the lessons apply to your life—home, school, troubled times, and so forth?

2. If the opportunity came your way, how would you teach these truths to someone else? What would you emphasize? Who is someone you know who could benefit from what you've learned? How would you communicate in a way that's clear?

FOR FURTHER STUDY

Matthew 11:29; 26:39
Romans 12:16
2 Corinthians 8:9
Titus 3:1-2
1 Peter 5:5-7
Numbers 12:3

NOTES

If you are watching the LifeTogether DVD, you may use this page to take notes.

WHEN PAIN LEADS TO GAIN

When my friends Brett and Dee Eastman became pregnant for the third time, they had no idea what was ahead of them. They learned that Dee was carrying triplets, the first shock of many.

The three girls were born several weeks premature and two of these beautiful babies were born with cerebral palsy. Brett and Dee were drowning in a whirlpool of diapers, feedings, sleepless nights, and nagging questions about their future. At least one, and possibly two, of the girls would never walk. As followers of Christ, Brett and Dee had experienced hurdles in their spiritual journey, but the triplets made the past pains seem like a party. This was definitely a season of intense pain for them.

My friends wrestled with God and their grief, and exhaustion took them to a place they had never previously experienced. God used this dark time to develop qualities in their life they didn't formerly have. As they grew spiritually, they began to feel a hope that was beyond what their own minds could understand. Brett told me that he learned to hang on to Bible passages (the ones you're about to study) like a drowning man would cling to a life preserver. The habit of making God's Word central to their lives carried Brett and Dee through their journey with pain. I know they wouldn't wish this type of heartbreak on anyone, but giving birth to triplets also gave birth to richer, deeper, and more committed followers of Jesus.

I've never experienced pain like the Eastmans' and you may not have either, but God can use any uncomfortable or painful situation you'll face the same way he did with Brett and Dee. It can make you more like Jesus.

Use this last session as a chance to share some pain that you've experienced (and maybe never shared before) and trust God to give birth to new depth, character, and joy in your spiritual life.

FELLOWSHIP: CONNECTING Your Heart to Others'

What has been one of the most difficult times of your life?

How did you make it through that tough time?

What did God do in your life as a result of the pain you experienced?

DISCIPLESHIP: GROWING to Be Like Jesus

When life gets tough, what do you normally do? Many people feel sorry for themselves, hang their heads, and wait for the pain to go away. In the life of a believer, God can use the pain to bring about life-change gain. Don't hang your head. Learn what God can and will do during difficult times.

²Consider it pure joy, my brothers, whenever you face trials of many kinds, ³because you know that the testing of your faith develops perseverance. ⁴Perseverance must finish its work so that you may be mature and complete, not lacking anything. ⁵If any of you lacks wisdom, he should ask God, who gives generously to all without finding fault, and it will be given to him. ⁶But when he asks, he must believe and not doubt, because he who doubts is like a wave of the sea, blown and tossed by the wind. ⁷That man should not think he will receive anything from the Lord; ⁸he is a double-minded man, unstable in all he does.

—James 1:2-8

Who what when, where why how +home

Key words or 3 statements

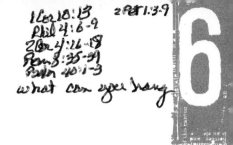

Life was especially difficult for the early Christians; they often endured persecution because of their beliefs. What does James say is the key for successfully navigating trials?

According to this passage, why should you have joy in the midst of trials?
How does joy help you through trials?

People often think of joy as an automatic, emotional response. How can you choose joy?

Where does wisdom come from? Why does God give it generously?

When you get wisdom from God, how does that help you get through trials?

9 Describe a time when wisdom helped you with a trial.

10 What are some ways you can know if you've made a wise decision?

11 Why is it necessary to "believe and not doubt" in order to get wisdom?

12 For what current trial do you need wisdom in order to respond well?

13 How do trials, perseverance, and wisdom relate to each other? Do trials automatically produce perseverance?

14 What are some practical ways you can work on your attitude in the midst of troubles?

MINISTRY: SERVING Others in Love

Take another opportunity to care for one another in the small group. Make sure you include everyone.

Write the name of every person in your small group next to one of the activities listed below. You may have more than one name on a line.

I made a new friend named _____.

_____ and I prayed together.

_____ helped me learn more about the Bible.

_____ challenged me to develop new spiritual habits.

_____ asked me about my spiritual goals.

_____ encouraged me to grow spiritually.

_____ laughed at something funny I said.

I gained insight through a conversation with _____.

_____ made me feel like I belong to this group.

I feel _____ knows me.

_____ listened carefully when I talked.

Share the names you wrote in the list above. Use this as an opportunity to thank the people in your group for contributing to the depth of your spiritual life.

EVANGELISM: SHARING Your Story and God's Story

You can't run from pain. Everyone goes through it—Christians and non-Christians! If you're not experiencing pain of some sort, some is waiting for you in the future. This isn't a prediction of bad news; it's a statement of reality, truth, and life. Life hurts, but in the midst of hurt God offers hope and healing.

How can your youth ministry become a place where you listen about the pain of others?

18

When you learn about someone's pain, how can you respond? What are some specific steps you can take to help others during their times of pain?

How can your response to pain become an evangelistic opportunity? What might the relationship between pain and evangelism look like?

19

WORSHIP: SURRENDERING Your Life to Honor God

Go personal

What's the next step for your spiritual journey?

◇ I'd like to start a new small group and lead it.

◇ I want to go through another book in the LIFETOGETHER series with this small group.

◇ I want to make another spiritual growth goal. My new goal will be _____.

◇ My next step is something else. I'd like to _____.

Go practical

Do you agree to continue meeting together? If yes, continue on with the remaining questions.

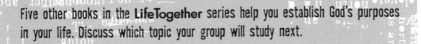

Five other books in the **LifeTogether** series help you establish God's purposes in your life. Discuss which topic your group will study next.

Starting to Go Where God Wants You to Be: 6 Small Group Sessions on Beginning Life Together

Connecting Your Heart to Others' : 6 Small Group Sessions on Fellowship

Serving Others in Love: 6 Small Group Sessions on Ministry

Sharing Your Story and God's Story: 6 Small Group Sessions on Evangelism

Surrendering Your Life to Honor God: 6 Small Group Sessions on Worship

You might have noticed this study guide, **GROWING to Be Like Jesus,** contained one session on each topic.

Turn to the **Small Group Covenant** (page 90). Do you want to change anything in your covenant—time, date, shared values, and so on? Write down the changes you agree upon. (Transfer them into your next LIFETOGETHER book.)

This is a good time to make suggestions for other changes—starting on time, paying attention when others are sharing, rotating leadership responsibilities, or whatever ideas you have—for improving the group.

Go prayerful
Finish your time together by thanking God for each person in your small group.

AT HOME THIS WEEK

Choose one or more of the following options.

Daily Bible Readings
Check out the Scriptures on page 106.

Memory Verses
Try memorizing a verse from page 110.

Journaling
Use **SCRIBBLE** pages, page 115-125

- 📖 Write whatever is on your mind.
- 📖 Read your journal entry from last week and write a reflection on it.

◪ Respond to this question: *Based on this study, how will I view pain and respond to it in the future?*

Wrap It Up
Write out your answers to session questions your group didn't have time to discuss.

LEARN A LITTLE MORE

Whenever you face trials
This passage doesn't give us helpful advice in case we face troubles; James knows that everyone will face troubles. The truth in this passage is like a parachute that slows our fall and keeps us from eternal harm. This world is far from perfect, and bad things will happen. The question is whether we'll endure them with God's help.

The testing of your faith
God doesn't make the pain. Some trials are so bad that it seems impossible to view them as character-building experiences. Just because God uses terrible events to accomplish good does not mean that he makes such tragedies happen. Evil and suffering remain mysteries. But knowing that God brings good out of bad gives us hope.

If any of you lacks wisdom
Wisdom is unusual insight—into what's real, how things work, what's important in life, and how to live well. We can either try to make sense of trials on our own or we can ask God to guide us. God may not answer all of our questions, but he'll give us wisdom into what's important and into how we can live well in the midst of pain.

Ask God
A stubborn heart can't learn. We can't learn anything—gain wisdom—if we're not firmly convinced that we need it. God doesn't override our ability to choose him and his ways, so he doesn't cram wisdom down our throats. We have to ask God because that's the only way we'll ever accept it.

FOR FURTHER STUDY

1 Peter 4:12-13
Philippians 1:29
Romans 8:17
2 Corinthians 1:5

NOTES

NOTES

APPENDIXES

PERSONALIZING THE LORD'S PRAYER

Our Father in heaven, hallowed be your name,
your kingdom come, your will be done on earth as it is in heaven.
Give us today our daily bread.
Forgive us our debts, as we also have forgiven our debtors.
And lead us not into temptation, but deliver us from the evil one."

Write out your prayer, Once an idea starts to flow, you can
finish a prompt with a few words or a paragraph or a page.

Our Father in heaven, hallowed be your name
Write something about God that amazes you. This is called
praise, worship, honor, or adoration.
Dear Father who...

Your kingdom come, your will be done on earth as it is in heaven
Acknowledge God's authority as the Creator and King.
I so much want to see your will be done in...

For some people, prayer is difficult to learn. They have a hard time knowing what to say. One way to begin thinking about prayer is to use Jesus' prayer as a model.

Give us today our daily bread

Write out what you'd like God to do for you or for others, known as supplication, intercession, or just plain asking for help!
Please give me and those I love...

Forgive us our debts

Write down any items you need to clear up with God. This is confession.
Forgive me for...

As we also have forgiven our debtors

Do you have any grudges or hurts to let go of?
I forgive...

And lead us not into temptation, but deliver us from the evil one

Draw from God's strength when you face temptations.
Please protect me or others from...

PRAYING THE SCRIPTURES

As a way of focusing on God's Word, read the Bible verses on this page out loud. Let everyone read a portion, have one person read one passage, or have one person read all the passages. While the verses are being read, the rest of the group closes their eyes to fully concentrate on the meaning.

God blesses those people who refuse evil advice
and won't follow sinners or join in sneering at God.
Instead, the Law of the Lord makes them happy,
and they think about it day and night.
They are like trees growing beside a stream,
trees that produce fruit in season and always have leaves.
Those people succeed in everything they do.

-Psalm 1:1-3 CEV

"Come, all you who are thirsty, come to the waters;
and you who have no money, come, buy and eat!
Come, buy wine and milk without money and without cost.
Why spend money on what is not bread,
    and your labor on what does not satisfy?
Listen, listen to me, and eat what is good,
    and your soul will delight in the richest of fare.
Give ear and come to me; hear me, that your soul may live.
I will make an everlasting covenant with you,
    my faithful love promised to David."

-Isaiah 55:1-3 NIV

Every part of Scripture is God-breathed and useful one way or another--showing us truth, exposing our rebellion, correcting our mistakes, training us to live God's way. Through the Word we are put together and shaped up for the tasks God has for us.

-2 Timothy 3:16-17 MSG

The law of the Lord is perfect, reviving the soul.
    The decrees of the Lord are trustworthy, making wise the simple.
The commandments of the Lord are right, bringing joy to the heart.
    The commands of the Lord are clear, giving insight to life.
Reverence for the Lord is pure, lasting forever.
    The laws of the Lord are true; each one is fair.
They are more desirable than gold, even the finest gold.
    They are sweeter than honey, even honey dripping from the comb.
They are a warning to those who hear them; there is great reward
    for those who obey them.

-Psalm 19:7-11 NLT

What God has said isn't only alive and active! It is sharper than any double-edged sword. His word can cut through our spirits and souls and through our joints and marrow, until it discovers the desires and thoughts of our hearts. Nothing is hidden from God! He sees through everything, and we will have to tell him the truth.

-Hebrews 4:12-13 CEV

PRAYER AND EVANGELISM

After your group has discussed the connection between prayer and evangelism, spend about five minutes writing your reflection here.

SMALL GROUP COVENANT

Read through the following covenant as a group. Discuss concerns and questions. You may modify the covenant based on the needs and concerns of your group members. Those who agree with the terms and are willing to commit themselves to the covenant as you've revised it should sign their own books and the books of everyone entering into the covenant.

> A covenant is a binding agreement or contract. God made covenants with Noah, Abraham, and David, among others. Jesus is the fulfillment of a new covenant between God and his people.

If you take your commitment to the Small Group Covenant seriously, you'll find that your group will go deep relationally. Without a covenant you may find yourselves meeting simply for the sake of meeting.

If your group decides to add some additional values (character traits such as be encouraging or be kind), write the new values at the bottom of the covenant page. Your group may also want to create some small group rules (actions such as not interrupting when someone else is speaking or sitting up instead of lying down). You can list those at the bottom of the covenant page also.

Reviewing your group's covenant, values, and rules before each meeting will become a significant part of your small group experience.

OUR COVENANT

I, _____ , as a member of our small group, acknowledge my need for meaningful relationships with other believers. I agree that this small group community exists to help me deepen my relationships with God, Christians, and other people in my life. I commit to the following:

Consistency I will give my best effort to attend every time our small group meets.

Honesty I will take risks to share truthfully about the personal issues in my life.

Confidentiality I will support the foundation of trust in our small group by not participating in gossip. I will not reveal personal information shared by others during our meetings.

Respect I will help create a safe environment for our small group members by listening carefully and not making fun of others.

Prayer I will make a committed effort to pray regularly for the people in our small group.

Accountability I will allow the people in my small group to hold me accountable for growing spiritually and living a life that honors God.

This covenant, signed by all the members in this group, reflects our commitment to one another.

Signature	Date
Signature	Date
Signature	Date
Signature	Date
Signature	Date
Signature	Date
Signature	Date
Signature	Date
Signature	Date
Signature	Date

SMALL GROUP
Roster

name	EMAIL

Phone	Address	School & Grade

Cliques arise naturally because we all want to belong—God created us to be connected in community with one another. The same drive that creates community creates cliques. A clique isn't just a group of friends, but a group of friends uninterested in anyone outside the group. Cliques result in pain for those who are excluded.

If you reread the first paragraph of the introduction "**Read Me First**" (page 9), you see the words *spiritual community* used to describe your small group. If your small group becomes a clique, it's an *unspiritual* community. You have a clique when the biblical purpose of fellowship turns inward. That's ugly. It's the opposite of what God intended the body of Christ to be.

- Cliques make your youth ministry look bad.
- Cliques make your small group appear immature.
- Cliques hurt the feelings of excluded people.
- Cliques contradict the value God places on each person.
- Few things are as unappealing as a youth ministry filled with cliques.

Many leaders avoid using small groups as a means toward spiritual growth because they fear the groups will become cliquish. But when they're healthy, small groups can improve the well-being, friendliness, and depth of your youth ministry.

> **Be wise in the way you act toward outsiders;
> make the most of every opportunity.**
>
> —Colossians 4:5

Here are some ideas for preventing your small group from turning into a clique:

Be Aware

Learn to recognize when people feel like they don't fit in with your group. It's easy to forget when you're an insider how bad it feels to be an outsider.

Reach Out

Once you're aware of a person feeling left out, make efforts to be friendly. Smile, shake hands, say hello, ask them to sit with you or your group, and ask simple yet personalized questions. A person who feels like an outsider may come across as defensive, so be as accepting as possible.

Launch New Small Groups

Any small group that has the attitude of "us four and no more" has become a clique. A time will come when your small group should launch into multiple small groups if it gets too big. The bigger a small group gets, the less healthy it will become. If your small group understands this, there will be a culture of growth instead of cliques. New or introverted people often are affected by cliques because they have a hard time breaking through the existing connections that the small group members already have. When you start new groups you'll see fellowship move from ugly to what God intended—a practical extension of his love.

Challenge Others

Small group members expect adult leaders to confront them for acting like a clique. Instead of waiting for an adult to make the move, shock everyone by stepping up and challenging what you know is destructive. Take a risk. Be a spokesperson for your youth ministry and your student peers by leading the way—be part of a small group that isn't cliquey and one who isn't afraid to challenge the groups who are.

By practicing these key ideas, your group will excel at reaching out to others and deepening the biblical fellowship within your church.

ACCOUNTABILITY QUESTIONS

During your small group time, you'll have opportunities to connect with one other person in the group—your spiritual partner. Relationships can go deeper if you have the same partner for the entire book or even the entire LIFETOGETHER series. Be as mellow as you want or crank it up to a higher level by talking throughout the week and checking in with each other about your spiritual journeys.

For those who want to go to a deeper level with their spiritual partners, here's a list of questions you can use as a guide for accountability. Depending on the time you have available, you might discuss all of them or only a couple.

The Wonder Question
Have you maintained an attitude of awe and wonder toward God?
(Have you minimized him? Placed him in a box? Forgotten to consider his character?)

The Priority Question
Have you maintained a personal devotional time (quiet time) with God?
(Have you allowed yourself to become too busy? Filled your life with too much activity?)

The Morality Question
Have you maintained integrity in the way you live?
(Have you compromised your integrity or the truth with your actions? Your thoughts? Your words?)

The Listening Question
Are you sensitive to the promptings and leading of the Holy Spirit?
(Have you drowned out his voice with too much noise?)

The Relationships Question
Have you maintained peaceful relationships and resolved conflicts to the best of your ability?
(Have you caused conflict, offended others, or avoided resolving tension?)

The Prayer Question
How can I pray for you this week?

SPIRITUAL HEALTH assessment

E valuating your spiritual journey is a good thing. Parts of your journey will take you to low spots, while others will lead you to high places. Spiritual growth is not a smooth incline—loopy roller coaster is more like it. When you regularly consider your life, you'll develop an awareness of God's Spirit working in you. Evaluate. Think. Learn. Grow.

The assessment in this section is a tool, not a test. The purpose of this tool is to help you evaluate where you're at in your faith journey. No one is perfect in this life, so don't worry about what score you get. It won't be published in your church bulletin. Be honest so you have an accurate idea of how you're doing.

When you finish, celebrate the areas where you're relatively healthy, and think about how you can use your strengths to help others on their spiritual journeys. Then think of ways your small group members can aid one another to improve weak areas through support and example.

FELLOWSHIP: CONNECTING Your Heart to Others'

1. I meet consistently with a small group of Christians.

1	2	3	4	5
poor				outstanding

2. I'm connected to other Christians who hold me accountable.

1	2	3	4	5
poor				outstanding

3. I can talk with my small group leader when I need help, advice, or support.

1	2	3	4	5
poor				outstanding

4. My Christian friends are a significant source of strength and stability in my life.

1	2	3	4	5
poor				outstanding

5. I regularly pray for others in my small group between meetings.

1	2	3	4	5
poor				outstanding

6. I have resolved all conflicts I have had with other Christians and non–Christians.

1	2	3	4	5
poor				outstanding

7. I've done all I possibly can to be a good son or daughter and brother or sister.

1	2	3	4	5
poor				outstanding

Take time to answer the following questions to further evaluate your spiritual health (after your small group meets if you don't have time during the meeting). If you need help with this, schedule a time with your small group leader to talk about your spiritual health.

8 List the three most significant relationships you have right now. Why are these people important to you?

9 How would you describe the benefit you receive from being in fellowship with other Christians?

Do you have an accountability partner? If so, what have you been doing to hold each other accountable? If not, how can you get one?

DISCIPLESHIP: GROWING to Be Like Jesus

11. I have regular times of conversation with God.

1	2	3	4	5
poor				outstanding

12. I'm a closer friend with God this month than I was last month.

1	2	3	4	5
poor				outstanding

13. I'm making better decisions this month when compared to last month.

1	2	3	4	5
poor				outstanding

14. I regularly attend church services and grow spiritually as a result.

1	2	3	4	5
poor				outstanding

15. I consistently honor God with my finances through giving.

1	2	3	4	5
poor				outstanding

16. I regularly study the Bible on my own.

1	2	3	4	5
poor				outstanding

17. I regularly memorize Bible verses or passages.

1	2	3	4	5
poor				outstanding

Take time to answer the following questions to further evaluate your spiritual health (after your small group meets if you don't have time during the meeting). If you need help with this, schedule a time with your small group leader to talk about your spiritual health.

What books or chapters from the Bible have your read during the last month?

18

What has God been teaching you from Scripture lately?

19

What was the last verse you memorized? When did you memorize it? Describe the last time a memorized Bible verse helped you.

20

MINISTRY: SERVING Others in Love

21. I am currently serving in some ministry capacity.

1	2	3	4	5
poor				outstanding

22. I'm effectively ministering where I'm serving.

1	2	3	4	5
poor				outstanding

23. Generally I have a humble attitude when I serve others.

1	2	3	4	5
poor				outstanding

24. I understand God has created me as a unique individual and he has a special plan for my life.

1	2	3	4	5
poor				outstanding

25. When I help others, I typically don't look for anything in return.

1	2	3	4	5
poor				outstanding

26. My family and friends consider me to be generally unselfish.

1	2	3	4	5
poor				outstanding

27. I'm usually sensitive to the hurts of others and respond in a caring way.

1	2	3	4	5
poor				outstanding

Take time to answer the following questions to further evaluate your spiritual health (after your small group meets if you don't have time during the meeting). If you need help with this, schedule a time with your small group leader to talk about your spiritual health.

28 If you're currently serving in a ministry, why are you serving? If not, what's kept you from getting involved?

29 What spiritual lessons have you learned while serving?

30 What frustrations have you experienced as a result of serving?

EVANGELISM: SHARING Your Story and God's Story

31. I regularly pray for my non–Christian friends.

1	2	3	4	5
poor				outstanding

32. I invite my non–Christian friends to church.

1	2	3	4	5
poor				outstanding

33. I talk about my faith with others.

1	2	3	4	5
poor				outstanding

34. I pray for opportunities to share about what Jesus has done in my life.

1	2	3	4	5
poor				outstanding

35. People know I'm a Christian by more than my words.

1	2	3	4	5
poor				outstanding

36. I feel a strong compassion for non–Christians.

1	2	3	4	5
poor				outstanding

37. I have written out my testimony and am ready to share it.

1	2	3	4	5
poor				outstanding

Take time to answer the following questions to further evaluate your spiritual health (after your small group meets if you don't have time during the meeting). If you need help with this, schedule a time with your small group leader to talk about your spiritual health.

38 Describe any significant spiritual conversations you've had with unbelievers in the past month.

39 Has your faith been challenged by any non-Christians? If yes, how?

40 What have been some difficulties you've faced with sharing your faith?

41 What successes have you experienced recently in personal evangelism? (Success isn't limited to bringing people to salvation directly. Helping someone take a step closer at any point on his or her spiritual journey is success.)

WORSHIP: SURRENDERING Your Life to Honor God

42. I consistently participate in Sunday and midweek worship experiences at church.

1	2	3	4	5
poor				outstanding

43. My heart breaks over the things that break God's heart.

1	2	3	4	5
poor				outstanding

44. I regularly give thanks to God.

1	2	3	4	5
poor				outstanding

45. I'm living a life that, overall, honors God.

1	2	3	4	5
poor				outstanding

46. I have an attitude of wonder and awe toward God.

1	2	3	4	5
poor				outstanding

48. I use the free access I have into God's presence often.

1	2	3	4	5
poor				outstanding

Take time to answer the following questions to further evaluate your spiritual health (after your small group meets if you don't have time during the meeting). If you need help with this, schedule a time with your small group leader to talk about your spiritual health.

Make a list of your top five priorities. You can get a good idea of your priorities by evaluating how you spend your time. Be realistic and honest. Are your priorities in the right order? Do you need to get rid of some or add new priorities? (As a student you may have some limitations. This isn't ammo for dropping out of school or disobeying parents!)

50

List ten things you're thankful for.

51

What influences, directs, guides, or controls you the most?

DAILY BIBLE READINGS

As you meet together with your small group friends for Bible study, prayer, and encouragement, you'll grow spiritually. No matter how deep your friendships go, you're not likely to be together for your entire lives, so you need to learn to grow spiritually on your own too. God has given you an incredible tool to help—his love letter, the Bible. The Bible reveals God's love for you and gives directions for living life to the fullest.

To help you, you'll find a collection of Bible passages that reinforce each week's lesson below. Every day *read* the daily verses, *reflect* on how the verses inspire or challenge you, and *respond* to God through prayer or by writing in your journal or on the journaling pages in this book.

Check off the passages as you read them. Don't feel guilty if you miss a daily reading. Simply do your best to develop the habit of being in God's Word daily.

☐ Week 1

2 Corinthians 3:18
Philippians 3:13-14
1 Thessalonians 3:9-13
Colossians 1:28
Colossians 1:9-10

☐ Week 2

1 Corinthians 3:16-17
Ephesians 5:18-21
2 Corinthians 3:17-18
Romans 8:15-17
1 Corinthians 2:12-16

☐ Week 3

Psalm 42:1
Psalm 37:4-5
Psalm 138:8
Psalm 147:17-19
Isaiah 50:4-5

☐ Week 4

John 16:23-24
Philippians 4:6-7
Proverbs 15:29
1 Thessalonians 5:16-18
James 5:16-18

☐ Week 5

Psalm 1:1-3
Isaiah 55:1-3
2 Timothy 3:16-17
Psalm 19:7-11
Hebrews 4:12-13

☐ Week 6

1 Corinthians 10:13
Psalm 40:1-3
Philippians 4:8-9
2 Corinthians 4:16-18
Romans 8:38-39

HOW TO STUDY THE BIBLE

The Bible is the foundation of all the books in the LIFETOGETHER series. Every lesson contains a passage from the Bible for your small group to study and apply. To maximize the impact of your small group experience, it's helpful if each participant spends time reading and studying the Bible during the week. When you read the Bible for yourself, you can have discussions based on what *you* know the Bible says instead of what another member has heard second- or third-hand about the Bible. You also minimize the risk of depending on your small group for all your Bible study time.

Growing Christians learn to study the Bible on their own so they can learn to grow on their own. Here are some principles about studying the Bible to help you give God's Word a central place in your life.

Choose a Time and Place

Since we're so easily distracted, pick a time when you're at your best. If you're a morning person, then give that time to study the Bible. Find a place away from phones, computers, and TVs, so you are less likely to be interrupted.

Begin with Prayer

Make an effort to acknowledge God's presence. Thank him for his gifts, confess your sins, and ask for his guidance and understanding as you study his love letter to you.

Start with Excitement

We easily take God's Word for granted and forget what an incredible gift we have. God wasn't forced to reach out to us, but he did. He's made it possible for us to know him, understand his directions, and be encouraged, all through the Bible. Remind yourself how amazing it is that God wants you to know him.

Read the Passage

After choosing a passage, read it several times. You might want to read it slowly, pausing after each sentence. If possible, read it out loud. Originally the Bible was heard, not read.

Keep a Journal

Respond to God's Word by writing down how you're challenged, truths you want to remember, thanksgiving and praise, sins to confess, commands to obey, or any other thoughts you have.

Dig Deep

When you read the Bible, look deeper than the plain meaning of the words. Here are a few ideas about what you might find.

Truth about God's character
What do the verses reveal about God's character?

Truth about your life and our world
You don't have to figure out life on your own. Life can be difficult, but when you know how the world works you can make good decisions guided by wisdom from God.

Truth about the world's past
The Bible reveals God's intervention in our mistakes and triumphs throughout history. The choices we read about—good and bad—serve as examples to challenge us to greater faith and obedience. (See Hebrews 11:1-12:1.)

Truth about our actions
God will never leave you stranded. Although he allows us to go through hard times, he is always with us. Our actions have consequences and rewards. Just like he does in Bible stories, God can use all of the consequences and rewards caused by our actions to help others.

As you read, ask these four questions to help you learn from the Bible:

What do these verses teach me about who God is, how he acts, and how people respond?

- What does this passage teach about the nature of the world?
- What wisdom can I learn from what I read?
- How should I change my life because of what I learned from these verses?

Ask Questions

You may be tempted to skip over parts you don't understand, but don't give up too easily. Understanding the Bible can be hard work. If you come across a word you don't know, look it up in a regular dictionary or a Bible dictionary. If you come across a verse that seems to contradict another verse, see whether your Bible has any notes to explain it. Write down your questions and ask someone who has more knowledge about the Bible than you. Buy or borrow a study Bible or check the Internet. Try these sites to begin with:

www.twopaths.com
www.gotquestions.org
www.carm.org

Apply the Truth to Your Life

The Bible should make a difference in your life. It contains the help you need to live the life God intended. Knowledge of the Bible without personal obedience is worthless and causes hypocrisy and pride. Take time to consider the condition of your thinking, attitudes, and actions, and wonder about how God is working in you. Think about your life situation and how you can serve others better.

More Helpful Ideas

- Take the position that the times you have set aside for Bible reading and study are nonnegotiable. Don't let other activities squeeze Bible study time out of your schedule.
- Avoid the extremes of being ritualistic (reading a chapter just to mark it off a list) and lazy (giving up).
- Begin with realistic goals and boundaries for your study time. Five to seven minutes a day may be a challenge for you at the beginning.
- Be open to the leading and teaching of God's Spirit.
- Love God like he's your parent (or the parent you wish you had).

MEMORY VERSES

The word *memory* may cause some people to throw this book and kick the dog. Throughout your school years, you have to memorize dates, places, times, and outcomes. Now we're telling you to memorize the Bible?! Seriously?

Not the entire Bible. Start with some key verses. Here's why: Scripture memorization is a good habit for a growing Christian to develop. When God's Word is planted in your mind and heart, it has a way of influencing how you live. King David understood this when he wrote; " I have hidden your word in my heart that I might not sin against you" (Psalm 119:11).

Challenge one another in your small group to memorize the six verses below—one for each time your small group meets. Hold each other accountable by asking about one another's progress. Write the verses on index cards and keep them handy so you can learn and review them when you have free moments (standing in line, before class starts, when you've finished a test and others are still working, waiting for your dad to get out of the bathroom…). You'll be surprised at how many verses you can memorize as you work toward this goal and add verses to your list.

Week 1

But seek first his kingdom and his righteousness, and all these things will be given to you as well.
—Matthew 6:33

Week 2

I pray that out of his glorious riches he may strengthen you with power through his spirit in your inner being, so that Christ may dwell in your hearts through faith.
—Ephesians 3:16-17

GROWING to Be like Jesus

"You are worried and upset about many things,
but only one thing is needed.
Mary has chosen what is better,
and it will not be taken away from her."

—Luke 10:41-42

"Be still, and know that I am God;
I will be exalted among the nations,
I will be exalted in the earth."

—Psalm 46:0

Do your best to present yourself to God
as one approved,
a workman who does not need to be ashamed
and who correctly handles the word of truth.

—2 Timothy 2:15

Consider it pure joy,
my brothers,
whenever you face trials of many kinds,
because you know that the testing
of your faith develops perseverance.

—James 1:2-3

JOURNALING: SNAPSHOTS OF YOUR HEART

In the simplest terms, journaling is reflection with pen in hand. A growing life needs time to reflect, so several times throughout the book you're asked to reflect in writing and you always have a journaling option at the end of each session. Through these writing opportunities, you're getting a taste of what it means to journal.

When you take time to write reflections in a journal, you'll experience many benefits. A journal is more than a diary. It's a series of snapshots of your heart The goal of journaling is to slow down your life to capture some of the great, crazy, wonderful, chaotic, painful, encouraging, angering, confusing, joyful, and loving thoughts, feelings and ideas that enter your life. Writing in a journal can become a powerful habit when you reflect on your life and how God is working.

You'll find room to journal on the following pages.

Personal Insights

When confusion abounds in your life, disorderly thoughts and feelings can become like wild animals. They often loom just out of range, slightly out of focus, but never gone from your awareness. Putting these thoughts and feelings on paper is like corralling and domesticating the wild beasts. Then you can look at them, consider them, contemplate the reasons they were causing you pain, and learn from them.

Have you ever had trouble answering the question, "How do you feel?" Journaling compels you to become more specific with your generalized thoughts and feelings. This is not to suggest that a page full of words perfectly represents what's happening on the inside. That would be foolish. But journaling can move you closer to understanding more about yourself.

Reflection and Examination

With journaling, once you recognize what you're to write about, you can then consider its value. You can write about your feelings, your situations, how you responded to events. You can reflect and answer questions like these:

- Was that the right response?
- What were my other options?
- Did I lose control and act impulsively?
- If this happened again, should I do the same thing? Would I do the same thing?
- How can I be different as a result of this situation?

Spiritual Insights

One of the main goals of journaling is to learn new spiritual insights about God, yourself, and the world. When you take time to journal, you have the opportunity to pause and consider how God is working in your life and in the lives of those around you, so you don't miss the work he's accomplishing. And journaling helps you remember.

What to Write

There isn't one way to journal, no set number of times per week, no rules for the length of each journal entry. Figure out what works best for you. Get started with these options:

A letter or prayer to God
Many Christians struggle with maintaining a consistent prayer life. Writing out your prayers can help strengthen it. Begin with this question: *What do I want to tell God right now?*

A letter to or a conversation with another person
Sometimes conversations with others can be difficult because we're not sure what we ought to say. Have you ever walked away from an interaction and 20 minutes later think, *I should have said...?* Journaling conversations before they happen can help you think through the issues and be intentional in your interactions with others. As a result, you can feel confident as you begin your conversations because you've taken time to consider the issues.

Conflict and pain
You may find it helpful to write about your conflicts with others, especially those that take you by surprise. By journaling soon after, you can reflect

and learn from the conflicts. You'll be better prepared for the next time you face a similar situation. Conflicts are generally difficult to navigate. Thinking through the interactions typically yields helpful personal insights.

When you're experiencing pain is a good time to settle your thoughts and consider the nature of your feelings. The great thing about exploring your feelings is that you're only accountable to God. You don't have to worry about hurting anyone's feelings by what you write in your journal (if you keep it private).

Personal motivation

The Bible is clear regarding two heart truths:

- How you act is a reflection of who you are on the inside **(Luke 6:45)**.
- You can take the right action for the wrong reason **(James 4:3)**.

The condition of your heart is so important. Molding your motives to God's desire is central to being a follower of Christ. The Pharisees did many of the right things, but for the wrong reasons. Reflect on the *real* reasons you do what you do.

Personal Impact

Have you ever gone to bed thinking, *That was a mistake. I didn't intend for that to happen!*? Probably! No one is perfect. You can't predict all of the consequences of your actions. Reflecting on how your actions impact others will help you relate better to others.

God's work in your life

If you write in your journal in the evening, you can answer this question: *What did God teach me today?*

If you journal in the morning, you can answer this question: *God, what were you trying to teach me yesterday that I missed?* When you reflect on yesterday's events, you may find a common theme that God may have been weaving into your life during the day, one you missed because you were busy. When you see God's hand in your life, even a day later, you know God loves you and is guiding you.

Scripture

Journal about whatever you learn from the Bible. Rewrite a verse in your own words, or figure out how a passage is structured. Try to uncover the key truths from the verses and figure out how the verses apply to your life.

SCRIBBLES

JOURNALING page

SCRIBBLES

SCRIBBLES

SCRIBBLES

JOURNALING page

SCRIBBLES

SCRBBLES

SCRIBBLES

JOURNALING page

SCRIBBLES

SCRIBBLES

JOURNALING page

PRAYING IN YOUR SMALL GROUP

A s believers, we're called to support one another in prayer, and prayer should become a consistent part of creating a healthy small group.

One of the purposes of prayer is to align our hearts with God's. By doing this, we can more easily think his thoughts and feel his feelings—in our limited human way. Prayer shouldn't be a how-well-did-I-do performance or a self-conscious, put-on-the-spot task to fear. Your small group may need time to get comfortable with praying out loud. That's okay.

Follow Jesus' Example

When you do pray, silently or aloud, follow the practical, simple words of Jesus in Matthew 6.

Pray sincerely.

"And when you pray, do not be like the hypocrites, for they love to pray standing in the synagogues and on the street corners to be seen by men. I tell you the truth, they have received their reward in full."

—Matthew 6:5

In the Old Testament, God's people were disciplined prayer warriors. They developed specific prayers to use for every special occasion or need. They had prayers for light and darkness, prayers for fire and rain, prayers for good news and bad. They even had prayers for travel, holidays, holy days, and Sabbath days.

Every day the faithful would stop to pray at 9:00 A.M., noon, and 3:00 P.M., a sort of religious coffee break. Their ritual was impressive, to say the least, but being legalistic has its downside. The proud, self-righteous types would strategically plan their schedules to be in the middle of a crowd when it was time for prayer so everyone could hear them as they prayed loudly. You can see the problem. What was intended to promote spiritual passion became a drama for the crowd.

The Lord wants our prayers addressed to him alone. That seems obvious enough, yet how many of us pray more with the need to impress our listeners than to communicate with God? This is the problem if you're prideful like the Pharisees about the excellent quality of your prayers. But it can also be a problem if you're new to prayer and concerned that you don't know how to "pray right." Don't concern yourself with what others think; just talk to God as if you were sitting in a chair next to him.

Pray simply.

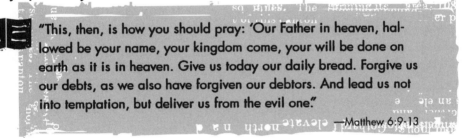

"And when you pray, do not keep on babbling like pagans, for they think they will be heard because of their many words. Do not be like them, for your Father knows what you need before you ask him."

—Matthew 6:7-8

The Lord doesn't ask to be dazzled with brilliantly crafted language. Nor is he impressed with lengthy monologues. It's freeing to know that he wants us to keep it simple.

Pray specifically.

"This, then, is how you should pray: 'Our Father in heaven, hallowed be your name, your kingdom come, your will be done on earth as it is in heaven. Give us today our daily bread. Forgive us our debts, as we also have forgiven our debtors. And lead us not into temptation, but deliver us from the evil one."

—Matthew 6:9-13

What the church has come to call **The Lord's Prayer** is a model of the kind of brief but specific prayers we may offer anytime, anywhere. Look at some of the specific items mentioned:

Adoration—hallowed be your name

Provision—your kingdom come...your will be done...give us today our daily bread

Forgiveness—forgive us our debts

Protection—lead us not into temptation

PRAYER REQUEST GUIDELINES

Because prayer time is so vital, small group members need to know some basic guidelines for sharing, handling, and praying for prayer requests. Without a commitment from each person to honor these simple suggestions, prayer time can be dominated by one person, be a gossipfest, or be a never-ending story time. (There are appropriate times to tell personal stories, but this may not be the best time.)

Here are a few suggestions for each group to consider:

Write the requests down.

Each small group member should write down every prayer request on the **Prayer Request Log** (pages 132-137). When you commit to a small group, you're agreeing to be part of the spiritual community, which includes praying for one another. By keeping track of prayer requests, you can be aware of how God answers them. You'll be amazed at God's power and faithfulness.

As an alternative, one person can record the requests and e-mail them to the rest of the group. If your group chooses this option, *safeguard confidentiality*. Be sure personal information isn't compromised. Some people share e-mail accounts with parents or siblings. Develop a workable plan for this option.

Give everyone an opportunity to share.

As a group, be mindful of the amount of time remaining and the number of people who still want to share. You won't be able to share every thought or detail about a situation.

Obviously if someone experiences a crisis, you may need to focus exclusively on that group member by giving him or her extended time and focused prayer. (However, *true* crises are infrequent.)

The leader can limit the time by making a comment such as one of the following:

- Everyone can share one praise or request.
- Simply tell us what to pray for. We can talk more later.
- We're only going to pray for requests about the people in our group.
- We've run out of time to share prayer requests. Take a moment to write down your prayer request and give it to me [or identify another person]. You'll get them by e-mail tomorrow.

3 ring binder for journal

Just as people are free to share, they're free to not share.

The goal of a healthy small group should be to create an environment where participants feel comfortable sharing about their lives. Still, not everyone needs to share each week. Here's what I tell my small group:

> As a small group we're here to support one another in prayer. This doesn't mean that everyone has to share something. In fact, I don't want you to think, *I've got to share something.* There's no need to make up prayer requests just to have something to say. If you have something you'd like the group to pray for, let us know. If not, that's fine too.

No gossip allowed.

Don't allow sharing prayer requests to become an excuse for gossip. This is easy to do if you all aren't careful. If you're not part of the problem or solution, consider the information gossip. Sharing the request without the story behind it helps prevent gossip. Also speak in general terms without giving names or details ("I have a friend who's in trouble. God knows who it is. Pray for me that I can be a good friend.").

If a prayer request starts going astray, someone should kindly intercede, perhaps with a question such as, "How can we pray for *you* in this situation?"

Don't give advice or try to fix the problem.

When people share their struggles and problems, a common response is to try to fix the problem by offering advice. At the right time, the group might provide input on a particular problem, but during prayer time, keep focused on praying for the need. Often God's best work in a person's life comes through times of struggle and pain.

Keep in touch.

Make sure you exchange phone numbers and emails before you leave the first meeting, so you can contact someone who needs prayer or encouragement before the next time your group meets. You can write each person's contact information on the **Small Group Roster** (page 92).

During the Small Group Gathering

- One person closes in prayer for the entire group.
- Pray silently. Have one person close the silent prayer time after a while with *Amen.*
- The leader or other group member prays out loud for each person in the group.
- Everyone prays for one request or person. This can be done randomly during prayer or, as the request is shared, a willing pray-er can announce, "I'll pray for that."
- Everyone who wants to pray takes a turn or two. Not everyone needs to pray out loud.
- Split the group into half and pray together in a smaller group.
- Pair up and pray for each other.
- On occasion, each person can share what he or she is thankful for before a prayer request, so prayer requests don't become negative from focusing only on problems. Prayer isn't just asking for stuff. It includes praising God and being thankful for his generosity toward us.

■ If you're having an animated discussion about a Bible passage or a life situation, don't feel like you *must* cut it short for prayer requests. Use it as an opportunity to add a little variety to the prayer time by praying some *other* day between sessions.

Outside the Group Time

You can use these options if you run out of time to pray during the meeting or in addition to prayer during the meeting.

■ Send prayer requests to each other via e-mail.
■ Pick partners and phone each other.
■ Have each person in the small group choose a day to pray for everyone in the group. Perhaps you can work it out to have each day of the week covered. Let participants report back at each meeting for accountability.
■ Have each person pray for just one other person in the group for the entire week. (Everyone prays for the person on the left or on the right or draw names.)

PRAYER REQUEST LOG

DATE	who shared	ReQuest	rEsponse/ anSweR

PRAYER REQUEST LOG

DATE	who shared	ReQuest	rEsponse/ anSweR

PRAYER REQUEST LOG

DATE	who shared	ReQuest	rEsponse/ anSweR

PRAYER REQUEST LOG

DATE	who shared	ReQuest	rEsponse/ anSweR

PRAYER REQUEST LOG

DATE	who shared	ReQuest	rEsponse/ anSweR

PRAYER REQUEST LOG

DATE	who shared	ReQuest	rEsponse/anSweR

LIFE TOGETHER FOR A YEAR

Your group will benefit the most if you work through the entire LIFETOGETHER series. The longer your group is together, the better your chances of maturing spiritually and integrating the biblical purposes into your life. Here's a plan to complete the series in one year.

> I recommend you begin with **STARTING** to Go Where God Wants You to Be, because it contains an introduction to each of the five biblical purposes (though it isn't mandatory). You can use the rest of the books in any order.

As you look at your youth ministry calendar, you may want to use the books in the order they complement events the youth group will be participating in. For example, if you plan to have an evangelism outreach in the fall, study **SHARING Your Story and God's Story** first to build momentum. Study **SERVING Others in Love** in late winter to prepare for the spring break missions' trip.

Use your imagination to celebrate the completion of each book. Have a worship service, an outreach party, a service project, a fun night out, a meet-the-family dinner, or whatever else you can dream up.

GROWING to Be like Jesus

Number of weeks	Meeting topic
1	Planning meeting—a casual gathering to get acquainted, discuss expectations, and refine the covenant (see page 90).
6	**STARTING to Go Where God Wants You to Be**
1	Celebration
6	**CONNECTING Your Heart to Others'**
1	Celebration
6	**SHARING Your Story and God's Story**
1	Celebration
6	**GROWING to Be Like Jesus**
1	Celebration
6	**SERVING Others in Love**
1	Celebration
6	**SURRENDERING Your Life to Honor God**
1	Celebration
2	Christmas break
1	Easter break
6	Summer break
52	One year

Dear Kathleen,

I just wanted to let you know how thankful I am for the dedication you showed me as my small group leader. I love telling people, "Kathleen is my small group leader — she's the best!" Next to God, you have had the greatest influence in my life. I want to grow up and love people like you, love Jesus like you do, love my future husband like you do, and be a small group leader like you.

What's amazing about you, is that all the girls in our small group felt like you liked them the most. We also felt your push. As I look back over my junior high and high school years, you loved me enough to challenge me to change. Thank you for always asking about my prayer life, my quiet times, my ministry, my heart. Thanks for seeing who I could be.

You've made a huge difference in my life. Thank you!

Love,
Sarah

Whether you are a student or a leader, when you're a part of a small group — investing your life in others — you're making a difference that will last an eternity. At Simply Youth Ministry we are dedicated to helping you do just that. For students, we've got tools like the *One Minute Bible*, that will help you grow in your faith. For leaders, we've got all kinds of resources that will help you simplify your ministry and save you time. For both of you, we have a deep appreciation for your commitment to serving Christ and loving each other.

doug fields'
simply youth ministry
simplifying ministry...saving you time.

toll free: 1-866-9-simply
simplyyouthministry.com

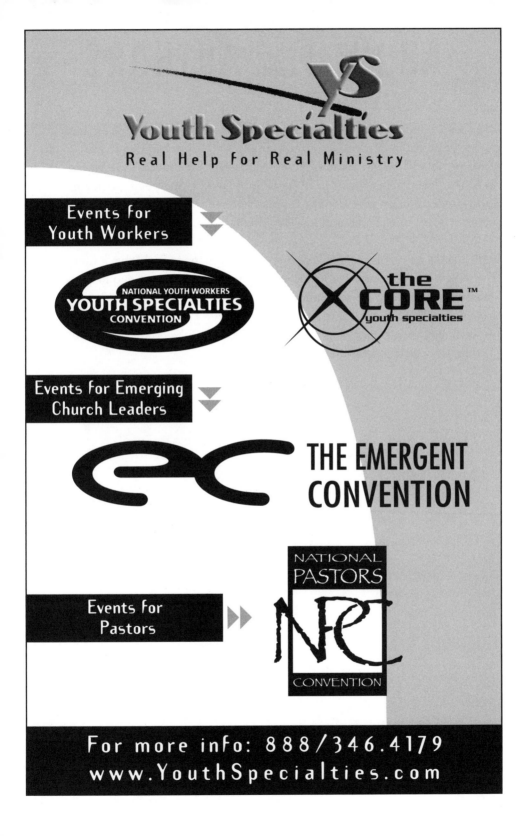

ABOUT THE AUTHORS

Doug Fields, a respected youth ministry leader for over two decades, has authored or coauthored more than 30 books, including **Purpose-Driven Youth Ministry**, **Your First Two Years of Youth Ministry**, and **Videos That Teach**. With an M.Div. from Fuller Theological Seminary, Doug is the youth pastor at Saddleback Church, president of simplyyouthministry.com, and a frequent presenter at Youth Specialties events. Doug and his wife, Cathy, have three children.

Brett Eastman is pastor of membership and small groups at Saddleback Church, where there are now over 1,500 small group leaders and a growing network of volunteer coaches and bivocational pastors. Brett created the Healthy Small Group strategy and he leads the Large Church Small Group Forums for the Leadership Network. Brett is coauthor of the DOING LIFE TOGETHER Bible study series. Brett and his wife, Dee, have five children.